Angolan Political Thought

Also Available from Bloomsbury

The Political Writings from Alienation and Freedom, Frantz Fanon
Maori Philosophy, Georgina Tuari Stewart
African Ethics, Luís Cordeiro-Rodrigues and
Jonathan O. Chimakonam
African Philosophy, Pascah Mungwini

Angolan Political Thought

Resistance and African Philosophy

Luís Cordeiro-Rodrigues

BLOOMSBURY ACADEMIC
LONDON • NEW YORK • OXFORD • NEW DELHI • SYDNEY

BLOOMSBURY ACADEMIC
Bloomsbury Publishing Plc, 50 Bedford Square, London, WC1B 3DP, UK
Bloomsbury Publishing Inc, 1359 Broadway, 12th Floor, New York, NY 10018, USA
Bloomsbury Publishing Ireland, 29 Earlsfort Terrace, Dublin 2, D02 AY28, Ireland

BLOOMSBURY, BLOOMSBURY ACADEMIC and the Diana logo
are trademarks of Bloomsbury Publishing Plc

First published in Great Britain 2024
This paperback edition published 2025

Copyright © Luís Cordeiro-Rodrigues, 2024

Luís Cordeiro-Rodrigues has asserted his right under the Copyright, Designs and Patents Act, 1988, to be identified as Author of this work.

For legal purposes the Acknowledgements on pp. viii–ix constitute an extension of this copyright page.

Series design by Charlotte Daniels
Cover image: African hieroglyphs with Africa Map, Adinkra symbols raster
(© Monika Hunackova / Alamy Stock Photo)

All rights reserved. No part of this publication may be: i) reproduced or transmitted in any form, electronic or mechanical, including photocopying, recording or by means of any information storage or retrieval system without prior permission in writing from the publishers; or ii) used or reproduced in any way for the training, development or operation of artificial intelligence (AI) technologies, including generative AI technologies. The rights holders expressly reserve this publication from the text and data mining exception as per Article 4(3) of the Digital Single Market Directive (EU) 2019/790.

Bloomsbury Publishing Inc does not have any control over, or responsibility for, any third-party websites referred to or in this book. All internet addresses given in this book were correct at the time of going to press. The author and publisher regret any inconvenience caused if addresses have changed or sites have ceased to exist, but can accept no responsibility for any such changes.

A catalogue record for this book is available from the British Library.

A catalog record for this book is available from the Library of Congress.

ISBN: HB: 978-1-3502-4540-2
PB: 978-1-3502-4544-0
ePDF: 978-1-3502-4541-9
eBook: 978-1-3502-4542-6

Typeset by Newgen KnowledgeWorks Pvt. Ltd., Chennai, India

For product safety related questions contact productsafety@bloomsbury.com.

To find out more about our authors and books visit www.bloomsbury.com and sign up for our newsletters.

My mother taught me that we can resist and overcome the most hurtful injustices and misfortune by choosing to be vulnerable through love and sincerity. She transformed the stones thrown at her into diamond castles. Like a lotus flower, she has always been able to struggle through the mud of life and blossom. This book is about what I hope to learn from you: the ability to dream about the beauty of Spring when the Winter storm is passing; the passion for justice under the cutting sound of indifference; the strength to act with love in the face of acid rain; the endless resilience to remain a poem amid a minefield. If only the whole world were like you.

Contents

Acknowledgements — viii

1. Introduction — 1
2. King Afonso I of Kongo: Slavery, power and a Christian revolution — 15
3. Queen Njinga: Resistance without ideology — 29
4. Lourenço da Silva Mendonça: Towards universalism and abolitionism — 47
5. Kimpa Vita and subversive Christianity: Challenging colonialism from within — 59
6. Creole anti-colonialist and proto-nationalist voices in Angola — 77
7. Mário Pinto de Andrade: Colonialism, African nationalism and liberation — 101
8. Pepetela: Angolanness, African personhood and transformative war — 121
9. Agostinho Neto: Revolution, art and liberation — 143
10. Angolan political thought and the indefatigable heartbeat of African philosophy — 157

Notes — 175
References — 179
Index — 201

Acknowledgements

Many people have been vital in enabling me to complete this book, and I am grateful to them for making my life more meaningful and, thereby, allowing me to engage in philosophical questions that matter to me.

I would like to thank Marko Simendic, Aribiah Attoe, Peter Ditmanson, Yunwoo Song, Bony Schachter, Yuan Wang, Adalberto Fernandes, Ada Agada, Esther Mijers, Jeremy Dell, Naomi Thurston and Motsamai Molefe for reading various parts of my book. I must also extend my thanks to Louise Chapman, who proofread the book.

I must also thank people who gave me invaluable writing and editorial suggestions, even though they have not read the book. This includes Haifang Liu, Matthew Festenstein, Mozaffar Qizilbash, Matt Matravers, Mihaela Mihai, Danny Singh, Monica Mookherjee, Thaddeus Metz, Cornelius Ewuoso and Abraham Olivier.

Work contained in this book has been presented at Hunan University, Zhejiang University, Sun Yat-sen University, Sichuan Normal University, Xiamen University, Peking University and the Guangdong University of Foreign Studies. I wish to thank Demin Duan, Jun Wang, Zhida Luo, Jianhong Chen, Jing Zhu, Zhou Zhenquan, Yanchao Zhang, Jiawei Xu, Kaili Wang, Jisen Liu and Weibing Chen for the invitations to present my research and the very insightful exchanges that arose as a result. Many thanks to the Bloomsbury editorial team and especially Liza Thompson, Katrina Calsado and Lucy Russell for their help.

My colleagues at Hunan University have been extremely supportive and have given me a wonderful environment to work in. I particularly wish to thank Yongming Xiao, Hanmin Zhu, Yuxiang Chen, Renren Chen, Hui Yin, Jun Zhang, Lu Yu, Daichun Yang, Qingliang Li, Beibei Zhan, Ying Zhang, Ji Wang, Xian Chen, Feifei Wang, Wei Li, Huanlin Zhong, Qingjuan Sun, Jordan Martin, Zhibin Chen, Ethan Yee and Hua Wei. Without the support of my assistants, Jiaji Lu, Fangling Li

Acknowledgements ix

and Anjie Zhao, I would not have been able to finish the book on time, and I am deeply thankful for their help.

Some friends outside the academic circle have been crucial for a peaceful environment and a feeling of fulfilment that was necessary for the process of writing. This includes Rafael Fidalgo, Pedro Ribeiro, Rita Grácio, Samir Sulemane, Ricardo Tavares, Catarina Rosa, Francisco Zurita, Simone Roger, Nelinha Ganhão Fernando Ganhão, Rui Lopes Pereira and Pedro Banza.

My deepest gratitude goes to those who fill my life with love: Catarina Banza Cordeiro, Ricardo Cordeiro Rodrigues, Yuxiang Dai and the late Otília Banza and Manuel Cordeiro. These people have helped and inspired me and made me grow.

All views expressed within this book are my own.

This research has been funded by Hunan University's Fundamental Research Funds for the Central Universities, fund number 531118010426. 本文受湖南大学"中央高校基本科研业务费"专项资 金资助 (531118010426).

Parts of Chapters 2 and 5 of this book have been previously published in the following article: 'Christianity in the Kingdom of Kongo and Western Theism: A Comparative Study of the Problem of Evil', *Philosophia Africana*, vol. 21, no. 1, 2022, pp. 13–27 (doi: https://doi.org/10.5325/philafri.21.1.0013). This article is reproduced here with the permission of The Pennsylvania State University Press, and I thank them for providing this permission.

Sections of Chapters 3 and 8 were originally submitted as assignments in 2019/20 at the University of Edinburgh. I thank the university for permission to reproduce this material here.

Introduction

The study of Africa has been politicized throughout the history of philosophy and African Studies (Mudimbe 1990; Eze 2010). Although there are now significant signs of change and increasing interest in African philosophy, African thinkers have been regularly dismissed as irrelevant and unsophisticated since the very beginnings of the discipline (Parris 2015; Mbembe 2017). The history of African philosophy is a history of its exclusion, its constant struggle for survival and its resistance against oppression. Precisely because of this history of exclusion, then, it is a political act to occupy the space of philosophy with the word 'African'. This book is a further occupation of this space that has been captured by an elite. It aims to amplify subversive voices from Africa that have been silenced and to go further than other authors pursuing the same goal. Many philosophers from Africa and of Africa have attempted to demonstrate the relevance of African philosophy for problems in philosophy today. I myself have done so (Cordeiro-Rodrigues; 2021b, 2018; Cordeiro-Rodrigues and Ewuoso 2021a, 2021b; Cordeiro-Rodrigues and Metz 2021). However, in this book, I wish to show that it is possible to write a history of African philosophy that reaches back beyond the twentieth and twenty-first centuries. My aim is to demonstrate that African philosophy is not relevant just today but that it has been relevant for a long time, despite its relevance having been suppressed. This book occupies a history – the history of philosophy – by claiming ownership to what has been stolen: the intellectual brilliance of African thinkers in history. I carry out this task by looking at the history of political thought in Angola, by which I mean the territory that constitutes Angola today as well as that which has been directly relevant to its contemporary territorial borders today. This book starts with an African who was born in the fifteenth century, King Afonso I of Kongo, but whose political relevance only emerged in the sixteenth century, and goes till the end of Portuguese colonialism in the twentieth century with the thought of Agostinho Neto, the first president of independent Angola. This research focus occupies an intellectual space not just because it carries out a history of African philosophy, but also because it focuses on a quite neglected form of African philosophy – namely, the African philosophy that hails from Lusophone Africa. Till now, very little has been done in this field. Most of the research concerns the work of Amílcar Cabral, who is from Guinea-Bissau, and occasionally some work regarding Mozambican intellectuals (Amilcar Cabral 2016, 1969; Rabaka 2009; Macamo 2015; Graness 2015; Martin 2012). The topic is not interesting just because of the absence of research on it. Angolan philosophy brings new ideas to the field of African philosophy and its history, and more specifically, it helps scholars to understand the history of African philosophy and offers innovative views on the concepts of 'African', 'war', 'personhood', among other important notions.

What is African philosophy?

Controversies related to African philosophy arise immediately with the very meaning of the term. What exactly is 'African philosophy'? The debate here mainly concerns the definition of the concepts of 'African' and 'philosophy'. Regarding the former concept, there are two broad positions. On the one hand, several authors take the view that a piece of writing may be considered 'African' only if it is written by an individual from Africa. According to this position, a scholar using concepts such as *ubuntu* and *ukama* but who is of European origin is not doing African philosophy. This is the view of Paulin Hountondji (1996: 66), for instance, who states, 'The essential point here is that we have produced a radically new definition of African philosophy, the criterion now being the geographical origin of the authors rather than an alleged specificity of content.' Notably, however, this definition entails that the writings of a person hailing from Africa who endorses, say, a pro-colonial approach, or who writes exclusively on European philosophy, must be considered African. Thus, oddly, the philosophy of someone doing Rawlsian political thought but with an African identity should be considered African philosophy.

By contrast, others use the term 'African' to designate theories that are grounded in African concepts and methodologies. Jonathan Chimakonam (2019), for instance, argues that it is the use of 'African methodologies' that determines whether a philosophy is African or not. Similarly, as we shall see later, Mário Pinto de Andrade considers that 'African' ought to be used to designate those who favour the liberation of Africa, independently of their ethnicity, geographical origin and so on. Although I favour this approach for its coherence and try to use the term accordingly throughout the present book, this has not always proved possible: different authors employ terms in distinct ways and the overriding need to avoid confusion has meant adopting their terminology where necessary. I try to avoid terms such as 'tribes', 'black' and 'white' due to the negative connotations they have today and try to use 'ethnicity', 'African' and 'European' instead.

There are good moral reasons to prefer the terms 'African' and 'Europeans' over 'black' and 'white' in this context. As Kwesi Tsri has argued, the term 'black' has such a long history of negative meanings that it is difficult to use it in a positive way. And the terms 'black' and 'white' are too closely associated with racial hierarchies (Tsri 2016b). He recommends the terms 'African' and 'European' instead. These terms are better because they avoid some of these problems. However, they are also imperfect, and I am not totally satisfied with using them. After all, the term 'African' has also been used in a negative way at times, and there is indeed a phenomenon that can be classified as 'Afrophobia' (Oro 2012). However, it is still a better term because one of the reasons for using these terms is that the individuals they refer to feel more respected in this way (Hardin 1995). Having said that, terms evolve and gain different meanings, and what may be justified to use now may not be justified to use in the future due to, say, some evolution of the meaning of the term. Take the example of the word 'queer', which was initially a negative term, but today, other things equal, there is nothing wrong in using the expression 'queer theory'. Ultimately, the individuals to whom one is referring are the ones who ought to choose how to be called. The plasticity of the terms needs to be done according to what is best for each situation – while sometimes the term 'African' is better, in some situations, 'black' may be a better term: say if the term 'African' is in some contexts exclusionary and, therefore, 'black' is better.

Having said this, I will sometimes need to use the terms 'black' and 'white' in this book as interchangeable terms with 'African' and 'European' mostly for a matter of conceptual clarity. Particularly, I will need to use the terms 'black' and 'white' when the authors themselves have used it or when I want to emphasize that what is at stake is the colour/racial hierarchy. This is most obvious in the chapters on Pepetela and creole proto-nationalism because racial hierarchies are one of the main themes they address. For instance, Pepetela uses the terms 'African' and 'Europeans', and while I am of course aware that these terms are problematic as ways to designate groups, I nevertheless repeat them for the purposes of making sense of the author's words regarding his positionality in the Angolan setting.[1]

Debates about the meaning of 'philosophy' are also divided into two main camps. Some scholars understand 'philosophy' analytically, as designating that which today is conceived as philosophy – namely an academic discipline with certain stylistic conventions of writing and methods of argumentation, carried out by professionals. Meanwhile, others consider philosophy to be any kind of critical wisdom about the world, including proverbs, myths and so forth. Again, my preference is for the second definition. In fact, the history of philosophy itself reveals its own changeability through time. The thinkers who are usually considered to be the first philosophers – Thales, Anaximander and Anaximenes – did not really write or think about the topics that contemporary philosophers write about, and indeed, they never used the term 'philosophy'.² Likewise, throughout this history, there is no shortage of unconventional texts and styles of writing, as the examples of Nietzsche, Wittgenstein and others demonstrate. Hence, I see no reason to endorse the narrow conception of philosophy. Part of the goal of this book, moreover, is to demonstrate that African philosophy has existed for a long time and that there is no need to limit consideration to contemporary writings.

Angolan thought and the history of African philosophy

The question as to when and where the history of African philosophy begins has perplexed African scholars for some time (Graness 2016). While several authors have, quite rightly, suggested that any such history should begin with Ancient Egypt (Asante 2000; Bernal 1987), this is not often borne out in the existing histories of African philosophy. Indeed, the histories that I am aware of all commence in the twentieth century, with the exception of the importation of a few thinkers from the Middle Ages, such as Zera Yaqob (Kiros 2004). I suspect that the reason for this is that very few Africans' writings from prior to the twentieth century have been preserved, and there has been a reluctance to use imperial sources to write a history of African philosophy. As I shall explain in the following sections, however, there are methodological tools that can be deployed to overcome the challenges of an imperial archive. Another reason why no continuous history of African philosophy exists is that there has been a reluctance to include certain scholars within the tradition. Saint Augustine, for instance, is often included as part of the history of Western philosophy but, as a recent study demonstrates, there are several aspects to his thought that, in fact, originate from Africa. While this by no means entails removing Augustine from the history of Western philosophy, it nevertheless questions his exclusion from African intellectual history (Hua 2022). My aim in this book is to attempt to overcome these forms of prejudice and to be inclusive in a systematic, rigorous and analytical fashion. It will be noticed throughout the book that I eschew such a binarism which separates what is African as diametrically opposed to the outsider. Instead, I prefer an approach that integrates and understands the world in the form of continuity.

Typically, the first steps of African philosophy are traced back to the work of Placide Tempels who reported on the Bantus, in particular his book *Bantu Philosophy* (1945 [2010]). Tempels's book expounds an ontology of the Bantu peoples and is best known for proposing vitality as a key concept of this. A similar work, Alexis Kagame's *The Bantu-Rwandan Philosophy*, appeared in 1956, in many ways pursuing similar ideas. The work of Tempels and Kagame is often classified as 'ethnophilosophy', a term that designates studies of cultural systems of thought. A little later, in 1969, the Kenyan philosopher John Mbiti published *African Religions and Philosophy*, providing a summary of key ideas in African religions. The rise of independence and anti-colonial political movements at around the same time sees the appearance of political writings by revolutionary leaders such as Kwame Nkrumah, Julius Nyerere, Nelson Mandela and Thomas Sankara, among others. These writings are marked by an anti-colonialist standpoint informed by socialist ideas.

This wave of political texts was greatly influenced by pan-Africanist ideologies and so, to a large extent, homogenized African cultures. By contrast, much of the writing that followed, from the 1970s to the 1990s, aimed to explore specific regional differences among African belief systems, including the work of Odera Oruka, Kwasi Wiredu and Kwame Gyekye. Subsequently, from the 2000s onwards emerges what we may call 'professional philosophy'. Many philosophers of this generation – such as Cornelius Ewuoso, Thaddeus Metz, Motsamai Molefe, myself and others – apply African concepts to traditional questions in philosophy, such as the problem of evil, virtue ethics, the justification of harm, abortion and so forth.

Only some of the authors I discuss here are easy to locate in the history of African philosophy as it is usually told. King Afonso I, Queen Njinga, Lourenço da Silva Mendonça, Kimpa Vita, Pedro da

Paixão Franco, António de Assis Júnior and the authors of the book *Voz de Angola Clamando no Deserto* all precede the period that is most often taken to encompass the history of African philosophy – the periods from which these figures date are mostly left blank in histories of the subject. Conversely, Mário Pinto de Andrade, Pepetela and Agostinho Neto fit perfectly well within the tradition of revolutionary writing initiated by Nkrumah and Nyerere. Much writing by Angolan intellectuals has appeared somewhat later than it might otherwise have done owing to the fact that Portuguese colonialists suppressed independence movements for longer than did colonizers elsewhere. Given that the focus of this study is on anti-colonial thought, I do not discuss the thought of Angolan intellectuals who address themes upon which philosophers such as Tempels, Wiredu, Metz and others have focused. However, as regards ethnophilosophy, there exist substantial texts on the cultures of Angola in Portuguese (such as Óscar Bento Ribas, José Martins Vaz and Joaquim Martins) that remain unknown to audiences of African philosophy who mostly read and write in English and French.

Methodological caveats

Several methodological challenges confront the study of the history of African philosophy. First, very few materials are available for consultation. The history of African thought has, in great part, been transmitted orally, and there are very few written sources by Africans dating from before the twentieth century. Ancient Egyptian sources provide one of the few exceptions to this rule, but besides these, there is very little that remains of African intellectual history prior to 1900. Second, many of the sources that are to be found are secondary and written by colonialists. Thus, the interpretation of these sources requires due consideration of the fact that they belong to an imperial archive. Third, as Leo Strauss has pointed out, many of the societies where philosophical texts have been produced are not liberal, and their authors may be routinely subject to censorship (Strauss 1988). Fourth, linguistic barriers exist: many available texts are written in old Portuguese, while relevant sources can also be found in English, Italian, French and Spanish. How then to address these issues?

With regard to matters of language, I have researched texts in Portuguese as well as Italian, French and Spanish and have translated when necessary to English. Most of the relevant sources regarding thinkers of the twentieth century are in contemporary Portuguese, but my efforts to understand sixteenth-to-eighteenth-century thought have required looking at sources in these other languages. Indeed, attending to a multiplicity of sources from different geographical origins and in different languages has been crucial for cross-checking evidence and reports that are frequently colonially biased or else laden with over-optimistic or even utopian perspectives on African history and philosophy.

This brings me to the problem of the imperial archive. There is no doubt that when consulting the works of Capuchin missionaries who wrote about Queen Njinga or Kimpa Vita it is not easy to discern what imperial ideology is and what is likely to be accurate. I would argue that it is not possible to fully resolve this conundrum, given that these are the available sources of evidence, and judgements as to what is likely to be true or not must, to a great extent, remain speculative. In order to properly evaluate this evidence, I have tried to become as informed as possible as to the context and linguistic circumstances of the time and to consider a variety of sources in order to provide the most accurate account possible (please see in each chapter how this was carried out). Although my engagement with these texts is rigorous, my aim is not simply to construct a philosophical anthropology. Sometimes, I employ concepts that may not have been used by a given thinker but that synthesize in a way that will be clearer to the contemporary reader what they are actually trying to say. And often the meaning is not obvious, and following Gadamerian hermeneutics, the whole can only be understood through the parts and the parts through the whole – which sometimes makes my interpretation less obvious, but I do not fail to support contextual evidence combined with interpretation of the text. For instance, in the chapter on the *Voz de Angola Clamando no Deserto*, I affirm that the authors were defending the value of the rule of law – indeed there is evidence, as I shall later demonstrate, that this is the case – despite their never using the term 'rule of law'. For the contemporary reader, however, the term 'rule of law' expresses what the authors themselves phrased in a way more suited to their immediate context and helps contemporary readers also to make more sense of what is being said.

Limited evidence is a problem but not one without a solution. After all, knowledge of the Presocratics is very much grounded in secondary sources and amounts to a great deal of speculation, yet a lack of evidence does not prevent classicists from studying them; instead, they routinely remind us that such enquiries must be carried out with caution (Kenny 2006; Barnes 1982). There is something to learn here from scholars of the classical period: whatever we can say about African philosophy prior to the twentieth century must be affirmed with caution, but we nevertheless can and should try to understand the past. The important thing is that this enterprise is carried out with caution and with the understanding that what we can say is limited and will be highly speculative.

As to censorship, the authors of the *Voz de Angola Clamando no Deserto* clearly faced a great deal – the fact that the first version of the book was anonymized is testament to this. More broadly, I am aware that many of the texts that I consider may hold hidden truths that are not obvious to the casual reader. Accordingly, my analyses seek when necessary to scrutinize texts for that which lies between the lines. I am very much persuaded by Leo Strauss's *Persecution and the Art of Writing* (1988), and where relevant, I employ it as a method of analysis in this study. Strauss allows reading between the lines: 'Reading between the lines is strictly prohibited in all cases where it would be less exact than not doing so' (Strauss 1988: 30). However, this reading is not totally free. According to Strauss, there are certain rules that ought to be respected to read between the lines:

> Only such reading between the lines as starts from an exact consideration of the explicit statements of the author is legitimate. The context in which a statement occurs, and the literary character of the whole work as well as its plan, must be perfectly understood before an interpretation of the statement can reasonably claim to be adequate or even correct. One is not entitled to delete a passage, nor to emend its text, before one has fully considered all reasonable possibilities of understanding the passage as it stands – one of these possibilities being that the passage may be ironic. (Strauss 1988: 30)

In addition, Strauss suggests that contradictions in the text are not necessarily a contradiction in the meaning of the text. The reader should presume that these are authors who have found creative ways to express their views; therefore, the type of text (i.e. whether it is a dialogue, a drama, a treaty, etc.) is relevant to know the real meaning. Sometimes mistakes might be intentional. Indeed, he states that 'The real opinion of an author is not necessarily identical with that which he expresses in the largest number of passages' (Strauss 1988: 30). The method permits less liberty than might appear at first sight. It is not that the reader can totally extrapolate the meaning and it has some limits to it. This becomes clear in my discussion of Assis Júnior: while some authors may wish to suggest that Júnior hid his real thoughts, I argue that there can be no reading between the lines in this case.

My approach combines a Straussian methodology with that of the Cambridge School of intellectual history, which offers a somewhat restrictive framework for the analysis of historical texts. Philosophers such as Quentin Skinner, John Dunn and John Pocock contend that scholars often assume that more can be said about authors from the past than what they have actually said (Dunn and Dunn 1996; Pocock 1989; Skinner 1969). Authors from the Cambridge School contend that there are strict limits to what we can say and strict methodological tools for doing so. This is particularly true in the case of Skinner, who claims that for those scholars interpreting texts, to do so accurately would require the reconstruction of the intentions of the author by following a variety of criteria. Skinner, along with the contextualists he criticizes, maintains the need to look at the religious, political and economic factors, the type of society and the historical period in which the author lived. And, yet, he claims, these factors are insufficient. The contextual approach makes the mistake of reducing authors' writings to a simple mirroring of their respective societies and class positions. Skinner contends that a piece of writing should be understood as a set of utterances formulated during a certain time period with the intention of communicating a certain meaning to a certain group of readers. Consequently, in addition to the context, a historian needs also to understand the intention of the author in writing their work. This intention needs knowledge of the context, but also knowledge of the linguistic tools used at the time, such that it is a requirement for scholars to understand the linguistic context to understand the text. As Skinner states, 'any statement is inescapably the embodiment of a particular intention on a particular occasion, addressed to the solution of a particular problem, and is thus specific to its context in a way that it can only be naive to try to transcend' (Skinner 1969: 88).

So in order to offer a plausible interpretation of what an author may have said, a scholar ought to have knowledge both of the author's socio-historical situation and the linguistic devices that the writer may have used at the time: to know these is to know the writer's intentions. Included in the knowledge of the linguistic uses of the time, for Skinner, is the personality and identity of the author, the people with whom they interacted, the author's audience and the relations between what the author actually said and what they may be able to say. In short, the text should be viewed as an intervention in the intellectual disputes of the time.

Strauss and the Cambridge School might look like an odd couple to put together. Probably, each sees very little merit in the other's approach. But I think there are good reasons to use both methodologies. First of all, I think the differences between these methodologies are highly exaggerated. The proponents of the Cambridge School may find Straussian methodology too flexible, but as I have explained in the previous paragraphs, it allows much less liberty than is usually assumed.

Secondly and relatedly, the vast period covered in this book requires a mixed approach. The lack of material in some cases forces the reader to take instructions from both schools. On the one hand, Angolan thought is unlike early modern English thought, with archival material easily available. On the other, it is not like the Presocratic philosophers and, therefore, allowing us a high degree of speculation.

There is no doubt that a mixed methodological approach will be contested by some. Hard-core contextualists will contest my view on the grounds that I am generalizing too much; hard-core textualists will contend that there is insufficient primary text to do such a work and that I rely too much on contextual evidence. Both criticisms assume, in my view, that the purpose of history is to do some form of historical realism, that is, the idea that the job of historians is to tell exactly what happened. However, historical realism has largely been abandoned in contemporary historiography. No serious historian thinks that it is possible to know exactly what happened. All that can be done is to find narratives which are plausible, and if the use of different methods helps us in this, there is no reason to be rigid about these. While this is not a book that merely tries to endorse a form of historical realism, the claims I make through the book are historically informed.

Outline of the argument

The argument of this book is that Angolan political thought has a long-neglected history and that a close analysis of this history will reveal its deep marking by the experience of oppression. As such, I contend that Angolan political thought is a philosophy of resistance and that, furthermore, it is possible to generalize this argument to African philosophy as a whole. By 'philosophy of resistance' I mean a philosophy driven and constituted by elements that challenge and subvert oppression. This does not necessarily need to be decolonial in the sense of aiming at totally dismantling and replace a colonial order with a more egalitarian system; but it is routinely anti-colonial to the extent that it resists colonialism and tries to subvert it. There is a certain degree of continuity in Angolan political thought if understood as a large array of resistance to colonialism. To demonstrate this, I have selected key figures of Angolan intellectual history for discussion. In Chapter 2, I outline the thought of King Afonso I of Kongo in the fifteenth and sixteenth centuries, while in Chapter 3, I outline the life and thought of Queen Njinga, who lived in the sixteenth and seventeenth centuries, and explain the philosophy underlying her actions. I contend that her philosophy can best be understood as a form of 'resistance without ideology'. Chapter 4 moves on to the seventeenth century to examine Lourenço da Silva Mendonça's arguments against slavery, while Chapter 5 takes as its subject Kimpa Vita, a key figure of the Kingdom of Kongo in the seventeenth and eighteenth centuries. I argue that Kimpa's life and actions suggest that she defended a form of subversive Christianity as a means to resist colonialism.

The end of the nineteenth century and the beginning of the twentieth is when proto-nationalism began its rise in Angola. In Chapter 6, I outline the views of several Creole proto-nationalists who espoused a timid anti-colonialism. Chapters 7, 8 and 9 then focus on Angolan political thinkers of the twentieth century. Chapter 7 outlines the philosophy of Mário Pinto de Andrade, an Angolan pan-African nationalist and progenitor of the nationalist movement in Angola. In Chapter 8, I explore the thought of Pepetela and argue that his theories of war, personhood and transformation were very much informed by his experience as a guerrilla fighter in Angola. Chapter 9 focuses on Agostinho Neto's intellectual development as the first president of postcolonial Angola, outlining his theories of military ethics, poetry and colonialism. Finally, Chapter 10 makes the argument that the aspects of Angolan political thought that I have explored may be generalized to African philosophy as a whole and concludes by exploring the relevance of African philosophy for today's political struggles.

2

King Afonso I of Kongo: Slavery, power and a Christian revolution

Introduction

The people of the Kongo migrated to West Central Africa around the fifth century (Fish and Fish 2002). However, the formation of the Kingdom of Kongo did not begin until the end of the thirteenth century, at which time the ancestors of Kongo's royal family ('*Ntinu Wene*', which, according to John Thornton, translates as 'King of the Kingdom') crossed the Congo River and engaged in a war, conquering Mpemba Kasi (Thornton 2020). The first record of Portuguese contact with western Central Africa came in 1483, when Diogo Cão reached the mouth of the Congo River (Fish and Fish 2002). According to these first records, western Central Africa was composed of small-scale states governed by a central authority (Thornton 2020). The Kongo Kingdom was, in fact, one of the largest such states in sub-Saharan Africa at the time. It is estimated that it encompassed about 115,000 square miles (Strauss 1988: 30). The history of the Kingdom of Kongo is marked by the treacherous politics of the royal elite and the various wars resulting from it (Thornton 1983).

The first five rulers of the Kingdom of Kongo were Lukeni lua Nimi (1390–1420), Nanga of Kongo (1420–35), Niaza of Kongo (1435–50), Nkuwu a Ntinu of Kongo (1450–70) and João I Nzinga a Nkuwu (1470–1506). Very little is known from their reigns, however, and most of what is known about João I Nzinga a Nkuwu comes from his son and successor (the protagonist of this chapter), Afonso I Mvemba a Nzinga (1506–42), who wrote letters to the Portuguese kings (Thornton

1998, 2020). Although the Christianization of the Kingdom of Kongo had begun earlier and Afonso I's father had adopted a Christian name, it was with Afonso I that Christianity spread widely throughout the Kingdom of Kongo (Heywood 2019).

King Afonso I is known by many names, including Mvemba a Nzinga, Nzinga Mbemba, Funsu Nzinga Mvemba and Dom Afonso. He was the sixth ruler of the Kingdom of Kongo from the Lukeni kanda dynasty. He was born with the name Mvemba a Nzinga and was the son of King Nzinga a Nkuwu, also known as João I of Kongo (officially the first Christian king of the Kingdom of Kongo). Afonso I's father ruled the capital M'banza Kongo in 1491, which is when he encountered the Portuguese. Afonso I was converted to Christianity, whereupon he was baptized and thus appropriated his Christian name. He studied with the Portuguese priests, saying that he had an avid interest in Christian doctrine. The letters of Afonso I of Kongo are one of the primary sources that detail the reality of Kongo both before and during Afonso's reign. In addition to giving an inside view of the reality of Kongo in the fifteenth and sixteenth centuries, his letters can also be read as putting forth a set of political statements and ideas (Thornton 2020, 1983, 1981; Jordan 1999; Balandier 1968).

The succession to the throne

At the time of Afonso I, the Kingdom of Kongo's political system was elective and not hereditary, such that, although Afonso I did have an advantage, he was not guaranteed the throne; he had to compete for it with his half-brother, Mpanzu, a Nzinga. Afonso's mother, Leonor Nzinga a Nzala, realized the threat posed by such competition and recommended that he move quickly to the capital city to ensure the attainment of the throne. His mother kept the death of João I a secret from Afonso, thus allowing him to mobilize everyone and to return to the capital Mbanza Kongo to assume power. The death of King João I was therefore announced only when Afonso was already in the kingdom with an army. Afonso became king in 1509 and reigned until 1542 or 1543 (Thornton 2020, 1981; Lagamma 2015; Balandier 1968). The succession was already marked by an ideological Christian vernacular. Even King Afonso I's own description of the final years of his father's reign signals the importance of Christianity to his belief system (Thornton 2020, 1981; Afonso, Jadin and Dicorato 1974; Balandier 1968; Brásio 1952). King Afonso contended that in the last years of his father's reign, an anti-Christian faction led by his half-brother Mpanzu a Nzinga (whose nickname, 'Mpanzu a Kitemu' means 'the furious') emerged. His half-brother did not support Christianity and headed a faction of traditionalists. Afonso I succeeded, and how he characterized his half-brother's attempt at the throne and subsequent defeat are revealing of the overarching ideas at the time. Notably, he accused his half-brother of creating an anti-Christian faction (Jordan 1999; Thornton 1981; Afonso, Jadin and Dicorato 1974; Brásio 1952). Furthermore, in the letters, the emphasis on the fact that Mpanzu a Nzinga was his half-brother signals that Afonso I was aware of European forms of succession and in particular the idea that half-brothers were not entitled to hereditary succession.

With Leonor's support, King Afonso I brought his supporters and weapons into the city disguised as food. Mpanzu a Nzinga did not expect this, but he was nonetheless able to mobilize an army. Afonso I won the ensuing battle, and as detailed in his letters, he described the victory as a miracle performed by the Virgin Mary and Saint James the Greater, contending that their ghosts appeared to Mpanzu a Nzinga and his men and frightened them into abandoning the battle. It is likely that Afonso I executed all his opponents after the war, including his brother (Thornton 1999; Afonso, Jadin and Dicorato 1974; Balandier 1968).

After winning the throne, Afonso I of Kongo felt secure in his position. Indeed, having defeated his main rival, Afonso I then began distributing power to his close relatives, thereby placing his most trusted allies in control of significant provinces. But this does not mean, of course, that his reign was peaceful. He attempted to expand his power throughout the kingdom and neighbouring areas, engaging in several wars, but he was also subjected to many assassination attempts (including from his Portuguese allies). But with his traditionalist rivals eliminated, Christianity cemented itself as the main religion in the Kingdom of Kongo (Thornton 2020).

By 1526, Afonso I's sons were in charge of all the key provinces. The exception to this was Mbata, where one of his enemies, Dom Jorge, was in power. In one of his letters, Afonso I requests King Manuel I of Portugal to unseat this rebel and replace him with his close relative, the Mwene lord of Mbata. The resistance by Dom Jorge was both religious and political. Indeed, when Afonso requested military support, he identified these enemies as anti-Christian (Thornton 2020; Lagamma 2015; Jordan 1999; Balandier 1968).

The easy victory Afonso I had over his brother led him to believe that he had a holy mission. Clearly, he found that one of the sources of legitimacy for his reign was his link to Christianity, an insight that can be seen in his use of self-descriptive titles in his letters. For instance, in a letter to Pope Paul III from 1535, he described himself as follows: 'Dom Affonso by the grace of God, King of Comguo, Jbu[m]go and Cacomgo, Emgoyo, above and below the nzary [River Congo], Lord of the Ambu[m]dos, and Amgolla, of Quisyma and Musuru, of Matamba, and Muyullu, and of Musucu, and the Amzicos and of the conquest of Pamzualu[m] bu etc.' (Thornton 2018: 18).[1]

This letter confirms an important idea about legitimacy for Afonso I: he saw Christianity as central to the victory and legitimacy of his power. The logic follows: he is king by divine rule because he fought the anti-Christians and won by means of a miracle. The ideological aspect is overwhelmingly present in the justification of his power in the kingdom, not just for people in the Kingdom of Kongo but also – and especially – for international allies (Balandier 1968).

King Afonso I of Kongo on slavery

There are several disputes about the accuracy of the historical descriptions of the relationships between the Kingdom of Kongo and the Portuguese in the sixteenth century. Historians such as James Duffy and Basil Davidson contend that the Kingdom of Kongo was developed such that when the Portuguese arrived they made an alliance with the ruler at the time, King Nzinga a Nkuwu (baptized as João I in 1491) (Davidson 1980; Duffy 1961).

Initially, the relationship was mutually beneficial. The Portuguese furnished the Kingdom of Kongo with technological and military resources that allowed the rulers to consolidate their power both within the kingdom itself and against their rival neighbours (Thornton 2020; Thornton 1999). In exchange, the Portuguese gained a significant advantage in the slave trade. Part of the success of this war was attributable to the support of the Portuguese, who gave Afonso I crossbows and muskets, sophisticated weaponry for the time (Thornton 1999). In the beginning, these weapons were used by the Portuguese mercenaries helping the Kingdom of Kongo, but the use of mercenaries was not adequate for Afonso I (Afonso, Jadin and Dicorato 1974; Brásio 1952), who complained to the king of Portugal that the mercenaries were incompetent cowards. The mercenaries were important and valuable for the goals of Afonso I, but they simply did not offer enough to allow Afonso I to deliver on his ambition. Hence, Afonso I wanted to acquire weapons as early as 1510 to avoid revolts inside the Kingdom of Kongo and also to deter its prominent rival neighbour from the South, the Kingdom of Ndongo (Afonso, Jadin and Dicorato 1974; Brásio 1952).

The change from a beneficial to a problematic relationship with Portugal is clear from Afonso I's letters, where in one of them he contends,

> Each day, the traders are kidnapping our people – children of this country, sons of our nobles and vassals, even people of our own family. This corruption and depravity are so widespread that our land is entirely depopulated. We need only priests and schoolteachers in this kingdom, and no merchandise, unless it is wine and flour for Mass. It is our wish that this Kingdom not be a place for the trade or transport of slaves. Many of our subjects eagerly lust after Portuguese merchandise that your subjects have brought into our domains. To satisfy this

inordinate appetite, they seize many of our black free subjects. ... They sell them. After having taken these prisoners [to the coast] secretly or at night. ... As soon as the captives are in the hands of white men they are branded with a red-hot iron. (Hilliard 1997: 357)

Some scholars and activists interpret the thought of Afonso I through the lens of human rights: someone who was opposed to slavery and keen to resist the Portuguese demands for slavery (Snethen 2009). This is probably false, for Afonso I's endorsement of slavery was not motivated as a lesser evil to sustain the economy of the Kingdom of Kongo as some scholars have suggested. At a certain point, Portugal and the Kingdom of Kongo agreed to give Afonso I a monopoly on all trade conducted on the African coast he ruled over, giving him extraordinary power and the possibility of establishing an independent and sovereign kingdom (Thornton 1981; Afonso, Jadin and Dicorato 1974; Brásio 1952). However, the Portuguese discovered that the Kwanza River could be navigated to the interior of the land where enslaved people could be captured. There they made connections with the ruler of Ndongo, Ngola Kiluanje, and began trading with him. This alliance between the Ndongo and the Portuguese mission in 1520 significantly threatened Afonso I's monopoly. Thus, Afonso I's main concern was his rights in Ambundu, where the Portuguese carried out clandestine trade. His letters are primarily complaints about the violation of this agreement. His main targets were Fernão de Melo's clients from São Tomé and António Carneiro from Principe, members of the royal household. His overriding complaint was that there were abuses of these people regarding the slave trade (Thornton 1981; Afonso, Jadin and Dicorato 1974; Brásio 1952).

In this regard, it is unlikely that Afonso I's primary concern was the welfare of fellow Africans who were enslaved. Slavery had existed in the Kingdom of Kongo before the arrival of the Portuguese, and as alluded to above, King Afonso I used it for his political gain.[2] His foremost concern was the loss of his monopolistic power over the several forms of trade that were conceded to him in agreement with Portugal. This led him to request the reorganization and replacement of the foreign representatives in the Kingdom of Kongo, threatening to expel all the Portuguese from his kingdom. According to Thornton, however, the 'all' in his letters refers only 'to include just the primary subjects of the king of Portugal, and meant only royal agents or clients of captains on São Tomé or Principe. Loyal Portuguese clients would no doubt be unaffected and remain in their posts' (Thornton 1981: 103).

It would be remiss, however, not to recognize that Afonso I had other concerns. There were many displays of disrespect and mistreatment engaged in by the Portuguese at the time. Also, the traditional forms of slavery from the Kongo were different from the ones imposed by the Portuguese. Moreover, it is true that at some point, the Portuguese monarchy lost control over those in the overseas territories, especially in Kongo and São Tomé. King Afonso I was also concerned about the violent behaviour of the Portuguese in trade, which included violating laws that protected the nobility of the Kingdom of Kongo. A Kongolese code prohibited the enslavement of some people, including nobles, but the Portuguese enslavers, buoyed by greed, broke this prohibition. As a response, Afonso I created a committee to inspect the slave trade. Moreover, he was concerned about the depopulation of his kingdom, for with the increase in the slave trade, the population had significantly decreased. Therefore, King Afonso I was not really concerned about opposing slavery *per se*, concentrating instead on fighting the quantities of slavery, nobles' enslavement and all deregulated forms of exchange undermining his monopoly (Encyclopaedia Britannica 2022; Thornton 2020; Lagamma 2015; Jordan 1999).

King Afonso I's Christian revolution

The Christian revolution in the sixteenth century was a critical event in the Kingdom of Kongo (Randles 2002). Afonso I waged several wars on the grounds of spreading the Christian faith and suppressing non-Christian factions, such that it is fair to say that he is one of the leading actors in spreading Christianity (as well as Portuguese culture) in the Kingdom of

Kongo (Thornton 2020). In addition to the religious wars he waged during his reign, he also created a network of Christian schools throughout the country, thereby allowing Christian beliefs to spread. He also built churches, institutionalized the Christian calendar and gave Christian titles to the kingdom's elites (e.g. Duke and Marquis). He also engaged in a variety of symbolic acts to instantiate Christianity as the main religion of the Kongo: the Kongolese nobles were baptized, Portuguese (Christian) names, titles, coats of arms and clothing were adopted and Christian festivals were celebrated (Thornton 2020, 1998; Heywood 2019).

Afonso I made prominent efforts to spread the Christian faith in the Kingdom of Kongo through education, and he actively participated in the teaching, and promoted the learning, of Christianity. According to Rui de Aguiarhe – the Portuguese royal chaplain who assisted him – Afonso I avidly studied theological textbooks. He aimed to expand the educated Christian elite, sending them to Portugal to study. Indeed, education in Christianity by the elites was crucial for Afonso I. He sent several nobles to Portugal (especially Lisbon) to learn about Christianity and the Portuguese social structure. Consequently, literacy became widespread among the Kongo elite, who, upon their return, continued the process of evangelization, opening schools to teach Christianity. Later, the educated elite published the Kikongo catechisms of 1557 and 1624 (Thornton 2020).

It is remarkable that the Kongolese nobility adopted Christianity so quickly. Thornton contends that part of the reason for this was that there were several economic and social structures shared both by the Kingdom of Kongo and European Christian kingdoms (Thornton 1981). Many of the religious beliefs in Kongo were similar to Christianity, such as the belief in a high God who is the creator (Tempels 2010; Lagamma 2015; Jordan 1999). Furthermore, the translations of the Christian doctrine into the local language of Kikongo were made equivalent to Kongo's cosmology. Emma George Ross observes that critical terms such as 'spirit', 'god' and 'holy' were carefully translated exactly for this purpose. Christianity was, therefore, not generally perceived as a different religion but simply as a branch of existing cosmologies (Ross 2002).

Several repressive measures were implemented to enforce Christianity. A law was passed stating that anyone possessing idols would be punished by death. But the measure was too harsh, and Afonso I had to revoke it later. Although people were still persecuted, the punishment was not as severe. Afonso I ordered that non-Christian religious symbols, buildings and infrastructure throughout the kingdom be destroyed and replaced by Christian churches. The endorsement of Christianity also served to increase participation in the international community and foster international relations, such as with the Portuguese Crown and the Vatican. Therefore, it was a link with a much larger world, not just the politics of the Kingdom of Kongo, and this is partly why Afonso I sent many of the nobles' children to study in Europe. In 1513, Afonso I sent an ambassador to Europe to pay homage to the Pope, which was the conventional way to become officially recognized as a Christian state. He also sent his son Henrique to Europe to have him ordained as Bishop, which found success in 1518. The goal was to make the church of the Kingdom of Kongo self-sufficient and independent from Portugal, but Afonso I failed to achieve this. The Portuguese interests interfered significantly because they wanted to rule over the Kongo's church. In 1534, the Pope made the colony of São Tomé an episcopal see, and the Kingdom of Kongo church became one of its branches (Thornton 2020, 1981; Thornton 2018; Randles 2002; Afonso, Jadin, and Dicorato 1974; Balandier 1968).

Afro-Christianity in the Kingdom of Kongo

How did Christianity look like in the Kingdom of Kongo? As briefly explained above, the formation of the Kingdom of Kongo dates back to the thirteenth century. Christianity adapted to the local conditions and developed some characteristics influenced by traditional African religions. For example, the Kongolese did not usually use the Portuguese word 'Deus' to refer to God. Instead, they referred to God in Kikongo, the language of the Kingdom of Kongo. Although the Kongolese believed in a God who shared many characteristics of the Catholic God (overall creator, supreme being, necessary being), they also retained local beliefs about God. For example, it is unlikely that they thought that this God was morally perfect and omnipotent. Regarding the attribute of omnipotence, African gods routinely have limited power to intervene in the world: they cannot reach everywhere even though they can reach farther than any other being.

Moreover, it is routinely the case in African religions that gods are understood as morally superior – wise, virtuous and morally better than all others – but not perfect (Bewaji 1998). In traditional African religions, God is typically seen as the most powerful being but not omnipotent and possessing the best moral character and the highest moral virtue but not morally perfect (Oladipo 2004). This is the case, for example, in the Yoruba religion. Indeed, as Olusegun Oladipo maintains, it is unlikely that Olódùmarè is considered all-powerful (Oladipo 2004). Likewise, referring to the Akan conception of God, Kwasi Wiredu suggests that he is not infinite: 'He together with the world constitutes the Spatio-temporal "totality" of existence … The notion of creation out of nothing does not even make sense in the Akan language' (Wiredu 1998: 29). Indeed, some African scholars do not agree that God is imperfect and limited (Gyekye 1995).

Several categories of beings are believed to exist in the African context, specifically in the Kongolese context. In addition to God, traditional Kongolese believe in the morally good and the morally bad living dead (Jordan 1999). There is a clear hierarchy among these beings. God is above all in terms of moral status, and below him are, in descending order, the good living dead, humans, the bad living dead, nonhuman animals and other things in nature. Note that ranking the various categories of beings in terms of power is not the same as ranking them in terms of moral importance. In terms of power, the evil living dead share the same rank as the good living dead (Cordeiro-Rodrigues 2021). In short, the living dead, good or evil, have strong powers, can intervene in the world and, thus, are more powerful than humans. But the evil living dead have a lower moral status than the morally good living dead and humans because moral status depends on an entity's capacity for social harmony. One interesting difference between Kongolese Catholics and their Western counterparts is that Nzambi a Mpungu is not usually engaged with the world. It is, indeed, believed that, after he created the world, he let it take its course and rarely intervened. He knows what is happening in the world and can change the course of events.

Nonetheless, he is generally not interested in doing so (Jordan 1999). The Kongolese hold a panentheistic cosmology according to which God is a force that is present in everything. Nzambi a Mpungu animates the natural occurrences of the world by being present in everything that exists (Jordan 1999). God is a force that runs through all objects, giving them life. The point is a constant flux, making reality dynamic, and if God withdraws it, everything disappears (Cordeiro-Rodrigues 2021).

Because God is a conscious force, it is possible to affirm that this view is pan-psychist – that is, there is consciousness in all objects (Agada 2019). So another important difference between western Christianity and Kongolese Christianity is that the latter embraces a form of panentheism according to which God and the world are distinct but highly interrelated: God is in the world, but not everything that exists is incorporated in the universe because God transcends it. The view is like pantheism but differs in that it does not hold that God is everything but only in everything, thereby maintaining that the identities of God and the world are distinct. Thus, for the Kongolese, there is a transcendent reality that is only God and not part of the world. For the Kongolese, God is not everything that exists but is in everything that exists as a force that gives vitality to all existence (Cordeiro-Rodrigues 2021). In the African context, panentheism is illustrated by the fact that God is sometimes characterized in anthropomorphic ways and usually described as having a body and that parts of the world are parts of this body. For example, the reason for lighting incense would be that this is the best way to feel the smell of God – both metaphorically and literally. These are parts where God is present and can free his scent, and thereby, his presence can be felt. Indeed, most rituals are carried out with the elements of nature precisely because to be in touch with these elements is to experience God in a more vivid and meaningful way (Mbiti 1990).

I can now summarize the significant differences between Kongolese Christianity and the mainstream Western theistic view. First, according to Western theism, God is morally perfect and omnipotent. In contrast, for Kongolese Catholics, God is not morally perfect but only morally better than all others. Second, in anticipation of what will be spelt out in more detail below, it is possible to say that God allows evil to take place in the mainstream Western theistic view, in which evil is outside God. In contrast, the Kongolese God embodies evil; evil, being a part of God, is suffered by God. Third, in the Kongolese case, God generally abstains from intervening in the world even though he is in everything in the world, something that does not hold in the Western theistic case.

The last point – about God's intervention in the world – raises the question, 'If God does not usually intervene in the world, are there any nonhuman entities that do?' African cosmology also accords great importance to nonhuman entities other than God. It is often understood that because God does not intervene much in the world, other nonhuman entities usually interact with humans – namely, the living dead. The living dead are those individuals from previous generations who have passed away but continue living on the earth, usually in areas close to their communities like forests (Metz and Molefe 2021). These living dead are the actual beings who routinely interact with humans (Metz and Molefe 2021). Some of them are morally good, and others are ethically bad. This is the case not only among the Kongolese, but also other Africans, such as the Akan, the Yoruba and the Igbo (Mbiti 1990). In the Kingdom of Kongo, God was expected to be one who could, through his emissaries, bring harmony amidst an endless civil war. And the evils brought by the Portuguese missionaries were precisely understood as forms of disharmony.

King Afonso I's political thought

There is little that can be said about King Afonso I's thought. Just like when studying Presocratics of whom we have little information, we can only speculate and affirm a little. Likewise, given the little information about King Afonso I, we are quite limited in what we can say. Historians have disagreed about King Afonso I's sincerity regarding his Christian beliefs. It is possible that he was a devoted Christian, but it is also possible that he was just very pragmatic, seeing in Christianity an ideology that could serve his ambitions for power. Independently of what his true religious beliefs and intentions were, however, it is certain that he saw the importance of legitimizing actions through ideology. Christianity played the role of justifying, both to the elites and the rest of the population, why King Afonso I was a legitimate king and why his actions were valid. Likewise, Christianity was instrumental in solidifying Afonso I as an important ally and collaborator of Portugal. He understood perfectly well the importance of ideology in politics; ideology is the means through which political goals can be achieved because it provides an ethos that enables political action to take place. This, in turn, was used to forward international relations, which King Afonso I thought were key for the stability of his kingdom and the spread of his power.

Education plays an important role too, for it is through education that people are acquainted with the ideology that will enable political action. King Afonso I emphasized the translation, reading and study of religious texts precisely because he viewed education as laying the foundation for everything else. This was especially relevant among the elites who needed to be aware of the ideology to know how to act. Moreover, this form of education was mostly grounded in religion and for religion (i.e. with the purpose of learning religion), and other elements of education were simply instrumental to this overarching study of religion.

Conclusion

This chapter studied the thought of King Afonso I of Kongo. It is clear from what has been argued that Christianity is key to understanding his thought. However, from King Afonso I's ideas, it is possible to understand that the form of Christianity was highly adapted to the circumstances and contexts of the time because he was trying, in this way, to Africanize some ideas with the aim of making it more attractive to local elites. But we also understand an idea which will become clearer throughout this book – namely, that the thought of *some* African leaders is sometimes not decolonial and is, in fact, complicit with European colonialism. As will be noticed later, sometimes this complicity is a form of avoiding greater evils, but other times, it is explored for the benefit of an elite with sacrifices from those who were worse off.

3

Queen Njinga: Resistance without ideology

Introduction

Queen Njinga/Nzinga[1] is undoubtedly one of the most important figures in the history of Angola and anti-colonial resistance, and yet she is not the unequivocal figure that one would perhaps expect. Many discourses on Queen Njinga are framed by a particular ideology that blurs the meaning of the historical evidence. On the one hand, conservative and colonial nostalgic readings mischaracterize her as cruel and portray her as the main perpetrator of the slave trade. Routinely, this negative image is used by apologists for colonialism to suggest that the Portuguese are not responsible for the atrocities committed in Africa. Indeed, as Alberto Oliveira Pinto shows in his analysis of Portuguese colonial literature, to call someone 'Njinga' or to suggest that one is related to her was often used as an insult (Pinto 2016). For instance, Manuel Maria du Bocage, the leading poet of the Romantic period in Portugal, used expressions such as 'the grandson of Queen Njinga' as an insult (Bocage 1870).

On the other hand, some readings overpraise Queen Njinga. One example is a recent UNESCO publication, in which Queen Njinga is portrayed as a liberator of the Africans (UNESCO 2014). Another example can be found in the writings of anti-colonialists, especially in the 1960s and 1970s, who often portray Queen Njinga as a saviour of the Angolan people (Mata 2012a; Centro de Estudos Angolanos Grupo de Trabalho História e Etnologia 1965). In 2003, a statue of Queen Njinga was even placed in the centre of Luanda, and since 1975, many streets in Angola have been named after her (Pinto 2016). Queen Njinga is so highly praised in anti-colonial circles that even the two main political parties of Angola (UNITA and MPLA), which disagree on almost everything, agree on the status of Queen Njinga as a national hero (Thornton 1991).

However, historical evidence calls for a more neutral approach: Queen Njinga resisted Portuguese colonialism and was an avid fighter who had some impressive achievements, almost beyond compare. But she was not exactly an African liberator because she did sometimes contribute to and collaborate with the slave trade and, on some occasions, acted ruthlessly towards her people. Furthermore, she routinely changed sides because her main aim went beyond liberating people; she quickly sided with the Portuguese, both as a strategy to aid her community and, most importantly, to retain power. This, of course, does not mean that her political philosophy is not relevant to anti-colonialism; it is relevant to the extent that it can provide a strategic approach to dealing with colonial and neocolonial settings. In this chapter, I shall defend the thesis that Queen Njinga mastered the *art of disobedience* and offered a way to oppose Portuguese colonialism, which can be characterized as resistance without ideology (i.e. a more strategic, pragmatic struggle that is not based on moral values). Given the historical circumstances, she continued a tradition of opposing colonial rule, but in a rather different way than before.

To progress this argument, I have divided this chapter into the following sections. In the first section, I outline the sociopolitical setting in which Queen Njinga was born, exploring some features of the Mbundu and the Kingdom of Ndongo. The next two sections describe Queen Njinga's life: the second section focuses on how she appeared on the political scene to become a relevant political actor; the third section explores the nature of her reign and the struggles that she had to face. The fourth section synthesizes Queen Njinga's political philosophy. Finally, the last section attempts to answer some possible objections to my interpretation of Queen Njinga's political theory.

The Kingdom of Ndongo: Queen Njinga's sociopolitical setting

According to historical records, the first Europeans arrived in central Africa in 1483 (Heywood 2019), with the Portuguese arriving in the Kingdom of Ndongo around 1560 (Thornton 1991). The Kingdom of Ndongo was not yet the largest state in terms of land mass in central Africa when the Portuguese arrived, but rather was the second largest, after the Kingdom of Kongo (Pantoja 2000, 2020; Thornton 1991; Miller 1975, 1976). Indeed, the Kingdom of Ndongo was only about one-third of the size of the Kingdom of Kongo (Heywood 2019; Centro de Estudos Angolanos Grupo de Trabalho História e Etnologia 1965). More precisely, the Ndongo Kingdom corresponds to the areas designated in Angola today as Kwanza North, Kwanza South, Malange, and Bengo (Heywood 2019; Pinto 2016). These two kingdoms (Kongo and Ndongo) were political enemies, and many of the wars and alliances that occurred with the Portuguese were also related to the pursuit of regional hegemony and competition between kingdoms.

The people of Ndongo were called the Mbundu; however, the meaning of the term 'Mbundu' is contested and requires clarification (Pantoja 2000, 2020; Miller 1975, 1976). The Mbundu often considered themselves a larger group distributed among other kingdoms. Ethnographers routinely consider the Mbundu to be an ethnically distinct group from the Kongo (who were northerners in relation to the Ndongo), the Lunda and the Lwena (who were in the east of Ndongo), and the Ovimbundu (in the south of Ndongo). This distinction is based on the linguistic patterns at the time, and it identifies the Mbundu with Kimbundu speakers, while separating them from Kikongo, Cokwe and Umbundu speakers. The distinction, however, is not clear-cut, because there is evidence of mixed vocabularies (e.g. Kikongo mixed with Kimbundu) (Miller 1976).

Nonetheless, following other scholars of West Central Africa, I refer to the Mbundu as those who are Kimbundu speakers, albeit those who were potentially speaking dialects mixed with other local languages (Pantoja 2020 2020; Miller 1976). It is important to also note that although there is a degree of commonality, the beliefs and value systems of those placed under the 'Mbundu' predication were somewhat heterogeneous. Furthermore, cultural similarities with other groups, such as the Imbangala, are also at stake (Miller 1976, 1972).

The people of Ndongo had an economy that heavily relied on agriculture and metal working (Fish and Fish 2002). But the key to their economy was slaveholding and slave trading (Heywood 2019). The slave trade was highly regulated, and enslaved people were often acquired in military excursions or as the result of punishment for crimes (Cavazzi 1965). In addition, there was a tax system stipulating that subordinates had to pay the king. The king's official residence was in the capital of the Kingdom of Ndongo, Kabasa, where many important officials also lived. Some key government officials at the time were the *tendala*, the king's principal advisor and head of the military, and the *makota*, who were also advisers to the king but occupied a lower level than the *tendala*. There were three principal kinds of *makota*: the *mwene lumbo*, the *mwene kudya* and the *mwene misete*. The first was responsible for managing the king's household, the second for regulating taxation and the third for managing the reliquaries from previous royalty (Heywood 2019; Cavazzi 1965).

The value system of the Kingdom of Ndongo was somewhat hierarchical, but its format changed throughout the centuries, particularly in response to the arrival of the Portuguese (Thornton 1991). Kings had a special status and were considered almost as deities: they were believed to have supernatural powers, such as omniscient knowledge and the power to fertilize the land and control the rain (Heywood 2019; Cavazzi 1965). With the coming of the Portuguese and disputes over slave trade routes, the Kingdom of Ndongo became more centralized. In the early sixteenth century, the king ruled along with the *makota*, who probably had the right to elect or veto the ruler as well as their own territorial rights. In the late sixteenth and early seventeenth centuries, although the *makota* still had some influence, they began to lose power, which became increasingly concentrated in the hands of the ruler (Thornton 1991).

Before the ascension of Queen Njinga, the Kingdom of Ndongo was mainly ruled by men. And even though some stories of origin mention a queen (Horo ria Ngola), they say that she was overthrown by wickedness and/or surrendered herself voluntarily to male power (Thornton 2020). This is not to say that women did not have an important role to play in the society of the Kingdom of Ndongo; some women did have important roles, but just not as queens. For instance, women from the elite – as Queen Njinga was – participated in political and social events, although not entirely as equals (Thornton 2020; Heywood 2019), while other women had roles in food collection (Pantoja 2020, 2000).

The founder of the Kingdom of Ndongo was Ngola Kiluanje kia Samba (who reigned between 1515 and 1556). Ngola Kiluanje kia Samba's strategy was to maintain internal cohesion and peace while expanding the kingdom's borders through military excursions in neighbouring states, primarily to protect his territory from the Kingdom of Kongo. He attempted to make alliances with the Portuguese and even sent two ambassadors, so as to compete with the Kingdom of Kongo, but his attempts failed. His successor, Ndambi a Ngola (who reigned between 1556 and 1561) had a reputation for being more brutal. One story says that he became king because of a hellish incursion against his siblings. He had three siblings, two of whom he killed, and the other escaped death only because he fled. Ndambi a Ngola was very suspicious of the Portuguese, for although he initially allowed Portuguese visitors into the capital Kabaza, he quickly changed his mind (Heywood 2019). His successor, Ngola Kiluanje Kia Ndambi (who reigned between 1561 and 1575) was somewhat aggressive towards the Portuguese, as he suspected that they intended to spy on the land, so as to conquer it. The first official mission from Portugal occurred in 1560, led by Paulo Dias de Novais, accompanied by Jesuits, traders and dignitaries. Dias de Novais became the first Portuguese governor of Angola and one of the main enemies of the Kingdom of Ndongo. Ngola Kiluanje Kia Ndambi arrested Dias de Novais in 1565/1566 and killed several Portuguese people (Heywood 2019; Pinto 2016; Cadornega 1681).

Ngola Kilombo kia Kasenda (Queen Njinga's grandfather) reigned between 1575 and 1592, the same period as the return of the Portuguese to the Kingdom of Ndongo. Although he was not a direct descendent with the right to the throne, he succeeded in carrying out a coup (Heywood 2019). Ngola Kilombo kia Kasenda was suspicious of the Portuguese intentions to expand but first attempted diplomatic means of resolution, sending ambassadors to Luanda. He had been apprehensive about the alliance between the Kingdom of the Kongo and the Portuguese from 1565 to 1574, which threatened his territory. His diplomacy was short-lived, as he eventually resorted to waging war by killing forty Portuguese. He made some alliances with the surrounding kingdoms, but despite initially being successful, these alliances quickly broke down (Heywood 2019; Pinto 2016; Cadornega 1681). There was a segregation of states, and some groups wanted to cooperate with the Portuguese to benefit from the slave trade. Several *sobas* (the name given to local rulers) became dissenters and switched allegiances (Centro de Estudos Angolanos Grupo de Trabalho História e Etnologia 1965). This was particularly the case for those *sobas* from the Hari lineage, who perceived themselves as the rightful inheritors of the Ndongo's throne on account of their claim as descendants of one of Ngola Kiluanje kia Samba's concubines. These switches of allegiances led to the erosion of the tax system, which as explained above, was one of the primary economic sources in the Kingdom of Ndongo (Heywood 2019; Pinto 2016). The Portuguese succeeded in the war and made significant advances throughout the 1580s.

Mbande a Ngola (who reigned from 1592 to 1617) inherited a destroyed, fractured kingdom replete with deep cultural and economic crises. Thus, nearly every politically relevant actor challenged Mbande a Ngola: his half-brothers, the *sobas* and the Imbangalas. The Imbangalas made alliances with the Portuguese, further eroding the

Kingdom of Ndongo by making significant advances in the southern part of the kingdom. The main reason for the disputes was control over slave trade routes; the more control over territories the Portuguese and their allies gained, the weaker the Kingdom of Ndongo became (Heywood 2019).

After Mbande a Ngola's death in early 1617, his son Ngola Mbande (Queen Njinga's brother) took the throne. Ngola Mbande, Queen Njinga, Kambu and Funji were all offspring of Mbande a Ngola's favourite concubine, Kengela ka Nkombe (Heywood 2019; Pinto 2016; Cavazzi 1965; Centro de Estudos Angolanos Grupo de Trabalho História e Etnologia 1965). Reports from the time suggest that Ngola Mbande was extremely cruel and did not consider any alternative means for achieving his ends, killing many of his rivals, including his possible successors. One of the leading biographers of Queen Njinga, Antonio Cavazzi, contends that when Ngola Mbande became king, he committed the following acts of violence: to avoid competition for the throne he killed Queen Njinga's son and made his three sisters infertile, mutilating their uteruses with boiling water and iron. He declared war on the Portuguese to eliminate external threats and to once again dominate the slave trade routes (Cavazzi 1965). Indeed, Ngola Mbande's situation was not easy because the governor Luís Mendes de Vasconcelos occupied the Pemba Real in Ilamba, a key area for the slave trade (Pinto 2016). Ngola Mbande did not wish to engage in diplomacy with the Portuguese, and Mendes de Vasconcelos attempted to conquer Ndongo in 1617, making significant advances and capturing two of his sisters (Kambu and Funji) and his main wife as well as conquering the capital Kabaza in 1620/1621 (Centro de Estudos Angolanos Grupo de Trabalho História e Etnologia 1965; Cadornega 1681). Ngola Mbande escaped, becoming a refugee in the Kwanza islands. In the meantime, the Portuguese attempted to put someone else on the throne to substitute Ngola Mbande, but this attempt ultimately failed because the population of the Kingdom of Ndongo did not recognize the new king (Heywood 2019; Centro de Estudos Angolanos Grupo de Trabalho História e Etnologia 1965).

Queen Njinga enters the political scene

Queen Njinga was born in 1582 and died in 1663; it was only in 1622 that she took on a more prominent role on the political scene. Before this, as a woman born into the elite of the Kingdom of Ndongo and because her father had a great appreciation for her, she was likely to have been engaged in the elite circles of the kingdom, learning religious rituals, political and military strategy and socializing at official ceremonies. But in 1622, while she was living in the Kingdom of Matamba, she took on a more significant role. Advised by the elders of his community, Ngola Mbande had decided to designate his sister, Queen Njinga, as his ambassador to negotiate peace with the new governor, João Correia de Sousa, in Luanda (UNESCO 2014; Cadornega 1681).

Njinga went to see the governor in Luanda. While receiving her, the governor attempted to humiliate Queen Njinga by making her sit on the floor while he sat on a chair. Queen Njinga immediately recognized this negotiating strategy, ordering an enslaved person to place herself in the position of a chair so that she could sit on her. The enslaved person immediately sat and Queen Njinga used her as a chair. This counterstrategy by Queen Njinga deliberately showed that she was an equal to the governor and would not accept being humiliated by him (Cavazzi 1965). During the negotiations, she assured the governor that her brother wanted peace and that they would cease military attacks, proposing to make alliances against common enemies. She promised to return the stolen enslaved people who 'belonged' to the Portuguese, but she refused to pay the annual tribute of 100 enslaved people to the Portuguese that other locals paid. Her justification was that this applied only to those who had been conquered and that her brother, King Ngola Mbande, was not a conquered subordinate. The Portuguese delegation was sceptical of Queen Njinga's intentions, doubting her sincerity to live in peace; thus, Queen Njinga went further to try and convince them, offering to study catechism and be baptized (Heywood 2019; Heywood and Thornton 2007; Cavazzi 1965).

When she returned from the diplomatic mission, Njinga's brother praised her for the successful negotiations. Queen Njinga was playing a political game, and, at the time, she already had ambitions for the throne. Although she was baptized, thus affording her a special status among the Portuguese, she persuaded her brother not to do the same (Cavazzi 1965). Indeed, when the Portuguese sent an African priest – father Faria Baretto – whom Ngola Mbande considered to be his subordinate, he refused to be baptized by him (Heywood 2019; Pinto 2016; Cavazzi 1965). Christian baptism was essential if one wished to be taken seriously by seventeenth-century Iberian monarchs. Thus, by being baptized, Queen Njinga put herself in a special, unique and, to a great extent, irreplaceable position to negotiate with the Portuguese (Miller 1976, 1975). At the same time, she ensured that she was responsible for various religious rituals within her community to gain the support and admiration of the Mbundu population (Cavazzi 1965). It was essential to play a double game, so that she could look like a legitimate leader, both for outsiders and members of the kingdom simultaneously.

In 1624, Ngola Mbande died and Queen Njinga ascended to the throne. Cavazzi contends that she confessed to him that she had poisoned her brother. As explained above, it was not part of the culture for a woman to become a leader, although women could have relevant political roles. However, Queen Njinga had influenced the key players and was able to successfully ascend to the throne. Before Ngola Mbande's death, she announced that she would be replacing him, thereby ensuring that the transition was created with the appropriate rituals supported by the relevant stakeholders. Moreover, as she was aware that she lived in a religiously driven society, she immediately took possession of all the royal symbolic objects that would entitle her to remain in power, thus becoming the queen of the Kingdom of Ndongo (Heywood 2019).

The reign of Queen Njinga

The reign of Queen Njinga coincided with many political crises in Portugal. After King Sebastião I of Portugal died in 1578, he left no heirs. This led to a political crisis that ultimately merged the Portuguese and Spanish thrones, with King Felipe II of Spain taking the Portuguese throne in 1580, thus also becoming Felipe I of Portugal (Crowley 2015; Kupperman 2012; Russell-Wood 2008; Bethencourt 2007; Charles Ralph Boxer 1969). Felipe I, also known as 'the prudent', was aware of the importance of solid national sentiment and wanted to avoid contestation. Thus, he decided that the Portuguese colonies should be kept under Portuguese power networks (Costa, Rodrigues and Oliveira 2014; Kupperman 2012; Charles Ralph Boxer 1969). Felipe I's successor, Felipe II, continued this policy for the same reasons, whereas King Filipe III, also known as 'the oppressor', took a different approach. When he came to the throne in 1621, he attempted to replace Portuguese with Spanish power in the colonies, which led to the deposing of the king in 1640 and ultimately to the separation of the crowns of Spain and Portugal (Crowley 2015; Costa, Rodrigues, and Oliveira 2014; Russell-Wood 2008).

At the beginning of Queen Njinga's reign, Dutch incursions against Portuguese colonies had begun, but they only conquered Luanda between 1641 and 1648. The expansion of the Dutch Empire was a significant threat to the religious and economic dominance of the Portuguese (Charles Ralph Boxer 1958; 1958; Crowley 2015; Kupperman 2012; Bethencourt 2007). Aware of the growing fragility of the Portuguese kingdom, Queen Njinga became more defiant, closing routes for the slave trade and attacking the Portuguese. In addition, the Portuguese broke the promise of withdrawing from Ambaca Fort, which further motivated Queen Njinga's defiance (Pantoja 2020, 2000). In response, the Portuguese used a variety of strategies to attempt to discredit her and cause her to lose internal power. The Portuguese tried but failed to discredit *Ngangas* (the *Ndongo* priests) by classifying them as arbiters of mere witchcraft, which would also go some way in undermining the Queen's power in so far as the priests had an important role in ceremonies that legitimized the ruler (Pantoja 2020, 2000). The governor de Sousa also decided to enthrone Hari a Kiluanje in 1626 to challenge Queen Njinga's legitimacy as ruler. Hari a Kiluanje was a descendant of the lineage that had opposed Queen Njinga's entitlement to the throne since the reign of her grandfather Ngola Kilombo kia Kasenda (Thornton 2020; Pinto 2016). De Sousa armed Hari a Kiluanje to form another front against the Queen (Heywood 2019; Cadornega 1681). He also added to this by attempting to disqualify her on the grounds of her gender.

This Portuguese policy led Queen Njinga to formulate a variety of counterstrategies. Queen Njinga was perfectly aware that the Mbundu saw the leader as a religious leader with supernatural powers and as a semi-deity. Hence, she promoted Mbundu spiritual beliefs and took charge of the public religious ceremonies, which placed her as the legitimate spiritual leader of the community. In short, the manipulation of Mbundu religion allowed her to influence the culture and further promote her leadership. Queen Njinga was also aware that her gender was a problem for her leadership and that de Sousa's strategy might eventually prevail (Miller 1976, 1975). Given this, she attempted to carry out her leadership role in such a way that she would be perceived as a man. She defied gender norms, rejecting feminine features unless they were convenient for her. She acted ruthlessly, killing anyone who defied her to better display her masculine traits. Notably, she had several male concubines dressed like women to humiliate them and then had them killed (Cavazzi 1965). She took the place of males in rituals where females were usually excluded. She performed the role of the opposite gender to maintain power.

Nonetheless, this performance was maintained only when it was convenient for her. Queen Njinga knew she needed to find allies, and one of the most powerful would be the Imbangala. She pretended to fall in love with one of the leaders, acting in more feminine ways to seduce the Imbangala Kasa, whom she eventually married. She had two primary goals: one was to kill her brother's son, who was sent to the Imbangala to be militarily trained and could be considered a legitimate heir to the throne; the other was to obtain a strong ally with military power – and the Imbangala were famous for their warrior skills. Thus, she combined Imbangala and Mbundu ideologies and rituals (e.g. eating human flesh) to have a more significant political reach (Cavazzi

1965), which brought her various benefits, including the conquering of Matamba in the early 1630s (Thornton 2020).

Queen Njinga also made alliances with the Dutch, who not only armed and protected her, but also attacked the Portuguese in Luanda. With a new player in the game, she took this opportunity to attack both the Portuguese and Hari a Kiluanje, who, as a consequence of Dutch attacks, received less protection from the Portuguese (Pinto 2016). Nonetheless, the alliance with the Dutch broke in 1648. Consequently, Queen Njinga had to find a new strategy, opting to cooperate with the Portuguese, who once again had the upper hand (Centro de Estudos Angolanos Grupo de Trabalho História e Etnologia 1965). She attained power over the Matamba and the areas between the Matamba and Ndongo to control the primary routes of the slave trade; she established good relationships with the Capuchins (who were the most influential religious order at the time); and she was baptized a second time, implementing Catholicism in her territories (Pinto 2016; Cavazzi 1965). After defying thirteen governors who ruled Angola between 1622 and 1663, she thought the best strategy to keep power was to be Catholic and to create ties with the Portuguese. She died as a Catholic, and after her death, her sister Kambu (baptized as Barbara) took the throne.

Ritual, religion and pragmatism

Taking this historical evidence on board, I would now like to tease out a political theory. My argument is inspired by Joseph C. Miller's interpretation of Queen Njinga's life (Miller 1976, 1975). According to Miller, Queen Njinga was not a legitimate heir to the throne and had to disrespect various Mbundu moral laws to gain and remain in power. Miller contends that there are three reasons for this. First, according to Mbundu lineage calculus, her claim to the royal title violated established Mbundu norms in so far as being a sister of the king was not sufficient grounds for being a legitimate heir to the throne. Although this variable would place her in the line of succession to the throne, there was no presumptive right to succeed as a sister and especially as the daughter of an enslaved woman. Succession to the throne was more connected with political standing, which may or may not be related to being kin. Furthermore, according to the Mbundu norms, it had to be a male, not a female, who would be most likely to gather support. Thus, it can be affirmed that her success was attributable to a coup and not to political legitimacy (Miller 1976, 1975). Adriano Parreira challenges this argument, contending that there is nothing necessarily problematic about the Mbundu having a queen (Parreira 1990). Although he is correct that, in theory, a woman could have been a ruler, as a matter of political practice, women rulers were uncommon, only to be found in distant history and myths of origin (Thornton 2020, 1991).

Second, her Christian baptism could be considered as sufficient to delegitimize her as an heir to the throne. On the one hand, the endorsement and welcoming of Christianity not only required one to engage in rituals disapproved by the Mbundu, but also went against Mbundu political and ideological preferences that restricted the access of Christians to their kingdom. On the other hand, it also allowed too much control of the slave routes, a policy many Mbundu people disagreed with and opposed.

Third, according to Mbundu norms, individuals were prohibited from showing hostility towards their leader; given that many suspected Queen Njinga of killing her brother, this would also have prevented her from attaining the throne (Miller 1976, 1975). Consequently, I (along with Miller) interpret Queen Njinga as more pragmatic and strategic than someone driven by Mbundu ideology. But what is this pragmatic and strategic political theory underlying Queen Njinga's thought?

Clearly, the means justify the ends for Queen Njinga. Throughout her life, she took different, even contradictory, identities, identifying as a Mbundu, a Christian, reverting back to a Mbundu, then identifying as an Imbangala and finally as a Christian once again. These identifications came along with incompatible behavioural traits and ritual practices that contradicted each other. It would be naive to affirm that she simply changed her mind often, for it is more likely that Queen Njinga conformed with the identity that served her better in a given context. The same can be affirmed with regard to gender; it would be an error to understand Queen Njinga as a proto-feminist concerned about women's rights or emancipation, for as Cavazzi contends, she was cruel to women in her kingdom (Cavazzi 1965). Her gender flexibility is perhaps more reasonably identified with the pragmatism in her understanding of politics. Depending on convenience and instrumental value, she could and did display either feminine or masculine behaviour, but more often, she attempted to be perceived as a male so that her leadership would not be questioned.

In relation to this, friendships and rivalries in the political arena ought to be understood flexibly. Queen Njinga was a political realist; she did not fall under the illusion that there were natural allies or natural enemies, but rather believed that political allegiances are such that they ought to be pursued in terms of what the goals are. In this regard, the identity of others was of little relevance to her, as she equally fought against Africans and Europeans, depending on what goals she wanted to achieve. Furthermore, she was betrayed by both Africans and Europeans, contributing to the fact that she did not consider the identity of the allies or enemies to be relevant for cooperation. Instead, what mattered was the goals of each at the time. Queen Njinga seemed to attach some value to family ties; she was deeply traumatized by the killing of her son and went to great lengths to save her sister (Cavazzi 1965). It might be contested that she did not value family given that she killed her brother and nephew, but I do not think these are proper counterexamples because not only are we not sure that she did so, but also her actions could have been potentially motivated by personal vengeance; they are more likely exceptions to how she perceived family relations.

Perhaps the most important idea to be extracted from Queen Njinga's ideology is that performance and the mastery of ritual are integral to political power. Queen Njinga deeply understood the Mbundu, Imbangala and Catholic rituals, which enabled her to negotiate with her opponents and to place herself in advantageous positions. She understood that ritual has critical symbolic importance for how individuals see others, subsequently influencing the decisions that they will make. Queen Njinga often played with the symbolic aspects of human interactions and acted in ways that sent a symbolic message to others. When she negotiated with the Portuguese, she was baptized because she knew how important this was to her opponents symbolically. Likewise, when she joined the Imbangala, she engaged in cannibalistic rituals, so that others saw her as a member of their community. Finally, she often changed names as a means by which to communicate with her allies, symbolically showing her identification with them.

The key lesson is that someone who is engaging in politics ought to be able to enact roles without being entirely consumed by them. Hans-Georg Moeller and Paul D'Ambrosio use the concept of genuine pretending to explain the *Zhuangzi*, but I think that it is also helpful here to understand the thought of Queen Njinga (Moeller and D'Ambrosio 2017). What is important is the action of taking on roles, learning them and mastering them, but simultaneously not being consumed by them. This idea implies that various virtues are required to succeed in politics. One is that mastering the art of deception is important for growing in the political realm. Queen Njinga routinely used deception techniques to achieve her goals. When negotiating with the Portuguese, she pretended to be strong when, in fact, the Portuguese had the upper hand. When attempting to seduce the Imbangala leader, she acted as if she was romantically attached to him when this was unlikely. When she could not fight the Portuguese anymore, she pretended to repent and accept the Christian faith. For Queen Njinga, one of the essential virtues in politics was to act deceptively. Another important virtue was knowing the enemy, understanding what is important to them and negotiating accordingly.

Finally, a degree of prompt spontaneity is necessary for succeeding in the political arena: in several situations, Queen Njinga was successful because she quickly understood and responded to what was at stake and acted accordingly. For instance, when she was negotiating on behalf of her brother with the governor, she promptly and spontaneously understood the humiliating gesture that attempted to place her in a vulnerable position and responded to it adequately.

Queen Njinga and Cavazzi's theory of the Portuguese empire

The above-mentioned account can be challenged by a more orthodox reading of Queen Njinga's foremost biographer, Antonio Cavazzi. Cavazzi travelled with other Capuchins to Luanda in 1654. It was not until 1658, however, that he met Queen Njinga when he went to replace Antonio Gaeta, another Capuchin missionary (Heywood 2019; Pinto 2016). In his *An Historical Description of Three Kingdoms: Congo, Matamba, and Angola*, he dedicates the last two volumes to the life of Queen Njinga of Angola (Cavazzi 1965). According to his description, the behaviour of the queen was explained primarily by the failure of the Jesuits to evangelize Africans in the right way as well as by the negative influence of Calvinism. His account of Queen Njinga's life can be rendered as a critique of how the Portuguese colonies behaved in Angola and its negative Jesuit influence.

Cavazzi also criticizes the baptism of Queen Njinga carried out in 1622 by a Jesuit Priest, contending that this baptism – which followed the methods of the Society of Jesus founded in 1540 (Manso 2016; Rubiés 2005) – was an inauthentic Catholic baptism, which mixed Christianity with local rituals (Cavazzi 1965: 36). Moreover, the baptism did not change the actions and beliefs of Queen Njinga. Therefore, according to Cavazzi, her sexual promiscuity, lack of scruples, cruelty and cannibalism were a result of the lack of authentic Christianity, which could have prevented such actions (Cavazzi 1965: 56). A transformation of Queen Njinga was possible only after a genuine conversion aided by the Capuchin missionaries and Gaeta. He contends that it was only because Gaeta taught and rebaptized her using the Capuchin way, which, in turn, followed the *Propaganda Fide's* guidance, that a change in Queen Njinga occurred. The influence was so strong that, according to Cavazzi, she even accepted monogamy, which was the most challenging aspect of the Christian doctrine for Africans (Pinto 2016; Cavazzi 1965: 89; Cadornega 1681). Cavazzi even blamed the Jesuits for Queen Njinga's alliance with the Dutch. He believed that the failed baptism led her to start a war with the Catholics and ally with the Calvinists against the Portuguese. Indeed, Cavazzi points out that two Jesuit priests, Coelho and Borges, attempted to convince Queen Njinga not to form an alliance with the Calvinists but failed – further proof, according to Cavazzi, that the Jesuits were not carrying out the conversion and religious influence in the correct way (Cavazzi 1965: 91–2). In short, Cavazzi believed that the Jesuit flexibility to adapt the teachings of the Bible to local cultures was not an acceptable way to convert non-Europeans; it could only lead to failed conversions.

Given the above, the contemporary reader may contend that the interpretation I offer in this chapter is too speculative; what Cavazzi suggests is that Queen Njinga had a conviction in her beliefs and her actions were more ideologically driven than driven by a pragmatic methodology to remain in power. However, I uphold that it is unlikely that Queen Njinga changed her mind so easily, quickly and conveniently. Cavazzi's reasons for describing the changes as ideological are bound up with the politics of the time. Rome was suspicious that the Jesuits were too focused on the commercial aspects of colonization and had neglected the religious aspects (Costa, Rodrigues and Oliveira 2014; Russell-Wood 2008; Bethencourt 2007; Boxer 1969), a suspicion shared by the governor of Angola at the time, Salvador Correia de Sá e Benavides. Furthermore, the Capuchins and the Jesuits competed for political power and local resources in Angola. The wars with locals damaged the Portuguese slave trade because cooperation was necessary to capture and enslave people (Caldeira 2013). This was an opportunity for the Capuchins to occupy the place of the Jesuits, and Cavazzi suggests a more substantial influence of Capuchins in the Portuguese Empire. For instance, Cavazzi describes how the Capuchin missionaries Boaventura de Corella and Francisco de Veas would have been able to persuade Queen Njinga to break her alliance with the Dutch, whereas the Jesuit priests failed. Taking this on board, I contend that the interpretation claiming that Cavazzi's account suggests that Queen Njinga was driven by ideology misses the fact that Cavazzi himself, as a Capuchin, had a political agenda. Although the political circumstances at the time suggest that he had an interest in conveying an ideological interpretation of Queen Njinga's actions, my view offers a more concrete way of understanding Queen Njinga's politics.

Conclusion

In this chapter, I have investigated the political theory of Queen Njinga, one of the most well-known agents of resistance against Portuguese colonialism in Angola. I have detailed how she is a controversial figure who has either been romanticized or denigrated, depending on the perspective being offered. I then provided a more realistic and historically informed understanding of Queen Njinga's political theory, claiming that she mastered the art of disobedience and offered a form of resistance without ideology. This, however, leaves a question open: given this characterization, to what extent is Queen Njinga relevant to those who uphold an anti-colonialist position? I argue that her role is vital because she offered a pragmatic and strategic approach to dealing with colonialism (and neocolonialism). Her strategies, independently of her intentions, were, in many cases, effective in resisting colonial rule, providing insightful lessons to those who wish to resist colonialism and its legacies. Angolan liberators were, therefore, to a great extent, rightly inspired by the leadership and anti-colonial practice of Queen Njinga.

4

Lourenço da Silva Mendonça: Towards universalism and abolitionism

Introduction

The forms of resistance to colonialism transformed significantly with Lourenço da Silva Mendonça, who offered a much more inclusive theory than the ones of the thinkers looked at in the previous chapters. Lourenço da Silva Mendonça was a seventeenth-century figure who has been largely neglected by the literature. Accounts of his life and thought are mainly gleaned from the work of two historians: Richard Gray and, more recently, José Lingna Nafafé (Gray 1997, 1987; Nafafé 2022 2019). The content of this chapter is largely inspired by the work of Lingna Nafafé. Although I was aware of da Silva Mendonça, information about his life was rather scarce (Mullett 1999; Gray 1997, 1987; Hastings 1996). The work of Lingna Nafafé made me realize that there was much more to be said about da Silva Mendonça, although I ultimately disagree with significant elements of Lingna Nafafé's interpretation. That is, I agree with most of Lingna Nafafé's narrative, and I owe much of this chapter to his work; however, I ultimately reject his interpretation of da Silva Mendonça's thought, and I will argue more specifically that da Silva Mendonça was selective in his antislavery stand and a proto-universalist.

da Silva Mendonça was born into a Mbundu family, probably in 1620; he had three brothers, and he died in 1698. His place of origin is likely to be Pedras de Pungo e Ndongo, in the Kingdom of Ndongo, where he lived until his early 20s (Nafafé 2022, 2019). Although this information is likely to be accurate, his date and place of birth are still disputed. Some accounts suggest that he was born in Brazil and had slave origins. Even if he was born in Brazil rather than in Africa, it is still possible that he had royal origins (Mattos 2006; Gray 1997, 1987), claiming ancestry connected to the Kingdoms of Kongo and Ndongo. As I pointed out in the previous chapter, some royals were sold as enslaved people against the will of the locals, which makes da Silva Mendonça's story more plausible and possible. Moreover, it is also suggestive that he had royal ancestors in so far as other Africans have recognized him as royalty (Nafafé 2022, 2019).

This chapter presents the political thought of da Silva Mendonça on slavery. I have divided the chapter into four sections. In the first section, I trace the family background of da Silva Mendonça and provide the historical context of his time. In the second, I describe his exile to Brazil, then to Portugal and Spain, and finally his trip to the Vatican. The third section offers an overview of the Atlantic Slave Trade. In the final section, I outline da Silva Mendonça's main theories. As will be noticed, he tried to resist colonialism, contrasting with the protagonists of previous chapters; however, his theory is much more inclusive and less preoccupied about the welfare of the elites.

The destruction of a kingdom: Filipe Hari I and João Hari II

Following the narrative of Lingna Nafafé, the destruction of Pungo-Andongo is relevant to da Silva Mendonça's story. But to contextualize da Silva Mendonça's life, it is first important to look at his family lineage (Nafafé 2022). His father was Dom Ignácio da Silva, who was the son of Ngola Aiidi, also known as King Filipe Hari I of Ndongo. In the history of the Kingdom of Ndongo, King Filipe Hari I is known for being the main rival to Queen Njinga for the throne (Cadornega 1681). King Filipe Hari I was Njinga's half-brother (Nafafé 2022); his mother (a 'mocama') was the third wife of their common father. A 'mocama' was a wife of a lower kind who was more like a household servant, which meant that although King Filipe Hari I had royal blood, he was not part of the highest nobility (Nafafé 2022).

The Portuguese preferred King Filipe Hari I over Queen Njinga for the throne. As explained in the previous chapter, Queen Njinga was largely defiant of Portuguese power. In contrast, King Filipe Hari I was generally submissive to the Portuguese and aligned with their interests. The Portuguese then lobbied for the election of King Filipe Hari I to the throne, as this would not only serve their interests better, but would also be an excellent way to intensify old African rivalries. It is said that João Correia de Sousa – the governor of Angola at the time – planned this as he saw Queen Njinga as an untrustworthy ally (Cadornega 1681).

King Filipe Hari I was elected to the throne on 12 October 1626, but not without contestation (Cadornega 1681). Queen Njinga did not accept King Filipe Hari I as the legitimate king, and likewise, King Filipe Hari I contested Queen Njinga's legitimacy. Each had sound reasons for claiming the illegitimacy of the other. As shown in the last chapter, Queen Njinga's gender and the suspicion that she killed her brother would have sufficed to render her an illegitimate heir. Likewise, King Filipe Hari I's ancestry disqualified him as a legitimate heir, as he came from a low-status mother (Nafafé 2022).

In addition, King Filipe Hari I was increasingly perceived by Queen Njinga, as well as by many Mbundu people, as a betrayer and puppet of the Portuguese; indeed, the reign of King Filipe Hari I did facilitate the advance of Portuguese colonization. Moreover, his reign was affected by an important controversy regarding tax. The Portuguese learned that the Mbundu people had a tax system, the *kabakula* tribute or *baculamento*, which was used in their politics, signalling a form of hierarchy (Cadornega 1681). The Portuguese wanted to introduce the *baculamento* as part of their relationship with the Mbundu people and demanded that all provinces under their control pay them 100 slaves as an annual tax. This was a way of exploiting local tributary customs. One fundamental problem that the Portuguese had with Queen Njinga was her refusal to pay the tax, and while King Filipe Hari I was also reluctant to accept this tax, he eventually yielded (Nafafé 2022).

This weak attitude of King Filipe Hari I disappointed many *sobas* (Birmingham and Birmingham 2000). *Sobas* were individuals with administrative powers in provinces who had noble blood and often owned a significant parcel of land (Cadornega 1681). Although generally they were delegated, they had a significant amount of autonomy and power over their regions; hence, the kings had to maintain positive relationships with them. Their disappointment with King Filipe Hari I therefore had a major impact, and while he became more defiant towards the end of his life, nothing significant changed (Birmingham and Birmingham 2000).

King Filipe Hari I died in 1664, and he was buried with royal honours (Cadornega 1681). He was succeeded by his son, King João Hari II. Despite the defiance seen at the end of King Filipe Hari I's reign, Portugal and the Ndongo had an alliance that had by that point spanned thirty-eight years. But, in an unexpected move, King João Hari II decided to end this harmonious relationship with Portugal. Given that King João Hari II was a graduate of the Jesuit College of Luanda, the Portuguese were expecting him to support the Portuguese regime (Birmingham and Birmingham 2000). King João Hari II undertook several actions in defiance of the Portuguese, including refusal to pay the *baculamento* and blocking trade routes to take control of trade, especially the slave trade. He also refused to aid the Portuguese in battles, and he and his brother Diogo Gola Calanga attacked several Portuguese-dominated zones, such as Dumbo Apebo. Finally, he attempted to revive Mbundu culture and politics by returning to ways and customs from before Portuguese influence (Cadornega 1681).

The *sobas* praised King João Hari II's defiance. From their perspective, this was a better approach to Portuguese colonialism than his father's. King João Hari II was therefore able to recover political alliances with many *sobas*. The Portuguese, on the other hand, had a different opinion. They thought this to be a great risk to the stability of the region, for not only was he disrupting the slave routes, but he could also influence other dominated areas to take up arms against the Portuguese. Thus, the Portuguese waged war in 1671 to recover their power and to send a political message. The war resulted in about two thousand deaths.

Initially, King João Hari II successfully fled with his family, but he was later captured and decapitated. His reign was short, ending in 1671.

Networking: From Brazil to the Vatican

The connections between the previous political events were made clearer because of new materials that Lingna Nafafé discovered, which aid in building a narrative of the life of da Silva Mendonça. The Portuguese wanted to stop the descendants of the Ndongo royal family from mobilizing people against the Portuguese, so they decided to send them away to Brazil. In total, there were sixteen members of the royal family sent to Brazil, among whom was da Silva Mendonça (Nafafé 2022). da Silva Mendonça lived in the city of Salvador, in Bahia Brazil, for eighteen years. He probably also lived in Rio de Janeiro in 1673 for six months. He is likely to have lived a good life in Brazil; as royalty, he had access to housing, education, food and clothing, for all his expenses were covered by the Portuguese Crown (Brásio 1982).

The goal of moving people to Brazil was to avoid political mobilization in the Kingdom of Ndongo after the defeat of King João Hari II. But, at some point, the Portuguese became increasingly concerned that da Silva Mendonça would run away to the Quilombo (free town) de Palmares. Quilombos were communities formed by individuals of African descent who had escaped from slavery. Generally speaking, these communities were independent, offered armed resistance and did not abide by the laws of the Portuguese settlers (Schwartz 1970).

Quilombo de Palmares was a community established by Zumbi dos Palmares, which was not far from where da Silva Mendonça lived. If da Silva Mendonça were to join, this would potentially mobilize more people owing to his royal blood: many slaves would see him as their legitimate king and would be motivated to join him. Moreover, if da Silva Mendonça took power, the Portuguese Crown would have needed to recognize Quilombo de Palmares as a kingdom. Thus, in 1671, they decided to send da Silva Mendonça to Portugal. He was sent to a monastery called the Convento de Vilar de Frades in Braga, north of Portugal, where he studied for four years. His brothers were also sent to Braga, but stayed in different monasteries (Nafafé 2022).

His experience in Brazil is very likely to have made a mark on da Silva Mendonça's life, for it was there that he was probably exposed to the evils of the slave trade. The province of Bahia where he lived is precisely where the Portuguese introduced sugar cane plantations and enslaved many Africans. Hence, when da Silva Mendonça moved to Portugal, he was already likely to have been strongly opposed to slavery. Indeed, it was initially in Portugal, and then in Spain, that da Silva Mendonça began lobbying to gain support for his ideology (Caldeira 2013; Pimentel 1999; Schwartz 1970).

Moving da Silva Mendonça to Portugal clearly backfired, as it gave him an opportunity to meet different people who supported his ideas. He developed important connections and met people in Portugal and Spain who wrote him recommendation letters. These recommendation letters are what gave him the legitimacy to prepare two petitions against slavery, which were to be presented in the Vatican.[1] Importantly, da Silva Mendonça was able to obtain two letters. One was a letter from Portugal written by a papal clerk, Gaspar da Costa Mesquita. In his letter, da Silva Mendonça was introduced as the legitimate representative of the *'pardos'* of Portugal, Castile and Brazil.[2] The other was a letter from Madrid, signed by Giacinto Rogio Monzon in 1682 and contained a similar description as the other letter. Monzon contended that da Silva Mendonça was the legitimate representative of an 'influential brotherhood of *pretos*'.[3] The connections and alliances he gained in Portugal and Spain gave him legitimacy, thus allowing him to give his cause a wider reach when he travelled to Rome in 1684 (Nafafé 2022).

The Atlantic slave trade

There is some evidence that the Atlantic slave trade already existed in the fifteenth century. Lagos in Portugal was one of the main ports for the deliverance of enslaved people, dating back to at least 1444. Nevertheless, most of the Atlantic slave trade occurred between the sixteenth and nineteenth centuries. Much of the trade was made possible by developments in seafaring technologies, which allowed the crossing of the Atlantic. The beginning of the Atlantic slave trade is attributed to the Portuguese in the sixteenth century, but other colonial powers such as Britain, Spain, France, the Netherlands and Denmark were also significantly involved. Indeed, up until the nineteenth century, all colonial powers engaged in slave trade (Bhattacharyya 2020; Black 2015).

The majority of enslaved people came from Central and West Africa and were captured by other Africans to be sold to Europeans (Sowell 2006). Chiefs were sometimes paid to provide people for enslavement; sometimes people were captured by slave missions and sometimes during periods of war. According to Birmingham, slave traders exchanged enslaved people for alcohol, weaponry, tobacco and clothes (Birmingham and Birmingham 2000). Obviously, the slave trade had a significant adverse effect on Africa, incentivizing locals to engage in the trade of enslaved people, which consequently resulted in an atmosphere of fear and violence.

The process of enslavement involved the capture and transportation of Africans, mainly to the Americas (National Museums Liverpool 2021). Enslaved people were initially caught from inner Africa and then marched to the coast. At this point, the enslaved people were chained in pairs at the ankles and fastened around the neck with ropes. It is estimated that around ten to fifteen per cent of enslaved people died during this process. Those who were less submissive were cruelly immobilized. During the journey, the slave traders refused to spend money on the slaves, giving them the bare minimum for survival, which resulted in starvation. The enslaved people slept on the floor and were whipped if they did not walk. Only after the slave traders gathered enough people would they move to the coast (Pimentel 1999).

With the establishment of sugar plantations in Brazil, the slave trade significantly increased. It is estimated that during the four-hundred years of Atlantic slavery, 12 million to 12.8 million Africans were shipped (Segal 1996) and that approximately 1.2–2.4 million died in transit (Manning 1990; Eltis and Richardson 1997).

In rather precarious conditions, the trip lasted about six months. Enslaved people were chained for the whole trip and kept in a small, overheated space with no ventilation. They did not have sufficient food or water, nor did they have toilets, which forced them to relieve themselves wherever they were chained. They then had to sit or lay in their own excrement. When they disembarked, they were divided into groups to be sold. Reports suggest that enslaved people looked at slave traders with horror and fear. The traders tried to fatten up those who looked more debilitated or to sell them more cheaply. During a purchase, it was common to ask questions about the origin, age and personality of the enslaved person, who was made to run, jump and scream. In addition, their teeth, eyes, muscles and genitals were inspected to ascertain their physical condition. Enslaved people were often provoked to see how they reacted and to assess what their personality was like. When purchased, slaves were marked with a burning iron to give them the buyer's brand. This would help with identifying them in the event that they ran away (Caldeira 2013; Pimentel 1999).

Enslaved people did various kinds of work, from manual labour, such as working on tobacco, cocoa, sugar and cotton plantations, to skilled labour, such as shipbuilding. They would also work in domestic settings as cooks, for instance (Pimentel 1999; Magalhães 1997). Enslaved women were often raped by their owners (Magalhães 1997). In all cases, they were the legal property of their owners and were sold in markets just like other goods. Enslaved people did offer resistance, however, by sabotaging work equipment, disrupting work rhythms and refusing to procreate, for instance; they also engaged in rebellious activity, escaping in groups or individually, organizing armed attacks and sometimes even going so far as to commit suicide.

Colonizers tried to justify slavery on the grounds of the fact that African culture already had slavery and that the Portuguese had a civilizing mission. On the one hand, slave apologists pointed out that slavery already existed in Angola before the arrival of the Portuguese. On the other hand, they thought that enslaving African people was necessary to civilize them (Pimentel 1999). Indeed, even Priest António Vieira, who was critical of enslaved people's treatment, defended slavery as a legitimate practice, contending that it could be understood as a way to evangelize Africans in a process of just war (Eisenberg 2003).

Lourenço da Silva Mendonça's views on slavery

da Silva Mendonça arrived in Rome in 1684 to confront the Vatican with the evils of slavery. It is unlikely he presented the case in person (Gray 1997; 1987), but his case was disclosed to Pope Innocent XI. The Pope, in turn, passed it to the '*Propaganda Fide*', which oversaw foreign issues. Da Silva Mendonça's speech took aim at kings, governors, priests, bishops and merchants. His goal was not to engage in the benign rhetoric of the time, insisting that the treatment of enslaved people was horrific and claiming to have first-hand evidence of this. He voiced many of the facts that I mentioned in the previous section.

He contended that enslaved people were captured by force and not in fair trade. He pointed out that their owners treated them with extreme cruelty, burning them with wax, lard and other materials. Furthermore, enslaved people were treated like cattle and forced to procreate. As a result of this abuse, they suffered depression and many ended up killing themselves. da Silva Mendonça insisted on the wrongness of perpetual slavery – the rule that made the offspring of enslaved people automatically slaves – contending that this rule made these peoples' lives hopeless. Moreover, it led many enslaved people to commit infanticide and abortion to save their offspring from suffering. da Silva Mendonça wanted justice, so he offered some remedies. He asked the Pope to punish and excommunicate those who perpetuated the slave trade.

I interpret this as da Silva Mendonça making a particular claim about specific victims of slavery rather than a universal declaration against all slavery. In other words, I do not think that he challenged the practice of slavery *per se*. As we saw in the chapters on Afonso I of Kongo and Queen Njinga, slavery was a common practice in Africa. Being a member of the royalty, he is likely to have enjoyed some benefits as an enslaver. Undoubtedly, the kind of slavery that existed in Africa was different from that in Europe and the Americas (e.g. there was no perpetual slavery), but it does not seem that da Silva Mendonça necessarily viewed slavery as morally wrong.

Lingna Nafafé views it differently, arguing that this is more of a universal claim against slavery.[4] Nonetheless, I disagree, because da Silva Mendonça insists on the question of baptism and, for that reason, seems to be demanding only the abolition of slavery of Christians. To begin with, da Silva Mendonça's argument does not seem to oppose slavery for conversion, signalling that he believed that Europeans had the right to convert Africans to Christianity; if slavery was necessary, then it was morally allowed.

Furthermore, when da Silva Mendonça mentions the question of baptism, he suggests that those who were baptized should experience the eternal glory and grace of God and would not lose their souls owing to the evils of slavery. Moreover, he argued that European *Christians* treated African *Christians*, New *Christians* and Indigenous *Christians* like animals. To show the wrongness of this act, he argued that *Christians* had a common identity sealed by baptism and that race should not get in the way of this. Ultimately, it appears that he wanted to abolish slavery for those who were Christian. Therefore, his point is likely to be that *Christians* have a common humanity that ought to be respected, which entails abolishing the enslavement of *Christians*. This seems to follow the thought of the Council of Trent, which saw the Church attempt to recruit new members in part by educating non-Europeans.

Also, da Silva Mendonça made an argument based on the philosophy of the Church at the time, contending that slavery violates eternal, natural, divine and human law. This is a typology that da Silva Mendonça takes from Thomas Aquinas such that it is important to clarify what Aquinas meant. Aquinas defined a law in general as 'a rule or measure of human acts, whereby a person is induced to act or is restrained from acting' (Aquinas 1981: 90), defining law as a 'dictate of practical reason emanating from a ruler' (Aquinas 1981: 91). According to this definition, a law is a rational command made by a legitimate authority of a community for the common good of that community.

In the *Summa Theologica*, Aquinas describes four kinds of law: eternal, natural, divine and human. Eternal law is the law of the universe that governs all the things in it. The community of the eternal law is composed of all the existing creatures with God's providence and creation promulgating the law (i.e. the law is communicated by giving these creatures capacities with a specific nature). Natural law is an extension of eternal law: 'The natural law is nothing else than the rational creature's participation of the eternal law' (Aquinas 1981: 91). It refers to the aspects of the eternal law that rational creatures can know and specifically to the kind of moral knowledge that rational creatures can know, what they are obliged to do or what they should not do. Natural law contrasts with divine law, where the latter is the aspect of eternal law unknown by reason and can only be attained through revelation. Finally, human law is the application of these to particular circumstances (Aquinas 1981).

The link that da Silva Mendonça makes between slavery and Aquinas' thought is quite ambiguous, however. He contends that abductions violate human free will and so are against natural law. Slavery also infringes natural law because it violates basic goods such as life. He upheld that slavery also violated human law because it goes against the law of the land of groups of people who have derived this law from natural law (Sunshine 2007). It violated divine law because it went against the scriptures of the Church; indeed, canon law expressed reluctance about slavery, claiming that it was impractical and unreasonable. Thus, according to this logic, when people engage in slavery, they are violating divine law too, and given that these are all instances of eternal law, there is consequently a violation of eternal law. In this context, da Silva Mendonça seems to use a concept akin to a 'crime against humanity'. This was indeed not common at the time, but it seems it appears frequently in the documents referring to him (Sunshine 2007). I believe that this 'humanity' refers to Christians, for the reasons I explained above regarding his concerns about enslaved Christians. Indeed, the very fact that da Silva Mendonça appeals to Aquinas suggests that he does not entirely disapprove of slavery because Aquinas himself did not oppose it.

Conclusion

This chapter had considered the context of the abolitionist debate, which is routinely located a century later from the time that da Silva Mendonça lived and which stems mainly from European discourse. However, da Silva Mendonça offered a moral and political theory against slavery a century earlier and from an African perspective, but his intervention did have an impact. Many Cardinals in the Vatican seemed to be unaware of the cruelty described by da Silva Mendonça, and the Vatican asked for witnesses to verify his story. The highest tribunal of the Roman Curia debated the matter, and the slave trade was officially condemned, at least in the form in which it appeared at the time. The Vatican decided to punish the wrongdoers, sending warning letters to the *nuncios* in Spain and Portugal, which improved shipment conditions, and promising to punish those who were found to perpetuate the cruelties of slavery. The thought of da Silva Mendonça is of great importance in Angolan thought, and I think it is a turning point vis-à-vis previous thinkers. My interpretation of the thought of King Afonso I and Queen Njinga is that their actions are, generally speaking, driven by self-interest – albeit as I also stated, it is not right to disregard other-regarding concerns of these thinkers. Nonetheless, with da Silva Mendonça, it is clear that there is a turn to a more universal concern with respect to others and a less self-interested political action. Likewise, in the next chapter, I will look at another political thinker who I believe continues this more other-regarding tradition – the prophet Kimpa Vita.

5

Kimpa Vita and subversive Christianity: Challenging colonialism from within

Introduction

Kimpa Vita was born in the Kingdom of Kongo in the late seventeenth century, nearly a century after Afonso I's reign, and she lived until the beginning of the eighteenth century (Pinto 2021a, 2021b, 2021c; Thornton 1998). Her Kikongo names were 'Vita', which was her family name, and 'Kimpa', which was her first name. She also had the Christian name 'Dona Beatriz'. Kimpa Vita was from a noble family, the Mwana Kongo ('child of Kongo'), and thus, her family was very different from that of lower-class women. Whereas lower-class women were usually responsible for agricultural work, Kimpa Vita had enslaved people do this. Moreover, as a noble family member, Kimpa Vita was socialized in an environment in which the politics of the Kongo were often discussed (Thornton 2020, 1998; Young 2011). Her social reality was the Christian Kingdom that was fragmented and disintegrating owing to a lengthy civil war (Thornton 2020, 1983). At the time of her birth, Alvaro X was reigning in the Kingdom of Kongo, but most of the relevant events in her life occurred during the reign of Pedro IV (Pinto 2021a; Thornton 1998). The Kingdom of Kongo had a strong Portuguese Catholic influence, and Kimpa Vita also saw herself as a Catholic. But her take on religion differed from the orthodox view of the time. Kimpa Vita claimed that when she was close to death, she saw Saint Anthony, who saved her, possessed her body and replaced her soul, such that Saint

Anthony was now inside her and speaking through her (Pinto 2021c; Thornton 2020, 1998).

This chapter will introduce the ethical and political relevance of this declaration of being possessed by Saint Anthony. As will become clear throughout the chapter, there is a significant change of paradigm in Kimpa Vita's thought. She defends a truly inclusive approach which aims at elevating all African subjects – something which is less clear in the protagonists of previous chapters. The next section will outline Kimpa Vita's context. The section after that will overview Kimpa Vita's declaration of becoming Saint Anthony. Then, I will summarize the status of women in Africa in the seventeenth and eighteenth centuries and explain why the negative portrayal of Queen Njinga and Kimpa Vita by the missionaries has a colonial framework. After this, in the light of the negative images of African women portrayed by missionaries, I will explain the importance of Kimpa Vita's thought with a special focus on the problem of evil.

Kimpa Vita's context: The disintegration of the kingdom of Kongo

After the death of Afonso I, one of his sons, Pedro, who was supported by a faction called '*kibala*' (court), succeeded to the throne. However, an armed section from *Nsi a Ngala* (the south coast) immediately overthrew him, replacing him with one of Afonso's grandsons, Diogo. The discourse of Christianization continued, and Diogo I continued the ideological discourse that othered his opponents as non-Christian. Like his grandfather Afonso I, Diogo I classified his opponents as infidels and pagans, attributing his victory to God (Thornton 2020). The following two rulers, Bernardo I of Kongo and Henrique I Nerika a Mpudi, did not reign for long as both were killed in war, and both failed in trying to expand the kingdom.

The succession after Henrique I Nerika a Mpudi was complicated. The person (Álvaro Nimi a Lukeni) left in power when Henrique was at war was not his son but rather his wife's (Izabel Lukeni Lua Mvemba) son. The reign of King Álvaro I was marked by subordination to Portugal. Facing a defeat against the Jagas, he asked for Portugal's help, but this came at the cost of having to submit to Portugal's power. His son and successor, Álvaro II, suffered several attacks but was able to maintain power.

Thornton describes the period that succeeded Álvaro II as chaotic (Thornton 2020; 1998). Álvaro II was unsure who should be his successor because his son had died. Bernardo II Mwanza a Mvemba, his brother, became king but did not reign for long. Álvaro III had a cruel reign, which brought more division and chaos to the Kingdom of Kongo. As a result, the rulers who came after this were either poisoned, challenged, betrayed or killed, and they generally did not hold power for very long (Thornton 2020, 1998, 1983; Heywood 2019; Fish and Fish 2002).

Kimpa Vita was born and lived in a warlike environment. She witnessed at least five great wars, which resulted in many deaths and enslavements, division and starvation. Her father is likely to have been called to fight in one of the wars in 1691. Wars were mostly an enterprise of the royal elite, and the population of the Kongo was exhausted from so many of them. Hence, Kimpa Vita encountered movements and individuals taking stands against war that later influenced her to also stand against war. Many of these anti-war movements were religiously inspired. Mafuta, for instance, claimed to have seen the Virgin Mary and also claimed that the Virgin Mary had told her that she had begged Jesus to be merciful with the people of the Kongo, because Jesus was angry with the Kongolese for failing to restore the capital city. Jesus was particularly angry with King Pedro IV who had an irreverent attitude but could have reoccupied the city. The movement was influential, and even Pedro IV's wife, Hippolita, became a follower of Mafuta. The situation was not easy for Pedro IV; he feared the movement growing and being taken over by his opponents for political gain. He asked one of his ecclesiastical advisors, Father Bernardo, for advice, who suggested arresting his wife to prevent her from becoming an engine for treason.

Pedro IV decided against this, however, leading to a temporary break in the relationship between Pedro IV and Father Bernardo (Thornton 2020, 1998; Young 2011).

It is claimed that Kimpa Vita herself also had visions at a young age. It is said that as a child she had a vision that two white children came to play with her and gave her gifts. In the period of the Kingdom of Kongo, having visions was a sign of spiritual abilities that entitled one to particular roles. Furthermore, in the Kingdom of Kongo, the colour white (*mpembe*) had a special meaning; specifically, while black was the colour of the human world, white was the colour of the spiritual world. Hence, the fact that she had a vision of white children was a sign of her sainthood. The fact that Kimpa Vita had these visions was understood as a sign that she was gifted and could become a '*nganga*', a Kikongo word meaning 'knowledge'. Hence, a *nganga* was an individual who could access the knowledge of the other or spiritual world through visions, trance experiences, dances and chanting, and this would bring a being from another realm into the *nganga*'s head who would then use the *nganga* to speak. Their function was to help people with their wisdom and capacity for fortune telling, advising individuals about disease, economics and life.

Often, *ngangas* had a special relationship with natural resources – for it is not uncommon in African religions to see spirituality in nature (Mbiti 2015, 1990). Rivers, for instance, were sacred places that signalled the boundary between the spiritual and human worlds (Thornton 2020, 1998; Young 2011). In African religions, the high gods are often more disengaged; they are creators, but they do not intervene much in the world. Supernatural entities (e.g. ancestors) and individuals with magical powers (e.g. the *ngangas*) have a much more prominent role in what happens in the world (Mbiti 2015, 1990). This was also true in the Kingdom of Kongo's culture; the Kongolese high god, Nzambi a Mpungu, was understood to be quite disengaged (Thornton 2020, 1998), such that the role of Kimpa Vita as a *nganga* was highly esteemed. Thus, she took on the role of helping the community with her *nganga* spiritual powers by interpreting dreams and communicating with the other world.

Becoming Saint Anthony

Although the role of the *nganga* was not necessarily a public one, as a *nganga*, Kimpa Vita was already well known in the political scene. The fact that she was identified as a *nganga* not only placed her in a relevant political and communal role, but also situated her as defiant of European Christianity. European missionaries saw *nganga* practices as witchcraft; moreover, because the *nganga* were priests, they were direct competitors to the European missionaries. Indeed, sometimes, European priests performed exorcisms on *nganga* as they thought they were possessed by the devil. Nonetheless, her defiant position became much more apparent after August 1704, during which time she was just twenty-one and having visions on her deathbed.

She claimed that she saw the image of Saint Anthony dressed as a Capuchin. He spoke to her, possessing her, replaced her soul and got inside her head (Young 2011), which cured her. Saying that a saint possessed her was an act of defiance to the European social order at the time, for it was not credible to Europeans in the seventeenth and eighteenth centuries that Africans could achieve any high spiritual status. In general terms, African inferiority was believed to preclude individuals from having any notable religious role.[1] Even Father António Vieira, who had a more open-minded view for the time, was not entirely convinced that Africans (and Native Americans) could achieve any meaningful spiritual status (D'Azevedo 2019). In addition, in the European imaginary, it was not believed that saints could possess individuals (let alone individuals from ethnicities they considered inferior) to communicate the truth. Broadly, they thought that these were signs of demonic possession rather than a holy event, and as demonstrated later, this was very much the European perception of Kimpa Vita. In short, divine words were not revealed through possession (Thornton 1998). Moreover, someone who is possessed is a threat to those with religious authority, because if they say things in the name of God, then those who are said to represent God surely lose authority.

Although the mere declaration of being possessed by a saint was an act of defiance, the most severe defiance came from Kimpa Vita's actual discourse. In this declaration, she claimed to be the firstborn of the Faith and Saint Francis as Saint Anthony. She said her mission was to fulfil God's project to preach to people, commanding her to restore the Kingdom of Kongo. The Kingdom of Kongo had been in a state of civil war since 1665, and the people were tired. In contrast, the royal family wished to continue pursuing power and control of the slave routes (Pinto 2021a, 2021c). Hence, the demands of Kimpa Vita went against the war and the perpetuation of slavery. There was a demand for restoring and repopulating the capital of the kingdom. This demand had one main target: Pedro IV, who, despite having the power and responsibility as ruler, failed to do this, such that Kimpa Vita insisted he return to São Salvador (Young 2011). As he did not, she attempted to repopulate it herself, with considerable success. After she took residence in a ruined cathedral in São Salvador, thousands of people followed her, a goal that Pedro IV failed to achieve (Young 2011). Jesus, she said, was angry about this, especially with Pedro IV. Those who opposed God's project would be punished. Saint Anthony told her that he had tried to get into some women's minds (literally) in Bula, Nseto and Soyo, but people did not accept his message before.

Kimpa Vita also accused one of the closest ecclesiastical advisors of the king, Father Bernardo, of jealousy and envy. The accusation itself, however, was not simply about holding these characteristics. For in the seventeenth and eighteenth centuries, the Kongolese believed that '*ndokis*' (witches) were selfish and greedy and would look for any means to achieve their ends (Thornton 2020, 1998). In this connection, the accusation against Father Bernardo was much more severe than a simple matter of character; it was a suggestion that he was a *ndoki*.

Notably, Kimpa Vita's accusation extended to the fact that Father Bernardo did not recognize that there were black saints. It was a general belief in European ideology at the time that blackness was a sign of sin, moral degradation and inferiority (Chimakonam 2018; Tsri 2016a, 2016b; Bethencourt 2014). This was particularly problematic because, according to Kimpa Vita, the history of Christianity was told incorrectly by Europeans, who neglected to say that it originated from the Kingdom of Kongo. According to Kimpa Vita, there were many black saints from Kongo. This also represented a challenge to the Kongolese understanding of colour, as white was the colour of positive spirituality. More importantly, the true version of the church was revealed to Kimpa Vita, wherein Jesus was born in the city of São Salvador in the Kongo. Furthermore, according to Kimpa Vita, Jesus was not baptized in Nazareth but rather in the northern province of Nsundi. She claimed that Mary was herself Kongolese and was a slave of the Marquis Nzimba Mpangi at the time of Jesus's birth. She further claimed that Saint Francis, the ideological father of Saint Anthony, was also Kongolese (Thornton 2020, 1998; Pinto 2021b, 2021c; Young 2011).

Kimpa Vita said that Saint Anthony had also revealed to her the true versions of the prayers '*Ave Maria*' ('Hail Mary') and '*Salve Regina*' ('Hail, Holy Queen'), reporting that the latter went as follows:

> *Salve* [Save] the Queen, mother of mercy, the sweetness of life, our hope. *Deus* [God] save you; we cry out for you, we the exiled children of Eve; we sigh for you, kneeling and weeping in this valley of tears. Therefore, you, our advocate, cast your merciful eyes on us and then show us Jesus, the fruit of your womb; Ehe, you the merciful, Ehe benevolent one! E sweet one! The perpetual Virgin Mary. Pray for us, *Santa* [Holy] Mother of Nzambi a Mpungu, so that we may be worthy of the promises of Christ. (Thornton 1998: 115)

In this prayer, Kimpa Vita used various Kikongo terms in place of the Portuguese. For instance, '*Nzambi a Mpungu*' is the Kikongo version of God. As Thornton has argued, the new version of the prayer is more like a commentary on the first version.

These acts of Kimpa Vita were a series of attempts to make Christianity more inclusive and disrupt power hierarchies that oppressed the people of the Kingdom of Kongo. Kimpa Vita wanted to Africanize – or more accurately, 'Kongolonize'[2] – Christianity, not only by making it accessible by rendering it understandable to those who pray, but also by bringing Kongolese elements to the prayer. She then also denies the power of sacraments – such as baptism – which she claimed were irrelevant; for what mattered most were the intentions of those communicating with gods. Moreover, even if someone communicates with gods or other spiritual entities, this does not give this individual a special positive status, for what God cares about most is the intention of the individual rather than the prayer or the consequences of the act. Hence, if one is baptized with bad intentions, it serves no purpose to God. What determines whether '*kindoki*' (witchcraft) is positive or negative is precisely the intentionality of the person performing it. Finally, she declared Saint Anthony to be the truest and most crucial saint to whom people should pray (Thornton 2020, 1998; Young 2011).

Christian missionaries, African women and the concept of evil

Grounded on this and the work in the chapter on Queen Njinga, I begin here by summarizing how African women were portrayed by Capuchins, before offering an exploration of the close connection between the concept of evil and the image of African women. The problem of evil is one that also has social ramifications, due to which it will certainly influence thought significantly. Thus, the introduction of this topic will help illuminate the importance of Kimpa Vita's work as a philosophy that resisted and subverted metaphysical and social oppression at the time. Queen Njinga is unanimously considered a national hero by most Angolan political factions who disagree about nearly everything else (Thornton 2020; Heywood 2019). The perspective is different in Portugal, where her name and image have negative connotations as she was one of the most important figures to resist Portuguese colonialism. Even today, the image of Queen Njinga is sometimes used by conservative politicians to evoke colonial nostalgia and to place blame for the slave trade on Africans themselves. These negative Portuguese discourses perhaps have their origin in the missionary writings of Giovanni Antonio Cavazzi, the main biographer of Queen Njinga. Cavazzi contends that Queen Njinga changed from the personification of every possible evil to a model Christian after her proper conversion to Catholicism. Cavazzi describes Queen Njinga as a cannibal, deceitful, sexually promiscuous, ruthless in her quest for power and willing to go to such unimaginable extremes as killing her brother, her nephew and anyone who had a different opinion from hers or could be construed as a potential opponent (Cavazzi 1965). All this changed by a miracle performed by Antonio Gaeta, the Capuchin priest who re-baptized Queen Njinga. Cavazzi describes how on the day of Queen Njinga's conversion, the sky changed colour; the whole of nature showed the premonition that something novel would soon occur.

Kimpa Vita also garnered a negative characterization. The Capuchin missionaries Bernardo da Gallo and Lorenzo da Lucca saw her as an affront to their power, such that they lobbied for her persecution, characterizing her healing practices as devilish witchcraft. Kimpa Vita's practices were inspired by the knowledge of the *nganga*, priests in the Kongolese traditional religion; yet da Lucca and de Gallo understood these practices as signs of possession by the devil. And the fact that Kimpa Vita said that Saint Anthony possessed her showed that the devil owned her. For not only did they not believe that saints could possess individuals, they believed that African inferiority precluded all Africans from achieving any level of holiness. Moreover, the new nativity story was a heresy that could originate only from the revelation of the devil. In fact, Father da Gallo suggested that the story had a Dutch origin, which at the time also implied demonic origin as the Dutch were, generally speaking, Calvinists (Boxer 1958).

What do these negative characterizations of African women tell us about the concept of evil at the time? The various concepts of evil have been used in ways that rationalize Portuguese colonialism as morally justifiable. Notably, the Capuchin entangled evil with the identity of African women, who were characterized in ways that required 'civilized intervention' from the colonizers, which went towards justifying colonialism. This entanglement, has consequently allowed colonial ideologies to be furthered by excusing colonizers' actions from the scope of evil, allowing a positive image of colonialism to be extracted from their negative characterization of African women.

It is important to clarify some critical theoretical points to progress this argument. First, I take the standpoint of neutralization theory on the problem being analysed. By this, I mean that those who commit acts of violence try to find justifications to rationalize their actions. They engage in acts that they feel violate some ethical norms but find ways to neutralize their guilt to protect their self-image. When individuals act in harmful ways, they often need to justify their actions to themselves and others (Cordeiro-Rodrigues and Achino 2017; Osofsky, Bandura and Zimbardo 2005; Sykes and Matza 1957). Second, as some postcolonial theorists have pointed out, colonialism has both a psychological and a material dimension. There is the aim to control and manage resources, but there is also an element of psychological satisfaction, which may be expressed as pleasure or relief from guilt and so on (Bois 2020; Said 2014; Nandy 2009).

In this regard, the characterization of Queen Njinga as sexually promiscuous, untrustworthy, cruel and cannibalistic set her in the position of a negative mirror wherein the colonizer's identity would reflect back positively. For the negative traits attributed to Queen Njinga are not simply about her, but rather function to enact an ideology wherein Africans and European colonizers appear as opposites on the moral barometer, thereby offering a rationalization of Portuguese colonialism. Attributing sexual promiscuity to African women allowed the colonizer to rationalize their mistreatment of them and, simultaneously, to absolve European males of their guilt regarding their treatment of these women (Davis 2019; hooks 2014). This is expressed by the fact that in Portuguese colonialism, African women were often considered unmarriable.

At the same time, European men routinely considered it reasonable and unproblematic to initiate sexual encounters or experiments with African women, which remained the case until the twentieth century (Figueiredo 2018; Henriques 2017). This was mainly because Portuguese European women did not usually travel to the colonies;

it was only men who travelled and settled there. Various colonial discourses emerged about Portuguese men's relationships with African women (Boxer 1985, 1969), who have often been characterized as sexually promiscuous. In the seventeenth century, black was considered the colour of sin, and African women were conceptualized as symbolic of this (Tsri 2016b; Bethencourt 2014). Such discourses about promiscuity allowed for the view that rape by European males was consent and African women were blamed for their fall into sin (Davis 2019; hooks 2014). Indeed, the negative attributes were all placed on African women, while European males were characterized as victims of their sinful seduction.

The demonization of Queen Njinga serves the goal of justifying colonial expeditions and promoting an image wherein colonizers could be positively reflected. In seventeenth-century Angola, the demand for slave labour had increased exponentially, such that the slave trade also intensified, with the control of slave trade routes becoming ever more critical (Heywood 2019). The Kingdoms of Ndongo and Matamba, where Queen Njinga lived, were strategically important areas for controlling the slave trade routes (Heywood 2019; Manso 2016; Bethencourt 2014; Cadornega 1681). Thus, the Portuguese (as well as the Dutch) attempted to gain control over these areas by intensifying their armed expeditions to Angola. And the negative characterizations of Queen Njinga allowed for the justification of these enterprises. Not only did the Portuguese colonialists appear as civilizing agents, but Africans appeared less than human, which allowed rationalization of their enslavement. By characterizing Africans in this way, the Portuguese – and, in particular, the ruler at the time – found a justification for the use of force. Portuguese colonizers waged war against Queen Njinga to gain control over the territory and to expand their colonies (Pantoja 2020; Thornton 1991).

This discourse on Queen Njinga also allowed the Capuchins to appear as civilizing agents of the uncivilized Africans. During this period, there were power disputes between religious orders, particularly between Jesuits and Capuchins. The Jesuits had controlled the slave routes for an extended period, and the Capuchins had gained power over them only recently. Hence, Cavazzi argues that in contrast to the Jesuits, the Capuchins succeeded in civilizing the Africans, in particular, Queen Njinga. Thus, Cavazzi portrays his Capuchin predecessor, Antonio Gaeta, as the person who, against all odds, could be relied upon to convert and civilize Queen Njinga. The overarching implication of this is that both the Capuchins and the Portuguese had a civilizing mission in Africa, such that colonialism required the guidance of the Capuchins but was fundamentally justified. This contributed to the view that the Capuchins and the Portuguese were the white saviours of Africans.

Likewise, the characterization of Kimpa Vita reflects a positive rationalization of Portuguese colonialism. To understand this, it is helpful to understand how Kimpa Vita's political theory disrupted colonial goals. By telling a new nativity story where (mainly enslaved) Africans were placed at the centre, the colonial discourse of a civilizing mission was undermined. Moreover, Kimpa Vita's discourse on Jesus made it morally unacceptable to make Africans slaves. She elevates the African subject by telling a story where the African subject is not of a minor status. Finally, if baptism rituals were meaningless, this rendered the role of missionaries irrelevant. Considering this, demonizing Kimpa Vita was instrumental to justifying colonialism; Fathers da Gallo and da Lucca characterized her as a fraud, demoniac and, thereby, dangerous, all because her position challenged the justifications of colonialism. For if Kimpa Vita's political theory was right, there was no place for a European, colonial civilizing mission, slave trade or for any of their religious rituals. She therefore also disrupts the power structures of her time; the ones responsible for slavery – the missionaries and the Kongolese King – are challenged in their religious legitimacy.

The problem of evil revisited

Kimpa Vita makes Christianity more inclusive. Previously, I demonstrated how her arguments try to include Africans more in it. I think it also aims at some metaphysical inclusion. The theory of Kimpa

Vita is a form of disruption of the dominant discourses of the time on what is evil. So it also has metaphysical implications for the problem of evil. I am not sure if these were intended or not because she never talks about it directly. But taking into consideration the religiosity of the society at the time, it may have been necessary to not simply take a political stand but a religious one. Also, the problem of evil does have social implications, and it is likely that Kimpa Vita understood this.

Philosophers have addressed the problem of evil for centuries, dating back to Plato (Cordeiro-Rodrigues and Chimakonam 2023; Hickson 2013). How can a morally perfect, omniscient and all-powerful God allow evil to exist? In Western Christianity, two philosophical issues have emerged regarding the problem of evil: the logical and the evidential. The logical problem of evil is that it is inconsistent to believe in a God who is omniscient, omnipotent and morally perfect while evil exists in the world. More particularly, the contention is that if evil does exist (and it does), there is no reason why God would let it exist. This is because he knows about it, has the power to stop it and is morally good enough to want to stop it. Hence, the argument goes that theists must give up either one of these characteristics or the existence of God altogether (Tooley 2020; Mackie 1955). Concerning the evidential problem of evil, the question is a little different. The issue is not so much about logical consistency. Instead, it is that the existence of God may be logically compatible with the existence of evil. Nonetheless, the quantity of evil in the world makes the existence of God questionable. Notably, even if God needs to have specific amounts of evil in the world, there is no reason he would allow the significant quantity of evil observable in the world. As these questions primarily emerge from the Western Christian tradition, it is no surprise that most philosophical enterprises take a Western point of view (van Inwagen 2008; Swinburne1998; Plantinga 1974).

The problem of evil is often thought to be simply a metaphysical problem without normative implications. However, this is not true. As explained in the previous section, concepts of evil helped justify colonialism. The problem of evil can be addressed with an oppressive metaphysics with real social consequences, neglecting some individuals who are morally relevant (Cordeiro-Rodrigues and Chimakonam 2023; Hickson 2013). The work of Kimpa Vita is, in part, a recognition that the problem of evil is also social. She does not address the problem of evil directly, but I do think that her views do have this implication. The views of Kimpa Vita – embodied in Kongolese Christianity – on the problem of evil overlap in many ways with those of Western Christian philosophers (after all, she is a Christian). Still, elements derived from African traditional religions make the Kongolese responses that she defends rather different from the Western ones. Notably, the African understanding of the world implies a different conception of God and a different outlook and solution to the problem of evil. Firstly, the discourses of Kimpa Vita offer an inclusive and decolonized view of evil, which contrasts with that of the missionaries. While missionaries exclude Africans from sainthood, Kimpa Vita elevates African individuals as potential saints and the descendants of Jesus, which reframes the problem of evil; evil can no longer be defined according to ethnicity. More precisely, what this implies is that the concept of evil cannot simply refer, or refer mainly, to blackness and sainthood to whiteness. Furthermore, if the African person becomes a subject worthy of moral consideration, then this implies that the experience of suffering of the African subject becomes relevant for considerations of evil. Part of what Kimpa Vita's view brings to light is the need to look at the problem of evil inclusively rather than as simply a European-centred one. According to Kimpa Vita, including the African subject's viewpoint is critical, for without it, any theory of evil (and good for that matter) is incomplete. The experience of slavery, the experience of Africanity, is relevant and informative. A new theodicy should include African epistemologies if it hopes to successfully comprehend evil (Cordeiro-Rodrigues and Chimakonam 2023). This, in turn, undermines the explanations of harm directed to Africans and particularly African women, as explained in the previous section. That is, this view undermines the missionary rationale that justifies slavery, rape and so on.

Secondly, in contrast with the Western theistic view, Kimpa Vita's theory, grounded on the Kongolese kind of Christianity outlined in Chapter 2, does not justify horrendous evils. Her view is that some evils in the world can be excessive. Horrendous evils such as slavery and the Holocaust are not morally justified as they are in some mainstream Western Christian views. This is because God is imperfect and, as such, He has limits to what He can do (Cordeiro-Rodrigues and Chimakonam 2023; Cordeiro-Rodrigues 2022b). For this reason, the Kongolese perspective defended by Kimpa Vita is morally more convincing than its mainstream Western counterpart. To understand my point, note that Western theists tend to deny the existence of excessive evil in the world. For example, Richard Swinburne and Peter van Inwagen, following Western Christian views, claim that there is no evidence that the evil in the world is excessive. The problem with this view is that it renders morally justified all the evils that happen in the world. According to this view, every evil is to a certain extent justified because it is allowed by a morally perfect entity to promote a greater good. The unintended implication is that horrendous evils such as slavery and the Holocaust are morally permissible since they are allowed by a perfectly good God. Western Christian theists do not explicitly state this, but this is the implication of their view. They must accept the undesirable view that horrendous evils are morally justified. They must accept the repugnant view that these horrendous evils are morally justified on the grounds of saving a few, as it is written in the Bible (Matt. 24.1–22) that only a few will be saved. The problem here is that Western Christian theists claim to ground their ideas in what they call Christian moral theory. As Eleonore Stump and Marilyn McCord Adams contend, theodicies and defences must be grounded in core Christian moral beliefs (Stump 2012; Adams and Adams 1991). From the perspective of these core beliefs, such horrendous evils as Nazism and slavery are not morally justified. Thus, the idea that all evils in the world are allowed by God to promote a greater good unwittingly leads some Western Christians into a contradiction.

This, of course, creates tension in the outlook of some Western Christian theists. On the one hand, horrendous evils such as slavery and the Holocaust are considered morally unjustified. On the other hand, they are morally justified because they promote a greater good (this is not an intended argument, but I think this is the implication). The end of encouraging a greater good justifies the means of the horrendous evils, according to philosophers like Stump, Swinburne or Plantinga. The Kongolese view (as defended by Kimpa Vita), in contrast, does not regard all evils as morally justified because it considers some evils excessive. Thus, in Kimpa Vita's version of the problem of evil, there are excessive evils in the world and things like slavery are simply not morally justified. For there are excessive evils in the world which result from God's incapability to address them. God for the Kongolese is imperfect and the existence of this evil is explained by this rather than by a mysterious God plan. Hence, her theory avoids the implication that things like slavery are, to some extent, morally justified because they result from the decisions of a perfect God. This is quite an innovative view that Kimpa Vita offers, and it is clearly a disruption that elevates African people in a way that other theodicies have failed to do. Kimpa Vita's theory implies that evil is not simply associated with blackness. Also, it does not accept that the harms inflicted on Africans ought to be morally acceptable. This disruption of the metaphysics at the time opens up a way for more social inclusion of African individuals.

Conclusion

In the history of Angola, Queen Njinga is routinely considered a symbol and prototype of African liberation. In Chapter 3, I adopted a neutral approach to present a more accurate description of Queen Njinga, independently of the admiration she rightly receives. Kimpa Vita is a neglected figure within African thought, but, as I have conveyed in this chapter, she had, in my view, a much more genuine concern for people, as well as a more inclusive political theory, than Queen Njinga. Kimpa

Vita offers a perspective on religions and social status that is inclusive of different classes, that eschews slavery and that centralizes Africans in ethical concerns, thereby making the African subject morally relevant. This is relevant for the decolonization of the discourse of the time, but also for its decolonization today.

6

Creole anti-colonialist and proto-nationalist voices in Angola

Introduction

The nineteenth century was a time of profound change. Portugal's political, social and economic structures were shaken, as were its colonial settings. At the beginning of the nineteenth century, Angola had many creole individuals (ethnically mixed people born during the colonial era) in positions of power. Nonetheless, the mass migration of European settlers to Angola had changed this. Creoles saw their power being overturned and so began to oppose it (Claro 2009; Corrado 2008, 2007; Gonçalves 1999; Tavares 1999; Guerra 1980a, 1980b). A native collective consciousness opposed to colonialism and monarchic power grew, perhaps for the first time, among Angolan creoles (Moreno 2014; Ribeiro 2012; Jacob 2010; Corrado 2008, 2007; Padilha 2008). The focus of this chapter is the writings of the creole elite who, in the late nineteenth and twentieth centuries, developed theories of proto-nationalism and anti-colonialism. The writings at this time were dispersed and written largely in the style of newspaper opinion pieces (Rodrigues and Candido 2018; Pinto 2017; Moreno 2014; Oliveira 2010; Gonçalves 1999; Tavares 1999). The primary sources used here are from various actors and require the inclusion of different views. I have chosen to analyse the underlying political theory of three of the most representative works from this period. I shall outline the theories of the authors of the book *Voz de Angola Clamando no Deserto* (Vários/União dos escritores Angolanos 1984), Pedro da Paixão Franco (1911, 1901) and António de Assis Júnior (2004, 1985, 1949). These three works are often considered the most representative of the proto-nationalist and anti-colonial thought of the Angolan creole elite in this period (Madureira 2021; Oliveira 2010; Claro 2009; Corrado 2008; Guerra 1980a, 1980b).

To explain their theories, I shall need to provide some context. In the first section, I thus explore the role of Social Darwinism in colonial Portugal throughout the late nineteenth and early twentieth centuries. After this, I explain the political turmoil in colonial Angola and the birth and role of the written press during that period. After providing this important context, I explain in the third section what led some members of the creole elite to write the *Voz de Angola* and what philosophical ideas can be found in this text. The penultimate section considers Paixão Franco's criticisms of the creole elite, and the last section analyses de Assis Júnior's political thoughts.[1]

Social Darwinism, Portuguese colonialism and Angola

One of the most famous figures in the biological sciences is Charles Darwin. His work has been extraordinarily influential and important for scientific inquiry. This is even more the case in the context of the nineteenth century when Darwin first published the *On the Origin of Species by Means of Natural Selection* in 1859. According to Darwin, there is a constant struggle for survival in nature: beings (plants, humans, non-human animals) continuously compete with one another. Owing to various factors, only a few can survive (the fittest), and consequently, there is a natural process of selection. Those that best adapt to their environment can survive to reproduce and pass their characteristics on to the next generation, while those who do not adapt do not survive or reproduce. Therefore, biological diversity results from this constant struggle and adaptation to the circumstances in which a being finds itself (Darwin 2020; Darwin and Francis 2017).

When Darwin wrote *On the Origin of Species*, his goal was to explain the biological processes that natural beings undergo. As a Victorian, it is likely that he held many racial prejudices and sought to defend the social hierarchies at the time. But he did not explicitly advance a social theory of evolution. In the late nineteenth century, however, some intellectuals influenced by Darwin's theory developed what today is called 'Social Darwinism' (Jackson and Depew 2017; Aschenbrenner 2015; Pereira 2010; Darwin 2009; Hawkins 2008; Jones 1980). Some of the most representative works of Social Darwinism are Joseph Fisher's 1877 article *The History of Landholding in England* and Herbert Spencer's works such as *Progress: Its Law and Cause* (1857). Social Darwinism can be considered the application of Darwin's ideas to social, political and economic reality, using the language of evolution (natural selection, adaptation, survival of the fittest) to explain what occurs (and how it occurs) in societies (Jackson and Depew 2017; Claeys 2000; Jones 1980).

The reason for the evolution of language can be explained by way of postcolonial theory. Edward Said, Ashis Nandy and other postcolonial theorists uphold that colonialism requires an ideological groundwork to justify itself. It needs to create an imaginary where those who are subordinated deserve or wish to be in such a position; furthermore, the ones who subordinate others need a theory to justify their unfair advantage, their higher rank in the hierarchy and so forth (Said 2014; Nandy 2009). The social and psychological function of Social Darwinism in Europe during the late nineteenth and early twentieth centuries was precisely to provide this ideological groundwork. Particularly, although Social Darwinism was a pseudo-scientific view (at least during the nineteenth and early twentieth centuries), it was understood to give a scientific grounding to racist views that placed white people at the top of the hierarchy (Jackson and Depew 2017; Aschenbrenner 2015; Darwin 2009; Boddice 2016; Sweet 2002; Jones 1980).

Early Social Darwinism was not homogeneous and had a variety of different supporters from distinct fields of thought. These various intellectuals applied it to different subjects, putting forward theories that were not necessarily contradictory but were not always shared by others. There were, however, some theories that were more popular and widely shared than others. Early Social Darwinism advances a variety of approaches that aim to justify colonial order – that is, that aim to provide a rationale for the subjugation of African people to European people. One popular theory linked to the justification of colonial order is the welcoming of competition. This view was defended because competition was seen as a natural (and thereby good) phenomenon that one should not interfere with. Competition is what brings the best to the fore, and interfering in it, so the Social Darwinists contend, means producing suboptimal outcomes. According to this view, colonial hierarchies are simply the result of competition and therefore represent an optimal, morally justified outcome. Another popular theory among early Social Darwinists was that the use of force and coercion was not ethically problematic. For them, this is just how nature is and is the necessary step for the fittest to emerge in society such that civilization can develop. It was also popular among early Social Darwinists that the hierarchy of European people dominating Africans was just the reflection of evolution, wherein the fittest get the most powerful positions in society.

According to this theory, the reason why colonial powers were more powerful was simply because they were innately better (survival of the fittest). Likewise, from this viewpoint, the colonizers' ability to accumulate wealth results from fitter social characteristics. Accordingly, this theory defends the idea that, eventually, other races – which they perceived as inferior – would disappear, and the fittest – which they believed was the white race – would be the only one to survive. From a Social Darwinist perspective, imperialism, racism and social inequality are morally justified. Hence, they often argued that there should be no laws to help the weak because they go against the evolution of civilization (Jackson and Depew 2017; Boddice 2016; Aschenbrenner 2015; Pereira 2010; Darwin 2009; Hawkins 2008; Claeys 2000; Jones 1980).

Social Darwinism was widespread among European colonial powers in the late nineteenth and early twentieth centuries, and Portugal was no exception. Some of the most well-known Social Darwinist views were defended by intellectuals such as Oliveira Martins (Martins

1921). Social Darwinism also deeply influenced Portuguese colonial legislation. From the 1880s, 'mixed-race' and 'black' people faced an increase in discriminatory practices, throwing much of the creole elite into unemployment, which was justified on Social Darwinist grounds. One example of this was the 1899 *'Regulamento do Trabalho dos Indígenas'* (Regulation for Indigenous Labour/Indigenous Labour Law), which decreed that all African people had the duty to work for the development of the territory. It also decreed that Africans could legally be forced to work even if they refused. This was justified because the labour was supposed to civilize African people. With a Social Darwinist explanation in hand, there were many justifications for Portuguese colonialism. Notably, many of these justifications focused on the civilizing mission of the Portuguese and the replacement of the creole elite by European settlers. Indicative of this was General Dantas Barracho's speech as a member of parliament in 1893, claiming that the 'white race' was superior and that 'black people' were lazy and morally inferior. He contended that the phenotypical characteristics of African people supported this view, concluding that forced labour was justified, so as to civilize African people (Moreno 2014; Oliveira 2010).

Literary and journalistic writings and anti-colonial resistance

In the middle of the nineteenth century, there were significant economic changes in the colonial world, particularly in Portugal. Portugal had faced successive crises throughout the century right up to the beginning of the twentieth century, including civil wars between 1820 and 1834 (Mesquita 2006a, 2006b). These civil wars greatly contributed to the bankruptcy of the metropole. Moreover, Brazil became independent in 1822, which led to significant economic losses for Portugal. Another relevant change was the prohibition of slavery. The initial legal enactment against slavery was carried out by Marquis Sá da Bandeira in 1836, who repressed the slave trade (Rosas 2018a; Corrado 2008).

Nonetheless, Marquis Sá da Bandeira's decree was not immediately enforced, and the slave traders strongly opposed it in Angola. The trade ceased only after a naval intervention by Britain. Later, between 1854 and 1858, Portugal enacted various laws to reduce slavery in Angola, and finally a proclamation declaring that all forms of slavery should be abolished appeared in 1878.

In 1884, the Berlin Conference took place, at which it was decided, among other things, that the sovereignty of colonial powers over African territories should be curtailed, including the limits of Portugal's claims over Angola's territory. Hence from the 1880s to the 1890s, there was a rush for territory in Africa. With the fear of expansion from other colonial powers into their territory, the Portuguese government gave many incentives to migrate to the colonies, putting substantial effort into occupying the colonial spaces. Nonetheless, in 1890, Britain presented an ultimatum to Portugal. Portugal claimed sovereignty over the land corridor that connected Angola and Mozambique (a project known as the 'Pink Map'). Britain's ultimatum succeeded, forcing Portugal to withdraw from Nyasaland (today known as Malawi) and Rhodesia (today known as Zimbabwe and Zambia). The success of the ultimatum was seen as a national humiliation that rendered the Portuguese monarchy fragile in an already unstable situation, owing to the many economic setbacks it had been facing (Rosas 2018a, 2018b).

These events led to significant changes in Portugal and its colonies. There was high unemployment, and many people had to move to the colonies to look for work. The European settlement started mostly in Luanda and Benguela. Contrasting with some other forms of colonialism (such as in Kenya), most colonizers in Angola came from economically poor backgrounds in the metropole. European settlers began migrating to Africa and occupying positions previously taken by the creole elite. One of the unique marks of Portuguese colonialism until the late nineteenth century was that it was a mostly male enterprise, a feature that, for instance, was not shared by Spanish colonialism. Consequently, many European settlers had relationships with African women, whose sons, the creoles, then occupied most of the critical posts in the colonies, given that there were insufficient numbers of European settlers and that the metropole did not want to give these positions to 'black' people (Boxer 1969).

But with the migration of European Portuguese to Africa, the privileged positions of the creoles came under threat. Furthermore, the prohibition of slavery changed the lives of the creole elite, who were highly economically dependent on this business. They had to change their businesses to other products, such as ivory (Caldeira 2013; Corrado 2008).

Given this environment, in Portugal and its colonies, the nineteenth century was marked by a wide contestation of the monarchical regime on various fronts, including the creoles who were discontented about losing their positions as well as those who had been made vulnerable owing to the economic crisis (Rosas 2018a). This contestation of the regime in the colonies came along with the explosion of the written press in 1845, much of which was anti-monarchic/pro-republican. However, there was also governmental press circulating. The first publication in Angola was put out by the government: the *Boletim do Governo Geral da Província de Angola*. The articles in it were primarily supportive of government policies (Hohlfeldt and Carvalho 2012; Jacob 2010).

This contrasted with the significant number of pro-republican newspapers that contested the regime at the time. Indeed, newspapers in the colonies became the primary vehicle for the transmission of literary, cultural and political ideas. In the case of Angola, the cities of Luanda and Benguela were the main centres of sociopolitical and cultural activity in the 1830s and 1840s. Newspapers had such an important role that, by the end of the nineteenth century, there were fifty-nine newspapers printed in Angola: forty-nine in Luanda, six in Mossâmedes, two in Benguela and one in Ambriz and Catumbela. Some of the main newspapers defending republicanism were *O Cruzeiro do Sul* (Southern Cruise) (1873), *O Echo de Angola* (The Echo of Angola) (1881), *A Verdade* (The Truth) (1882), *O Futuro d'Angola* (The Future of Angola) (1882), *O Pharol do Povo* (People's Lighthouse) (1883), *Arauto Africano* (African Herald) (1889), *O Desastre* (The Disaster) (1889),

O Polícia Africano (The African Police) (1890), *A Província* (The Province) (1893), *Propaganda Colonial* (Colonial Propaganda) (1896) and *Propaganda Angolense* (Angolan Propaganda) (1897). Although the press was prolific and there was a free press law in the 1850s, there was also significant censorship, particularly towards those newspapers edited by creole Angolans. Indeed, the free press law did not refer to the freedom to publish what one pleases. Instead, 'free press' referred to the possibility for newspapers to be privately run along with the official government bulletin (Hohlfeldt and Carvalho 2012; Jacob 2010; Corrado 2008, 2007).

In connection with racial disputes, these newspapers can be divided into two kinds. On the one hand, there were the European settlers' newspapers publishing racist articles in defence of colonialism and white supremacy; on the other, there were newspapers run by creole elites which present some of the first expressions of anti-colonial and proto-nationalist sentiments. In many newspapers run by European settlers, the repression of African people and the diminishing of the powers of creole people were defended. The creole elite of Angola reacted to this by publishing articles in the creole-run newspapers that contested racist social injustices and promoted debates over the colony's independence. The newspaper *O Echo de Angola* (Echo from Angola) (1881–2) was the first newspaper to be run entirely by Africans, but the most influential publication among creole elites was *O Pharol do Povo* (People's Lighthouse), despite lasting for only two years (1883–5). Most newspapers were short-lived because they had to close down as a result of censorship and political pressure. Many of the articles published in *O Pharol do Povo* advocated republicanism, independence of Angola and anti-colonialism, although it was highly censored. For instance, one of its republican journalists, Arantes Braga, was imprisoned for forty days for sedition. Despite censorship and the hostile environment, Angolan creoles took the opportunity given by the free press law and the importance of journalistic venues to express their dissent from the regime and defend local culture and value systems (Hohlfeldt and Carvalho 2012; Jacob 2010; Corrado 2008).

Furthermore, creole journalists edited journals to defend the economic and political interests that they felt were under threat in Angola. In nineteenth- and early-twentieth-century Angola, journalism was a space of political debate and resistance. But it was not the only form of resistance; indeed, all forms of literary writing were used as means of resistance. In 1896, the *Associação Literária Angolense* (Angolan Literary Association) was created by Augusto Ferreira, Francisco Augusto Taveira, Apolinário Van-Dúnem and Manuel Augusto dos Santos. This was a space for cultural exchange and production, allowing anti-colonial and proto-nationalist ideas to flourish. Indeed, these names partially make up a vital generation who later created two newspapers, the *Almanach-Ensaios Literários* (Literary Essays Almanac) (1901) and *Luz e Crença* (Light and Belief) (1902), which were influential in contesting colonialism (Hohlfeldt and Carvalho 2012; Jacob 2010; Corrado 2008, 2007).

Voz de Angola Clamando no Deserto: Anti-colonialism and proto-nationalism of the Creole Elite

The racial tensions in Angola were multifarious during this time. Still, an article published in number five of *A Gazeta de Loanda* (Luanda's Gazette) in 1901, written by a Portuguese resident, further provoked these tensions, stoking the indignation of the creole elite. The article was published anonymously under the title '*Contra a lei, pela grey*' ('Against the Law, for the People'), and it promoted many racist ideas. I quote two of the most outrageous passages: 'The harsh punishment of a white for a small offence to the black challenges racial hierarchies and the autonomy of the nation' (Anonymous 1901, my translation).[2] And

> to place the iron of the King in a black that killed, stole, harmed or offended public morality with actions or words is not a punishment; rather it is to give him an incentive to crime ... so what is the ideal life of a black besides eating without working? ... What is his law, his way

of life besides that? We are not in favour of physical punishment ... but a small tap never killed anyone. (Anonymous 1901, my translation)[3]

The author claimed that 'black people' (which also referred to mixed race people) were lazy and did not want to work. Furthermore, the author upheld that 'black people' are not exactly human, suggesting they are between animality and humanity. Consequently, the author argued that 'black people' ought not to be imprisoned.[4] According to the author, imprisoning African people gives other African people the chance to be lazy. Indeed, the author said that because African people are lazy and prison offers them the opportunity to be lazy, imprisoning them is, in fact, an invitation to crime. Instead, the author suggests corporal punishment or deportation as this is more appropriate and effective to their non-human nature. In addition, the author claims that the law should apply differently to African and European settlers; equality of treatment is counterproductive because it challenges the superiority of the 'white race', even if the same crime is committed. It is notable that the author believes that the law should function differently according to who the perpetrator and victim of the crime are: if the victim is a European settler (or, in his words, a 'white person'), then the punishment ought to be harsher; whereas if the aggressor is a European settler, the penalty should be lighter. Thus, according to this view, there should be separate legal systems for Africans and European settlers (Anonymous 1901).

This article provoked many strong responses. The backlash by the creoles was so significant that the same anonymous author felt compelled to write another article to explain that he did not mean to refer to the educated creoles but rather to the uneducated, uncivilized Africans (Moreno 2014). The most famous of these reactions are found in the anti-colonial and proto-nationalist writings in a volume entitled *Voz de Angola Clamando no Deserto* (Voice of Angola Crying/Calling in the Desert) (Vários/União dos escritores Angolanos 1984). Indeed, the book is sometimes considered the engine of anti-colonial Angolan political activism in the twentieth century. The book was published with the first volume of the *Almanach-Ensaios Litterarios*, which was edited by one of the book's authors, Francisco Castelbranco. Initially, one thousand copies of *Voz de Angola* were published anonymously in 1901. This was self-funded by the authors and anonymous donors. A second edition with a print run of 5,000 copies was published only in 1984 by the *União dos Escritores Angolanos* (Angolan Writers Association). The initial publication was anonymous to avoid retaliation; nonetheless, one of the copies had the names of the authors such that it is possible to identify them. There were eleven authors in total: the priest Antonio José do Nascimento (author of *Solemnia Verba*); Pascoal José Martins, or 'Sá' Martins (*'Á Contra lei, pela grey'*); Francisco Castelbranco (*'Á Gazeta Civilisadora d 'África'*); Mario Castanheira Nunes (*'Réplica'*); Carlos Saturnino de Sousa e Oliveira (*'Ex digito gigas'*); Augusto Silvério Ferreira (*'Agora nós'*); Carlos Botelho de Vasconcelos (*'Um protesto'*); José Carlos de Oliveira Jr. (*'Preconceitos'*); Eusébio Velasco Galiano (*'Quis eritis?'*); João de Almeida Campos (*'Confrontos'*); and Apolinário Van Dúnem (*'É o cúmulo das infâmias'*) (Moreno 2014; Hohlfeldt and Carvalho 2012; Oliveira 2010; Vários/União dos escritores Angolanos 1984).

Many of these names were involved in the anti-regime newspapers mentioned above. The *Voz de Angola* includes articles by intellectuals from different parts of Angola. Indeed, it is the first known publication to unite Luanda writers and writers from inner Angola/Golungo (north of Angola), Benguela (west of Angola) and Bengo (east of Angola). The diversity of authors signals the unity between creoles against the Portuguese system. The *Voz de Angola*, however, did not just comprise these authors' articles; it also included a compilation of writings from pre-published pieces by various authors who supported the political theory the book hoped to advance. The choice of making it anonymous brought conflict within the group. Pedro da Paixão Franco, whom I shall discuss in the next section, thought that it should not be anonymous, so his article was not published (Corrado 2008).

Because of the many different voices behind the authorship of the book, the political ideas it contains are multiple, although it is possible to identify a cohesive set of political ideas spanning the entire text. Many of the ideas are criticisms of the Portuguese metropole's colonization ideology. One of the marks of colonialism in general and Portuguese colonialism in particular is that it is justified in terms of a mission to civilize Africans. The authors of the *Voz de Angola* contest this ideology in various ways. They challenge that Portuguese colonialism had brought any civilization at all to Angola. According to some authors in the *Voz de Angola*, Portuguese colonialism has made Angola undeveloped, rather than developed as presupposed, under the headers of civilization, culture and progress. This argument is often tied in with the idea that Portuguese colonialism has undercut the possibility of Africans having equal access to education. Indeed, the authors often criticize the Portuguese colonial government for restricting the education of Africans. They claim that Portuguese colonialism has resulted in different systems for African and European settlers, wherein education was not a priority (Vários/União dos escritores Angolanos 1984).

Another way they challenge the idea that the Portuguese can civilize Africa is by pointing to the uncivilized behaviour of the Portuguese settlers themselves, demonstrating that they are actually incapable of civilizing Africans. More specifically, the Portuguese colonialists' enslavement, forced labour, exploitation and general inhumane treatment of African individuals suggest that the Portuguese colonialists were not best placed as agents of civilization. For the authors of the *Voz de Angola*, servitude is an enemy of progress, and to the extent that Portuguese colonialism emphasizes servitude, it cannot enhance progress. In fact, many of the criticisms that can be found in the *Voz de Angola* are directed at the Indigenous Labour Law mentioned above. They contend that this law is just disguised slavery (Vários/União dos escritores Angolanos 1984).

Another sign of the colonizers' lack of civilization was the disrespect for the law that many demonstrate. Remarkably, the lack of respect for anti-slavery laws by the colonizers acted as a sign of lack of civility, especially when compared with other European countries that abolished slavery. Likewise, some authors of the *Voz de Angola* claimed that there was more crime in Portugal than in Angola, which suggests a profound disrespect for the law and a sign of a deep lack of civilization (Vários/União dos escritores Angolanos 1984).

Moreover, some claimed that the Portuguese colonialists came from less educated classes in the metropole, which would make them unqualified to civilize the colonies. Indeed, the authors of the *Voz de Angola* tend to understand racism as a form of ignorance; therefore, they contend that the author of the opinion piece in the *Gazeta de Loanda* is likely to simply be uneducated. According to some of the authors of the *Voz de Angola*, these arguments demonstrate that if anyone is to blame for the lack of development and civility of some Africans, it should be the Portuguese colonizers themselves. It is, therefore, a hypocritical position to claim that the Portuguese are or could ever be civilizing agents (Vários/União dos escritores Angolanos 1984).

A key normative idea can be identified in this criticism of the article from the *Gazeta de Loanda*. For the creole elite, access to education was necessary for the development to which Africans were supposedly entitled, and yet the Portuguese colonizers curtailed it. This creole elite contends that the key differences between people amount to education, not to race. Indeed, a discriminatory tone towards the uneducated is sometimes noted in the text, even though the authors blame the colonizers for such a situation. Furthermore, the authors of the *Voz de Angola* insist that the act of barring Africans from education is not innocuous, staking the claim that Portuguese colonizers are afraid of educated African people because once they become educated, they can understand the injustices they have undergone and thus reclaim their rights. According to various authors of the *Voz de Angola*, the absence of educational institutions in Angola was a mechanism to allow for control over the local populations, such that education was therefore at the basis for liberation, a liberation that the Portuguese colonizers desperately attempted to undermine (Vários/União dos escritores Angolanos 1984).

The critique of education is also used to contest the dominant theory of Social Darwinism at the time (Corrado 2008). The authors of the *Voz de Angola* contend that it is not true that Africans are naturally inferior to European settlers, but that the lack of education they had received – owing to colonial policies – led to those differences. The authors of the *Voz de Angola* could not avoid some prejudice and paternalism regarding some Africans, however, whom they called 'uncivilized' owing to their lack of exposure to European values. It was the educated creole elites that they claimed to be equal to European settlers, not all Africans. Hence, the criticisms here aim at elevating creoles, but simultaneously endorse negative views about some Africans whom they considered inferior (Vários/União dos escritores Angolanos 1984).

At this point, it may be important to make an observation that the reader may also have noticed: were these intellectuals really anti-colonialists? Sometimes they seem to argue in favour of colonialism, praising European culture; at other times, they seem to be advancing an Africanization of society. Hence, it is difficult to understand exactly what they wanted. This confusion is legitimate because the texts do indeed often point in different directions. These texts need to be read in the context of the time – namely, one in which creoles were anxious about their identity, trying to find themselves and most of the time writing from within a ghettoized context (Laranjeira 1995; Hamilton 1975). It is no wonder that we therefore encounter some confusion.

The authors of the *Voz de Angola* disagree on what should be done concerning the problems caused by colonialism. It is not unanimous whether the attitude against the colonizer is to claim total independence from the metropole or simply a higher degree of autonomy or just a set of more egalitarian policy reforms. The nationalist sentiments here are divided, but they are not divided in terms of being a national of Angola. All the authors in the *Voz de Angola* feel that they are 'sons of the country' (i.e. they understand themselves to be not Portuguese but Angolan: an identity distinct from the metropole). The book's subtitle, *Naturals de Angola* ('Originally from Angola'), is an identarian affirmation that is not necessarily independentist but is undoubtedly anti-colonial and republican. It is important to note that in these texts, anti-colonialism does not mean a complete rejection of the colonial experience. Indeed, many authors not only see some benefits from colonialism, but also despise those who have not adopted some European modes of living (Vários/União dos escritores Angolanos 1984).

The pro-republican element, however, must be distinguished from the European republicanism of the time. In broad terms, and in contrast to the authors of the *Voz de Angola*, European republicanism was procolonialist, racist and proto-fascist (Rosas 2018a). Indeed, the article from the *Gazeta de Loanda* is understood by the authors of the *Voz de Angola* as symptomatic of how society at the time (both the monarchist and republican sectors) understood racial relations. The article in the *Gazeta de Loanda* is just one instance of the propaganda emerging from republicans and monarchists who generally had an anti-African sentiment (Moreno 2014; Oliveira 2010).

Another essential idea conveyed in the text is the affirmation of the value of Africanity. It is, the authors contend, the duty of African people to demonstrate their clout. Some authors do so by defending the value of dignity, upholding the idea that there are no human races, only human species, such that everyone should be treated equally. This appeal often comes with a religious claim that Catholicism does not differentiate people according to colour: everyone is the same in the eyes of God, and so humans laws should follow suit. Biblical references heavily influence the title and style of the book. The connection to a voice crying/calling in a desert appears with respect to Isaiah in the Old Testament. Isaiah predicts the coming of the Messiah and expects that great punishment will fall upon those who treat the poor and weak unfairly. This signals that Catholicism underpins the reasoning of the text, grounding its espousal of equality and dignity of all humans in religious values. Hence, the appeals to the Bible as an authority for dignity and equality are not surprising (Corrado 2008).

Some authors adopt a more secular perspective while defending Africans. For instance, although there is no specific mention of African value systems, they are indirectly referred to through the use of Kimbundu (the dominant language among Africans in Angola) terminology. Using Kimbundu terminology is not only a way to show their Angolan identification, but also a means by which to demonstrate that their identity is valuable and should be promoted. Especially telling of this context was the repression of African languages in Angola (Oliveira 2010); the use of Kimbundu was a contestation against the repression of Africanity. Another secular argument in the text shows the contribution of African individuals to development and cultural production, both in Angola and worldwide. In the case of Angola, some authors claim that African people have contributed substantially to the colony's development but that many European settlers have unfairly benefited from this labour. In other texts, it is shown how not only Angolans, but also African people from all over the continent have produced intellectual work (Vários/União dos escritores Angolanos 1984).

Moreover, from a secular viewpoint, some authors of the *Voz de Angola* cite work in anthropology and other social sciences to show that African people and European people are equal. Indeed, they not only contend that there are no pure 'racial kinds', but also that if there were, the Portuguese colonizers would not be one of them given that the history of Portugal is made up of an array of different ethnicities. They claimed there is no indication that African people are inferior; more precisely, they contended that African people are not physically, morally or intellectually inferior (Vários/União dos escritores Angolanos 1984).

Finally, the text also promotes the idea of legal equality as well as the need to preserve and value the rule of law. The article's title in the *Gazeta de Loanda* challenges the legal system. The title '*Contra lei, pela grey*' ('Against the Law, From the People') reverses the maxim by King John II in the fifteenth century, which stated '*pela lei, pela grey*' ('for the law, from the people'). The maxim of the king suggests that royal authority (or the law) should have the support of the population and that the power of nobility should be limited. Law needs to have the support of popular will and be respected (Corrado 2008).

In contrast, the article in the *Gazeta de Loanda* promotes disrespect for the law and a change to the current regulation. It advocates for being selective about who is most relevant for law-making, claiming that the European settlers should be given priority. Hence, the articles in the *Voz de Angola* claim that the law should be inclusive of both African and European settlers: it should be equal for all, with punishment and sanctions distributed according to the nature of the crime rather than according to ethnicity. Thus, if European settlers harm Africans, they ought to be punished. Punishment should also be proportional to the crime; rather than having laws that are excessive or lenient in terms of punishment, they ought to follow a reasonable understanding of the offence and apply a penalty accordingly. As I stated above, many of these arguments are grounded in religious justifications and use the rationale that everyone is equal under the laws of God and so should be equal under the laws of man (Vários/União dos escritores Angolanos 1984).

Pedro da Paixão Franco: A Pariah among African intellectuals

Unlike the authors of the *Voz de Angola*, Pedro da Paixão Franco was an African intellectual who was not mixed race. He was born in Luanda in 1869 and was the son of an African family from Dondo. Politically speaking, he was extremely active. For instance, he co-founded the newspaper *O Angolense* (The Angolan) with the African intellectuals Eusébio Velasco Galiano, Francisco das Necessidades Ribeiro Castelbranco and Augusto Silvério Ferreira. Paixão Franco was a very well-educated man for his time, who clearly had knowledge of literary culture from Angola and beyond as well as of world history (Portal de Angola 2016; Corrado 2008).

Paixão Franco had a very strong personality and routinely conducted his activism publicly, which is part of the reason why he often had conflicts with other intellectuals at the time. His famous work is the two-volume book *A História de uma Traição* (*The History of a Betrayal*).

In this work, he mostly criticizes those whom he thought were his friends. He is critical of the co-founders of the newspaper for not assuming equal authorship of an article that they published claiming that the discharge of a native from a job was unjust. The governor-general denounced this article as defamatory, and only Paixão Franco took responsibility for the article (Paixão Franco 1911).

In fact, it seemed that for Paixão Franco to take responsibility for one's ideas was very important. He collaborated in the production of the *Voz de Angola*, investing money in it as well as writing an article for it. This article by Paixão Franco, however, was not published in the final version. In contrast to the other authors, Paixão Franco wanted his name to appear in the publication of the *Voz de Angola*; this disagreement about the anonymity of the articles eventually led to the rejection of his article and to a break with the other authors (Oliveira and Severo 2019; Corrado 2008).

Much of Paixão Franco's political thought can, in fact, be characterized as trying to render his own position as opposed to the elitism of the creoles at his time, although he often falls into similar problems. He criticized his fellow collaborator Francisco Castelbranco (a creole) in *O Angolense* for being a hypocrite. As explained earlier, creoles were losing power, although they were still in a better position than people like Paixão Franco who were not mixed race and came from an underprivileged background. Paixão Franco was, then, critical of Francisco Castelbranco on the one hand for promoting equality, but on the other for enjoying the benefits of the colonial system as well as for excluding 'black people' from his concept of equality. He accused creole elites as simply being concerned with their loss of privilege and charged them with stimulating racism against non-creole Africans (Paixão Franco 1911, 1901).

Moreover, he criticized creole intellectuals for missing the point regarding what really matters. He did not think that race was the main site of inequality, but class. The political thought of the creole elites was, therefore, also discriminatory in another sense: it neglected the situation of the European working class who also suffered. The core value to be praised, according to Paixão Franco, is freedom, and this should be the same for everyone, regardless of the colour of their skin or their social class.

Ironically, however, Paixão Franco seems to sometimes fall into the same kind of racism that he accuses the creoles of. He was very fond of education, routinely arguing that education is crucial for development and liberation. Nonetheless, this position leads him to be very critical of undereducated Africans. He uses pejorative terms like 'savages' for those Africans who have not endorsed, and developed through, the learning of European customs and culture. He accuses them of being uncivilized and inferior, displaying a paternalistic attitude towards them (Paixão Franco 1911; Corrado 2008).

António de Assis Júnior: Cultural hybridism and African citizenship

Another representative work of the period analysed in this chapter is that of Angolan António de Assis Júnior. His work represents a generation that lived through the end of slavery and experienced the politics of the first republic and quasi-fascist dictatorship of *Estado Novo*. As explained above, Angolan literature at the end of the nineteenth and early twentieth centuries was relatively interventionist, which is also the case in de Assis Júnior's work (Corrado 2008; Hamilton 1975).

De Assis Júnior was born in Golongo Alto, Angola, in 1877 and died in Lisbon in 1960. Although he was not licensed, he practised law. Working as a district solicitor, he mainly took on cases related to the rights of local African individuals. He often advised local Africans about land expropriation and became known as 'the natives' lawyer'. In addition to practising law, de Assis Júnior was a writer and journalist. As a journalist, he was the director of *O Angolense* (The Angolan), which defended Angola's autonomy (Guerra 1980a, 1980b). As a writer, he wrote three important books: *Gramática de Kimbundu-Português* (*Grammar of Kimbundu and Portuguese*), *Relato dos Acontecimentos de*

Dala Tando e Lucala (*An Account of the Events that Occurred in Dala Tando and Lucala*) and *O Segredo da Morta, Romance de Costumes Angolenses* (*The Secret of the Dead Woman, a Novel on Angolan Culture*). Indeed, de Assis Júnior was very active in the African cultural scene. He was the founder of the *Liga Nacional Africana* (African National League) and was one of its leaders in 1930, 1931, 1933 and 1935 (Claro 2009; Corrado 2008; Hamilton 1975). His books display an exciting array of social, economic and political ideas, but the anti-colonialism present in his work is very moderate. He does not challenge Portuguese sovereignty and even praises some colonial legacies. Indeed, de Assis Júnior takes offence at being accused of endorsing independentist ideas in his *Account of the Events that Occurred in Dala Tando and Lucala*, considering the concept of Angolan independence as unfeasible. In fact, he understands that someone from the creole elite like himself would not see his situation improve in an independent and free Angola.

However, it is questionable whether or not de Assis Júnior was being sincere in these works (Júnior 2004, 1985). For he was not only the director of an independentist newspaper, he also had connections with various individuals who defended the independence of Angola (Guerra 1980a, 1980b). In any case, even though it is ambiguous whether he was simply avoiding censorship, there are at least three ideas that are clear in his texts. First, he is critical of the crimes committed by Portuguese colonizers to protect Portuguese sovereignty. He accuses some Portuguese colonizers of abusing the idea, so as to abuse Africans. Second, and relatedly, his writings promote social, economic and political reforms in the regime even if they do not challenge colonial rule. He considered that the citizenship of Africans was not respected and routinely violated. He was arrested under false charges in 1917 and accused of being the leader of an independentist conspiracy in Dala Tando (Guerra 1980b). However, his personal experience does not simply provide material about himself; the report he offers illustrates the wider situation of Africans in Angola. Notably, it shows how some Portuguese colonizers misused legal devices for the sake of abuse and how rights were easily violated in the Portuguese colonies (especially

Angola) with respect to the African people. He promoted the idea that African people ought to have the same civil and political rights as white people, reporting that, in the process of being arrested, he had been the victim of rights' violations in various ways, as usually happens with Africans. More precisely, he criticizes how he was treated, demonstrating that Africans in Angola have the right to be reasonably heard in any public proceeding and the rights to due process, fair trial, presentation of evidence, transparency and independent, impartial judgement. Africans are not, in short, treated as full citizens of Angola, but they are entitled to full citizenship (Júnior 1985). Third, even if Angola is not to become independent, the influence of Portuguese colonialism is not, for de Assis Júnior, negative. In *The Secret of the Dead Woman, a Novel on Angolan Culture*, he defends cultural hybridity. This book, like many texts from the time, is not entirely anti-colonial in the sense of opposing the colonialists' presence. Still, it contains a mix of nationalist and independentist feelings, without having a complete disregard for Portuguese colonial rule and influence. Indeed, it includes several passages praising what might be called a 'Euro-African' culture. He praises European values, despising those who have not endorsed some basic European legacies. The distinction between the civilized and uncivilized Africans in the work of de Assis Júnior is closely connected to his idea of Euro-African culture: those who endorse only African culture are considered rude (Corrado 2008; Júnior 2004).

All this being said, there is nonetheless an appraisal of African, specifically Angolan, traditional culture. Indeed, endorsing African cultural elements is a form of legitimate resistance against colonialism for de Assis Júnior. In *The Secret of the Dead Woman, a Novel on Angolan Culture*, he praises local Angolan customs, culture and characteristics, suggesting that endorsing elements of African religion in order to resist colonial Catholic influence is the right thing to do (Guerra 1980a). The novel does not present Angolan culture as exotic and mysterious, however, which was the colonial perception of Angola at the time. Although there is some mysticism in de Assis Júnior's description, he resists characterizing Angolan culture as alien and exotic (Guerra 1980a;

Hamilton 1975). More specifically, by positively describing Angolan culture and using Kimbundu, he demonstrates the inherent value of Angolan culture, although the culture that is valued is, admittedly, quite selective; de Assis Júnior includes only those African cultural values that he considers morally right and civilized. In short, his ideal culture is a Euro-African one (i.e. a culture that exists between European and African cultures). Individuals should attempt to participate in the two coexisting cultures and thus become culturally hybrid.

Conclusion

In this chapter, I have looked at the political ideologies of Angola's late nineteenth- and early twentieth-century creole elite. This elite played a vital role in the Angolan colony, occupying critical administrative positions and running important businesses. But the situation changed significantly by the mid- to late nineteenth century. European settlers were becoming increasingly powerful, thus placing the Angolan creole elite in a vulnerable position. The creoles began contesting the European settlers' dominance in the Angolan colony, and the political theory emerging from this contestation was the subject of this chapter. The ideas propounded by the creole elite all vary slightly, but they have some fundamental points in common; for instance, they all hold a republican perspective that challenges monarchy, racial hierarchies and the diminishing of African culture. Furthermore, they all have a sense of the creole elite being natives from the land of Angola, of having a different identity from the people from the metropole. Not all creoles defended Angolan independence, but all challenged colonial rule in some capacity; sometimes, this challenge argued for a simple reform of policies, whereas in other, more extreme, scenarios it encompassed an independentist perspective. Despite his disagreements with the creole elite, Paixão Franco, who was not a creole, very much endorsed similar views but seemed to be more concerned about class inequalities than the creoles. The importance of these thinkers in the history of African thought cannot be underrated. They were the first to voice proto-nationalist views, and as such, they significantly influenced subsequent intellectuals. Particularly, they laid the foundation for Angolan nationalism, which only developed later in the twentieth century and whose most important intellectual is Mário Pinto de Andrade, the protagonist of the next chapter.

7

Mário Pinto de Andrade: Colonialism, African nationalism and liberation

Introduction

The name Mário Pinto de Andrade has marked Angolan history. He was initially a member of the Angolan Communist Party (PCA) and later became the first president of the Movement for the Liberation of Africa (MPLA). Later still, he became distanced from the MPLA owing to certain disagreements (Kajibanga 2000; Espírito Santo 2000; Lopes 2000; Geraldo de Oliveira 2000). Nonetheless, Pinto de Andrade is undoubtedly one of the main representatives and precursors of Angolan nationalism (Espírito Santo 2000; Kajibanga 2000; Tindó Secco 2000; Faria 2000; Kandjimbo 2000; Nazareth Soares Fonseca 2000; Mata, Padilha and Parente Augel 2000; Pinto de Andrade 2000; Mata and Padilha 2000; Lopes 2000; Bonavena 2000; Geraldo de Oliveira 2000). He became known for his political activity against Portuguese colonial power in the 1950s and 1960s. His name, political activities and ideas are often associated with African nationalism and African poetry (Bonavena 2000; Pinto de Andrade 2000; Nazareth Soares Fonseca 2000; Pinto de Andrade 1997, 1953a; Pinto de Andrade and Ollivier 1974).

In this chapter, I outline some of Pinto de Andrade's main ideas in political philosophy. I begin by explaining what Pinto de Andrade understood as colonialism, how it functions and how Portugal had carried it out. He offers a critique of colonialism in general as well as of specific features of Portuguese colonialism in particular (Pinto de Andrade 2000, 1997, 1988, 1986, 1980, 1978, 1975, 1953a, 1953b;

Ferreira 1982; Pinto de Andrade and Fele 1955). The next section describes Pinto de Andrade's conception of African nationalism. As will become apparent throughout this chapter, African nationalism is the alternative to colonialism and the solution that Pinto de Andrade offers to construe a postcolonial Angola (Pinto de Andrade 2000, 1997; Bonavena 2000; Ferreira 1982). The third section explores Pinto de Andrade's views on modes of liberation, investigating his views on just war theory and poetry as an instrument of liberation (Pinto de Andrade 2000, 1988, 1980, 1978, 1975; Tindó Secco 2000; Kandjimbo 2000; Nazareth Soares Fonseca 2000; Mata and Padilha 2000; Lopes 2000). The final section addresses some possible objections to my interpretation.

What is colonialism?

Pinto de Andrade's conception of colonialism covers both its material and psychological aspects. In terms of content, colonialism operates by eroding the socio-economic institutions of the colonized subjects and building new ones that serve the colonizers' interests. Hence, precolonial economies are often replaced by colonial ones unless the precolonial economy serves a colonial purpose (Pinto de Andrade 2000, 1997, 1986, 1953a; Pinto de Andrade and Ollivier 1974). This means that the economy of the colonized country is reduced to very few industries, to the extent that whatever goods are produced are made in mass. The profits generated in a colonial economic regime often go to the metropole or the colonial authorities (Pinto de Andrade 1997; Pinto de Andrade and Ollivier 1974). Moreover, colonizers impose their economy through exploitation and violence. Pinto de Andrade means a few different things by 'exploitation'. It occurs when individuals are paid less than they are entitled to for their labour. Indeed, the wages of colonized subjects in colonial economies tend to be significantly low with respect to the work they do (Pinto de Andrade 1997, 1986, 1953a; Pinto de Andrade and Ollivier 1974). Exploitation is also used in a more orthodox Marxist sense, to signify profit. Pinto de Andrade was at one point a member of the PCA, so he was exposed to and significantly influenced by Marxist ideology. He refers to violence committed when colonized subjects are forced to work, contending that they are threatened with physical violence or hunger. Indeed, this is not the only violence that colonized subjects suffer, but through the lens of the economy, this is what Pinto de Andrade means (Pinto de Andrade 1997, 1977; Pinto de Andrade and Ollivier 1974).

According to Pinto de Andrade, the economic elements of colonialism can, therefore, be summarized in terms of two key ideas. One is that colonial economies involve stealing. Colonizers are not entitled to the profits of their colonies in at least two ways. First, they should not be able to politically rule and decide what industries should exist in a colonized country. This is a form of appropriation, as the resources of that country belong to the native people. Second, colonizers are also not entitled to these profits insofar as they obtain them through exploitation. That is, given that exploitation is morally wrong, whatever results from it is also ethically wrong. Hence, because the profits of colonial economies are founded on exploitation, they are a morally wrong way to obtain entitlements, and individuals are not entitled to things obtained via immoral means.

The other aspect of colonial economies involves a significant degree of 'unfreedom'. By unfreedom, I do not simply mean the restriction of any freedom; any political regime requires some restriction of some kinds of freedoms. Even traffic rules, which are generally accepted as a necessary measure, involve limitations of freedom. Instead, by unfreedom, I mean the *illegitimate* restriction of forms of freedom that, morally speaking, should not be restricted; unfreedom is thus a restriction pursued through illegitimate means. For Pinto de Andrade, the economic imposition of a particular form of industry, the forms of forced work and exploitation and the morally wrong appropriation of resources by the colonizer entail unfair restriction of colonized subjects' freedom to engage in their culture, social life, ways of living and chosen economic activities. In fact, for Pinto de Andrade, colonialism is at its core a system premised upon the disruption of life and the ability to flourish. Thus, restricting colonized subjects' freedoms is a way to undermine and disrupt their ability to flourish, to prevent them from living their lives as they wish (Pinto de Andrade 1997, 1986, 1953a; Ferreira 1982; Pinto de Andrade and Ollivier 1974; Pinto de Andrade and Fele 1955).

This brings us to the other aspect of colonialism – namely, its psychological impact on individuals. According to Pinto de Andrade, the process of subjugation outlined above requires that individuals be indoctrinated by an ideology that justifies colonial rule. The method of domination consists in dehumanizing the colonized subject, making her appear more like an animal than a human. It mischaracterizes the colonized subjects, predicating them with homogeneous negative traits such as laziness, barbarity, lack of civilization and lower ability to reason. It is a process that removes individuality and does so by negatively characterizing people, forcing the colonized subject to be a *consumer* of the colonizer's culture; for it is only by adopting the colonizer's culture that the colonized subject can lose her bruteness and lack of humanity. According to Pinto de Andrade, colonialism humiliates colonized subjects and their culture in order to stamp out their supposed primitivity (Silva 2017; Pinto de Andrade 2000, 1997, 1988, 1980, 1978, 1975, 1953a, 1953b).

This process serves at least three purposes: it serves the self-justification of the colonial elites' control of their abuses of power over the colonized subjects. That is, the psychological aspect of colonialism is a form of justifying one's actions to eliminate feelings of guilt as well as a means of influencing others to act in ways that further the elites' purposes. The process also serves to indoctrinate the non-colonized masses of a country to believe that the actions and policies of the colonizing elites are morally justified. Indeed, the function of eliminating guilt is important here too, although, as a Marxist, Pinto de Andrade understood ideology to go from top to bottom (i.e. it is a superstructure that results from the actions of those who have power). In addition, it humiliates and indoctrinates the colonized subjects in a way that not only scares them away from taking action against colonialism, but also contributes to making them believe that they are inferior (Pinto de Andrade 2000, 1988, 1986, 1953a, 1953b; Pinto de Andrade and Ollivier 1974; Pinto de Andrade and Fele 1955). Both the economic and psychological aspects of colonialism are encoded in the legal system. Moreover, both aspects have different manifestations at different times and in the different geographical locales in which colonialism occurs. Given his nationality, Pinto de Andrade was more interested in explaining how these specific characteristics of colonialism manifested in the context of Angola. Regarding the economic aspects, he upheld the fact that the Portuguese appropriated all manner of resources from Angola from the time of their arrival, including financial and human resources. The relationship changed from slavery to forms of exploitation and forced labour. For instance, the Colonial Act of 1930 and other laws enacted by the proto-fascist regime *Estado Novo* facilitated these forms of exploitation, forcing colonized subjects in all the former Portuguese colonies, including Angola, into manual labour.

Furthermore, it facilitated the appropriation of the colonies' economic resources into the metropole, given that it further centralized the economy in the metropole, limiting the colonies' financial freedom. Another way this economic domination was present in Angola was through the forced industries that the Portuguese colonial government imposed. Notably, many colonized subjects were forced against their will to plant and produce cotton to serve the interests of the metropole. However, Pinto de Andrade also points out that Portugal was just a second role player or underdog in the economic system. Imperialism is larger than merely Portugal, and indeed, for Pinto de Andrade, Portugal was simply a sub-power subjugated to other world powers such as the United States. As various scholars have pointed out, the Portuguese Empire was, for most of its history, a form of sub-power dependent on and vulnerable to other empires (Pinto de Andrade 2000; Pinto de Andrade 1997; Pinto de Andrade and Ollivier 1974; Pinto de Andrade and Fele 1955, 1953a).

Concerning the psychological aspect of Portuguese colonialism, Pinto de Andrade notes that it has changed over time and is more focused on what has become known as 'Lusotropicalism'. Before the Second World War, Portuguese colonial politics were, in general terms, very much like any other colonizers' colonialism (Pinto de Andrade and Fele 1955): namely, they mainly consisted in engaging in explicitly racist discourse that justified Portuguese presence in the colonies as a civilizing mission. Nevertheless, these discourses changed throughout the world after the Second World War. The project of racial purity indicative of Nazi Germany made the discourse on racial superiority politically unacceptable. Furthermore, there were emerging movements in Africa for liberation and civil rights movements in North America that put pressure on regimes with racially driven politics. Consequently, there was significant political pressure on the Portuguese proto-fascist government to give up their colonies and enable independence.

However, the *Estado Novo* refused to do so, instead deciding to significantly change its discourse and policy to mitigate tensions with international and national actors in opposition to the regime. Notably, it adopted the thought of the Brazilian social scientist Gilberto Freyre for its official address. Freyre held the theory that, unlike other colonialisms, the nature of Portuguese colonialism was not brutal and exploitative (Freyre 1936). Unlike Spanish colonialism, for example, Portuguese colonialism engaged in harmonious relationships, social engagements, miscegenation, cultural adaptation and integration with the culture of the colonies. The *Estado Novo* developed certain policies to justify the veracity of this idea. The official discourse now was that Portugal had a relationship of friendship and mutual understanding with the colonies. Therefore, unlike other colonial powers, it had a moral justification to be there. Accordingly, the Colonial Act was annulled and some institutions that promoted the colonies' cultures were formed. Moreover, the official discourse changed the term 'colonies' and began using the term 'overseas province' to distance the *Estado Novo* from the brutal legacy left by colonialism (Rosas 2018a, 2000, 1986; Trindade, Louçã, and Rosas 2016; Castelo 1998; Pinto de Andrade and Fele 1955).

Pinto de Andrade pointed out that this peaceful relationship with the colonies was false. The relationship of Portugal with the colonies was not one of friendship and harmony – far from it – for it was one of brutality, violence, slavery, forced labour, exploitation and overarching abuse. It is also not true that African people were treated equally in Portuguese colonies. Pinto de Andrade upholds that not only were there various laws that treated African and European people in Africa differently, but also that a significant proportion of the European population believed in African inferiority. The education system, for instance, differentiated African and European people, deliberately making African people illiterate.[1] African cultural elements were often prohibited and considered to be subversive. He also contended that miscegenation, if true, was not the result of some sort of friendship or equal treatment, but rather was simply circumstantial. Portuguese colonies did not have many women, so interracial sex was allowed in the colonies for the purposes of having a labour force, a theory corroborated by Boxer(1969) and Pinto de Andrade and Fele (1955). Moreover, Pinto de Andrade notes that there had been massive European immigration to the colonies in the twentieth century, so as to outnumber and weaken African presence in Angola. He argues that the Lusotropicalist perspective of Portuguese colonialism simply served the purpose of mitigating tensions in an emerging postcolonial Angola by attempting to indoctrinate international actors and internal rebels (Pinto de Andrade and Fele 1955).

African nationalism

In the 1950s and 1960s, the idea that African nations should be independent and autonomous grew exponentially, with many organizations and political parties forming around this idea (Bjerk 2017; Wilson et al. 2015; Birmingham 1998; Nkrumah 1996, 1974; Nyerere 1969). Pinto de Andrade was particularly representative of this, becoming one of the first Angolans to defend a form of African nationalism (Espírito Santo 2000; Kajibanga 2000; Faria 2000; Kandjimbo 2000; Nazareth Soares Fonseca 2000; Mata, Padilha, and Parente Augel 2000; Lopes 2000; Bonavena 2000). He understood African nationalism to be an antithesis of colonialism; in terms of values and outcomes, whatever African nationalism stands for is the opposite of colonialism. This makes African nationalism an ideology and movement that is defined in terms of its negative other; hence, from a colonial perspective, it can function in a reversed way as a positive image of negative colonialism (Pinto de Andrade 2000, 1997, 1953a; Birmingham 1998; Nkrumah 1996, 1974). According to Pinto de Andrade's conception, African nationalism is defined by six features. First, the core goal of the movement is the positive affirmation of African identity. This affirmation, in turn, requires a definition of what it means to be African. Second, it promotes a belief that African people have the right to self-determination. Third – at least in the case of Angola – there is the contention that this belief is not just an abstract ideal but rather a project with concrete policies: a feasible and desirable goal for Angola to become an independent, postcolonial country. Fourth, the view that a postcolonial Angola ought to contain institutions that reflect African identity is propounded. Fifth, African nationalism should not undermine but instead foster cooperation with other African countries. Sixth, there should be an understanding of how African nationalism is formed (Pinto de Andrade 2000, 1997, 1988, 1980, 1975, 1953a; Pinto de Andrade and Ollivier 1974).

The positive affirmation of African identity means being proud of precolonial values, one's body and cultural productions. Pinto de Andrade continuously emphasizes that freeing oneself from colonial rule means endorsing modes of living, cultural expression and social interaction that were in place before Portuguese colonialism arrived in Angola. Pinto de Andrade is not uncritical of precolonial values, however, and does not endorse a total inscription of the precolonial because he recognizes that they sometimes imply unfair hierarchies. However, as a general rule, a return to a precolonial value system is what should be enacted (Pinto de Andrade 1997, 1953a; Pinto de Andrade and Ollivier

1974). Sadly, Pinto de Andrade does not go into detail about what such a precolonial value system would be like, but he does sometimes mention forms of precolonial communal agriculture, similar to what other African liberators, such as Julius Nyerere and Kwame Nkrumah, have envisioned (Fouéré 2015; Nkrumah 1996, 1974; Nyerere 1969). For Pinto de Andrade, pride in being African is not about being ashamed and simply accepting one's African body; it is about being proud of one's history and cultural heritage. The affirmation of African identity also means, in contrast to being a cultural consumer (as was the case during colonialism), that Africans should become cultural producers (Pinto de Andrade 1980, 1978, 1975, 1953b; Ferreira 1982).

Although Pinto de Andrade is the primary representative of these ideas in Angola and perhaps their main precursor, his ideas were not as innovative as they might seem initially. Considering the work of thinkers from Africa and the African diaspora, such as Kwame Nkrumah, Aimé Cesaire, Frantz Fanon and Thomas Sankara, among others, it is worth noting that these thinkers had already defended this. Pinto de Andrade was, in some ways, borrowing these ideas and adapting them to the Angolan context. Nevertheless, something that is perhaps different in Pinto de Andrade's account is what he means by 'black' or 'African' (Pinto de Andrade 1953b). For him, to be black or African is not related to one's place of birth, ethnicity or melanin, but rather to a state of mind (an idea that Pepetela would later endorse, as we shall see when exploring what it means to be Angolan). In his edited collection *Poesia Negra de Expressão Portuguesa* (*Black Poetry of Portuguese Expression*), Pinto de Andrade does not only include poems written by black people; instead, what falls under the term 'black poetry' is all the kinds of works that challenge the ways in which colonialism mistreats Africans. What he calls 'black poetry' is anti-colonialist, denounces racism and promotes uplifting the condition of Africans. When discussing the future of Angola in his later works, Pinto de Andrade again uses the term 'African' to refer to those who wish to build a postcolonial and independent Angola (Pinto de Andrade 2000, 1988, 1980, 1975, 1953a, 1953b; Ferreira 1982).

This point about what it means to be African is reinforced in Pinto de Andrade's theory about the self-determination of African countries. In his book *Origens to Nacionalismo Africano* (*Origins of African Nationalism*), he propounds the idea that African countries, particularly Angola, ought to be independent and form their own governments independent of Portuguese colonial rule and avoid neocolonial forms of interference, primarily from the economic dependence of former colonizers (Pinto de Andrade 1997). Nonetheless, when defending this self-determination, he makes it clear that this kind of nationalism is not exclusionary; it is not based on ethnicity, perceived colour or place of birth. Nor does he view identity as a stable and unchangeable category. Instead, he emphasizes that those who are African and belong to Africa – and especially to Angola – are those who genuinely wish to build a postcolonial nation. The category of 'African' is not defined in terms of ethnicity; it is ideological and can mean different things at different times, depending on what anti-colonial goals are being furthered. In short, to be African is to have an anti-colonial state of mind that is also reflected in one's actions. The point is emphasized by the fact that Pinto de Andrade stresses how a part of independence signals the 'right to personality, which is not in the domain of physical characteristics but the ideological domain (Pinto de Andrade 1997, 1980, 1978, 1975, 1953b; Pinto de Andrade and Ollivier 1974).

The concrete policies suggested by Pinto de Andrade consist in a significant redistribution of resources. The economic structures of colonialism based on exclusion, theft and the monopolization of resources, forced labour, exploitation and so on are all to be reversed (Pinto de Andrade and Ollivier 1974). African nationalism demands that resources in African land and the profits gained from these through African labour belong to Africans. This entails removing colonial power in key Angolan industries they hold, refusing to send profits to the colonial power, choosing and designing what industries to engage with, abolishing forced labour, paying fair salaries for one's work, setting out legal equality among citizens and heavily investing in education. From Pinto de Andrade's point of view, these goals are possible and not just utopian dreams. He contends that Portuguese colonialism has built industries of cotton and diamonds that Angolans ought to seize, so as to use them to further the economic and political power of a postcolonial Angola on the international stage (Pinto de Andrade 1997; Pinto de Andrade and Ollivier 1974).

The new postcolonial Angola should not simply mirror Portuguese colonialism. Instead, it should Africanize institutions; it should seize the legacy of colonialism and transform it into an African value system. Pinto de Andrade does not give many examples of what this means. Still, one example, already mentioned above, is that the relationship between agriculture and the environment ought to follow precolonial values. Another example he provides relates to how work in the social sciences is conducted. Pinto de Andrade rightly points out that the colonial social sciences exoticized and diminished African cultures (Pinto de Andrade 2000, 1988, 1986, 1953a; Silva 2017). The *Cadernos do Ultramar* (a publication from the *Estado Novo*) and the pseudo-anthropological work carried out at the time routinely mischaracterized indigenous Africans as inferior (Noronha 1935; Archer 1935; Dias 1935). By Africanizing knowledge, Pinto de Andrade sought to undo this, in turn achieving African liberation. According to him, social sciences are never neutral and should not be. Hence, the social sciences in Africa should aim at improving African peoples' welfare (Silva 2017; Pinto de Andrade 2000, 1988, 1977, 1953b).

The kind of African nationalism that Pinto de Andrade endorsed was ultimately not akin to European nationalism, wherein relations are understood as a zero-sum game; there are intense rivalries between countries, which imply privileging and excluding those who are considered foreign nationals. For Pinto de Andrade, African nationalism goes along with the Pan-African ideal, which is based on solidarity and brotherhood/sisterhood with other Africans to develop a community with a shared prosperous future and a rejuvenation of African cultures by recovering old African ways, eliminating colonial legacies from institutions and minds. Nationalism in Africa, therefore, ought not to be based on rivalry but joint development and growth (Pinto de Andrade 1997; Pinto de Andrade and Ollivier 1974).

Finally, what, according to Pinto de Andrade, led to the rise of African nationalism? Often the maxim 'where there is power, there is resistance' is attributed to Michel Foucault. Pinto de Andrade was potentially one of the first to suggest this idea when he wrote about the factors that give rise to African nationalism. Even though he opposes colonial rule, Pinto de Andrade contends that the repression of it creates a sense of identity that perhaps did not exist before. Through a common feeling of repression, those who are subject to colonial cruelty form a collective consciousness through common feeling and a sense of repression such that they formulate a common identity. The Marxist influence on Pinto de Andrade's ideas here is undeniable. For just as the working class develops a class consciousness by way of exploitative conditions in the capitalist system, colonized subjects develop their consciousness and rebel against a system that represses them (Pinto de Andrade 1997, 1986, 1980, 1978, 1975, 1953a, 1953b; Pinto de Andrade and Ollivier 1974; Pinto de Andrade and Fele 1955).

Liberation, war and poetry

Two questions often posed are what the morally permissible means for liberation are and what the most effective means would be. Pinto de Andrade also wrote about this, offering a sophisticated understanding of the means for release. One legitimate and necessary means for liberation is war (Pinto de Andrade 1980, 1978, 1975; Pinto de Andrade and Ollivier 1974). Indeed, he believed colonial rule should be overcome at any cost: 'This [colonial settlement] demands an opposition by every means necessary in every front' (Pinto de Andrade 1974: 90). Moreover, in the face of Portuguese colonialism, Pinto de Andrade did not think it was possible to become independent without the use of force. The Portuguese colonial government and bourgeoisie would not peacefully pass power over to Angolans; therefore, it was necessary to remove this power by force. Again, the Marxist influence on Pinto de Andrade is apparent here; developing the ideas of Marx, Lenin and Stalin contended that the capitalist system could not be overthrown without the forced appropriation of the means of production by the working class and that the bourgeoisie would make efforts to undermine the revolution. Likewise, Pinto de Andrade thought that colonized subjects ought to engage in war to appropriate the resources and political power of their countries and should be wary of the Portuguese bourgeoisie's attempts to undermine this revolutionary process (Pinto de Andrade 1997, 1953a; Pinto de Andrade and Ollivier 1974). Given that, as explained above, Pinto de Andrade considers it essential for Angolans to appropriate the colonial industries built by the Portuguese, he may indeed be conflating the colonial subject with the working classes. He also notes, however, that liberation and war would provoke some colonized subjects to oppose liberation, for some benefitted from the colonial system and would fight for it (Pinto de Andrade and Ollivier 1974). This perspective is also a Marxist-influenced one. Mao Zedong, for instance, in his famous *Analysis of the Classes in Chinese Society*, claims that some individuals who belong to revolutionary classes will potentially oppose revolution if they feel that they can get more benefits from a capitalist or feudal system (Tse-Tung 2014; Mohanty 1978). Given that, according to Pinto de Andrade, China was one of the first supporters of Angolan independence and the MPLA, it is likely that this idea has Maoist roots.

Pinto de Andrade notes that war will have a negative economic impact on Angola and will bring more repression, which is an inevitable adverse outcome of war. However, he does not consider these sufficient reasons not to wage war against the Portuguese (Pinto de Andrade and Ollivier 1974). First, waging war will force the Portuguese to sit at the negotiation table because if the economy is significantly damaged, they will have no choice but to change from a stance of strict non-negotiation to one of negotiation. This was especially the case according to Pinto de Andrade because the Portuguese colonial economy was highly dependent on Angola. This tactic has been the archetype of many liberation movements in Africa, which have learned war strategy mainly from the experience of the Algerian National Liberation Front. Second, the moral permissibility of war should not be measured by the short- or mid-term goals but by long-term goals. If only the short-term goals were relevant to evaluate the moral permissibility of war, it would be impossible to justify it, given that the power of colonized subjects is insufficient to achieve any pertinent goals in the short term; this criterion would favour the colonizer such that Pinto de Andrade rejects it. Instead, he believes that war's moral legitimacy should be measured by its long-term possible achievements (Pinto de Andrade and Ollivier 1974). This perspective is, in fact, common among African revolutionaries: Nelson Mandela and Amílcar Cabral are two prominent examples of African revolutionaries who maintained this perspective (Cordeiro-Rodrigues and Chimakonam 2020; Cordeiro-Rodrigues 2018; Cabral 2016, 1969; Mandela 1995, 1967).

African arts, and particularly poetry, also have a fundamental role in the process of liberation. A significant part of Pinto de Andrade's political activity was to engage in the editing and publishing of artistic works created by Africans. But two questions arise at this point: why does poetry have a unique role for Pinto de Andrade? And why exactly is it worthwhile to carry out *liberation* through poetry? In answer to the first question, from Pinto de Andrade's point of view, traditionally, poetry is at the centre of most of African culture; most fundamental cultural activities (dances, funerals and birth rituals), as well as ways of learning and transmitting knowledge, are carried out through poetry. So even if other arts are relevant, poetry is present in most African artistic expressions, social interactions and ways of life such that it occupies a key position in African culture (Pinto de Andrade 2000, 1988, 1980, 1978, 1975, 1953a, 1953b; Geraldo de Oliveira 2000; Kandjimbo 2000; Lopes 2000; Tindó Secco 2000).

This explanation of the role offers a first answer as to why poetry can achieve liberation. According to Pinto de Andrade, a significant aspect of freedom is the return to precolonial values and ways of living; hence, engaging and producing African poetry is a form of recovering older values corrupted by colonial powers, and this becomes identical to the recovery of African culture. In addition, engaging with African poetry is in itself an act of defiance against colonialism (Pinto de Andrade 2000, 1980, 1978, 1975). Recall that Pinto de Andrade views colonialism as the dehumanization of people that creates a negative image of the colonized subject, both to the oppressor and the oppressed. This imaginary negative image often fabricates the colonial subject's alleged bruteness. Promoting African poetry is important precisely because it dissipates this negative image of the colonized subject as a brute. The divulgation defies the colonial order, for the existence of African poetry demonstrates that Africans can produce sophisticated cultural artefacts. This recognition of Africans' work contributes to eliminating the negative images that colonizers and colonized subjects may have of African people. In other words, the divulgation of African poetry has a role in antiracism and anti-colonialism to the extent that it defies the idea that Africans are simply consumers of culture and showing them to also be producers. The very title of one of Pinto de Andrade's edited collections is also therefore a subversive act of defiance: *Black Poetry of Portuguese Expression*. This title defied the Portuguese colonial order because the terms 'black' and 'African' were considered subversive (Ferreira 1982; Pinto de Andrade 1980, 1975, 1953b). As mentioned above, Portuguese colonialism after the 1950s was attempting to pass off the idea that all colonies were provinces of Portugal and the preferred classification for cultural productions by Africans was 'Portuguese Literature in Africa' or 'Overseas Portuguese Literature'. Poetry not only shows others the humanity of Africans, but also helps people to emancipate themselves from the self-loathing instilled by negative images of inferiority (Ferreira 1982).

Poetry was also crucial because it had a role in denouncing the atrocities of Portuguese colonialism. Africans living under Portuguese colonial rule could communicate the exploitation and abuses of the Portuguese in Africa through the medium of poetry. This was particularly important given the 'Lusotropicalist' discourse adopted by the *Estado Novo*, in which the Portuguese were good colonizers. Pinto de Andrade's edited collection *Antologia Temática de Poesia Africana I* (*Thematic Anthology of African Poetry I*) does precisely this; it gathers the poems of various poets to express the condition of colonized subjects under Portuguese colonialism (Pinto de Andrade 1975). Poetry also has the political role of motivating colonized subjects to enter the armed struggle. The *Thematic Anthology*'s second volume, for instance, is fully dedicated to the armed struggle against the Portuguese: this collection is a call to arms (Pinto de Andrade 1980).

Pinto de Andrade vacillates, however, on who precisely should be motivated by poetry. While in the first volume of the *Anthology* he seems sceptical that the masses can be motivated, in the second volume, he is convinced that poetry will influence groups to join and support the war. Independently of his position, and it seems to change, Pinto de Andrade always views intellectuals as having special duties; they are the ones who ought to educate and motivate the masses to understand and liberate themselves from their oppressed condition. From Pinto de Andrade's viewpoint, the intellectual is, in short, the agent of history motivating the working classes to take action (Ferreira 1982; Pinto de Andrade 1980, 1975, 1953b).

Ideology, exoticism, pro-colonialism and misinterpretation

In this section, I wish to address some possible objections to my interpretation of Pinto de Andrade's thoughts. These objections share the idea that what I present is misleading, because it would lead to implications that Pinto de Andrade would not accept or because events in his biography demonstrate otherwise. One objection is that I strongly classify Pinto de Andrade as Marxist. Often, my interpretation of his work is influenced by the presupposition that he is taking inspiration from Marxist standpoints. The objection could be raised that there are doubts about whether he was a Marxist. Although Pinto de Andrade was a member of the PCA, he later left it for the MPLA, which was not as heavily inspired by Marxism as the PCA (Espírito Santo 2000; Lopes 2000; Kajibanga 2000; Faria 2000).

A second possible objection is that if the interpretation I offer about Pinto de Andrade's thought is right, then there are internal contradictions in his discourse, indicating that my understanding is mistaken. More precisely, I contend that Pinto de Andrade accuses colonial social sciences of wrongly exoticizing Africans, but at the same time, I uphold that he defended the Africanization of institutions. The Africanization of institutions seems to presuppose an exoticized view of Africa wherein it perceives Africans as different. And, yet, I simultaneously maintain that Pinto de Andrade was against colonialism. This occurs, more specifically, when I contend that he is an anti-colonialist while also claiming that independence is possible only because Portuguese colonialism built the necessary socio-economic infrastructures and institutions conducive to independence. By affirming that Pinto de Andrade upheld this latter position, I am contradicting myself, because I am simultaneously claiming that he defended colonialism and that he opposed it.

Finally, another objection is that my interpretation of what Pinto de Andrade means by 'African' is too far-fetched. The definition of being African as an anti-colonial state of mind does not seem to fit any ideas of African nationalism. This interpretation ought to be abandoned as it is an anachronistic interpretation that Pinto de Andrade could not have held.

In response to the first objection, note that the change from the PCA to the MPLA does not signal a shift in ideology, but rather confirms the Marxist drive underlying Pinto de Andrade's thought and political action. There was a switch to the MPLA because it could encompass a wider group of anti-colonial factions and could therefore more effectively fight against colonialism. The MPLA was the main uniting force during the Angolan war against Portuguese colonialism. Thus, the change in party signals a pragmatic decision rather than an ideological shift. In addition, the MPLA is inherently Marxist in its ideology, and the Soviet Union was counted among its prominent supporters (Chabal et al. 2002).

Pinto de Andrade did not exoticize the African and the objection that my interpretation of his work implies this would be to misunderstand my point. Notably, the fact that Pinto de Andrade recognizes specificities of African culture does not signify an exoticization of what it means to be African. To exoticize a group of individuals, it is necessary to exaggerate and reify imaginary characteristics. The mere fact that a difference is noted is not the same; exoticization is the act of understanding and formulating an image of the negative other, which is not what Pinto de Andrade does. Instead, he develops an argument showing that institutions and modes of living in Africa ought to reflect the needs and desires of Africans and not the colonizers.

This brings me to the objection that my interpretation results in Pinto de Andrade being portrayed as pro-colonialist, which he obviously was not; therefore, I attribute false beliefs to him. My argument does not imply this, because there is a difference between generally claiming that colonialism is good and claiming that one should take advantage of some elements of colonialism that helped to develop the colonized country. In short, recognizing that colonialism has brought economic development in some areas is not an endorsement of colonialism. Economic development is not good in itself. Still, it also matters how it came about and it is possible to recognize that economic growth was achieved, but that the way in which it was achieved was not good. In addition, Pinto de Andrade is defending the use of colonial economic infrastructures given the context of a globalized world; his approach is non-idealistic in the sense that he does not imagine an ideal state of affairs where Angola can build its future by itself and ignore all other international actors. He is being pragmatic about what Angola should do. This does not rule out that he may have believed (and he did) that the world would have been better if European expansion – thereby globalization – had never occurred and that individuals had been left alone.

Finally, my interpretation of what Pinto de Andrade understands by 'black' and 'African' is not an anachronism. Like Pinto de Andrade, as we will see in the next chapter, Pepetela has a similar perspective on what it means to be Angolan. Furthermore, the discourse of the MPLA at the time Pinto de Andrade was writing was focused on the idea that ideology defines one's identity and that other categories ought to be eliminated. Other thinkers, such as Nelson Mandela, also attempted to stop ethnicity as the driving factor of group-belonging. Thus, my interpretation of Pinto de Andrade's concepts is not anachronistic and fits the language and ideology of his social circles.

Conclusion

In this chapter, I have outlined the key ideas of the Angolan political activist and political thinker Pinto de Andrade. I contended that three critical sets of ideas could be found in his works. First, Pinto de Andrade considers colonialism to be an unfair form of governance that ought to be challenged. Furthermore, he contends that colonialism pervades both the material and psychological. He also argues that African nationalism should be the aim in a postcolonial Angola. After independence, he believes that Angolan institutions should reflect African values (i.e. that they should be Africanized). His idea of what it means to be African and to Africanize is not based on an ethnic or biological perception of Africans, but rather on ideological markers. In addition, he also explains how African nationalism originates, defending the view that the repression of colonial powers contributes to a sense of common shared identity by colonized subjects. The third key idea relates to the morally justified means of liberation. Pinto de Andrade considers war against colonial powers to be morally justified. Furthermore, he holds that poetry has a political function in liberating minds, denouncing colonial abuses and mobilizing the masses.

8

Pepetela: Angolanness, African personhood and transformative war

Introduction

Pepetela is one of the most prominent Angolan writers and has won many international awards for his novels, including the Prize Camões in 1997, the highest literary prize for Lusophone writers, and the Prince Claus Award in 1999, the most prestigious prize for literature in the Netherlands. His work has been translated into seventeen languages and is widely acclaimed because it is an important expression of a different form of literature. He is part of the first generation of Angolan postcolonial writers. His work is crucial in understanding power relations between other groups, addressing the problems and consequences of colonization, the challenges of decolonization and the history of Angola. Pepetela is not simply a writer telling stories; a significant aspect of his work is military fiction, which is written by a person who took part in a war and who has thus lived and experienced war. Hence, he is often called the 'guerrilla-writer' (Unimessantos 2018; Chaves and Macêdo 2010).

Pepetela's work tends to be divided into three phases: the first phase contains his early fiction, written between 1969 and 1980, which focuses on the Angolan liberation and civil wars, revealing strong support for The People's Movement for the Liberation of Angola (MPLA). The second phase shows some disenchantment and criticism of the MPLA, stretching from the 1980s to the early 2000s. The third phase covers a diverse array of other topics (Mata 2012b).

It is understood that the core of Pepetela's political thought is contained in his earlier work and that his later work is less ideologically focused and based more on previously defended ideas (Mata 2012b). The focus of this chapter is thus to outline the main political ideas present in Pepetela's early writings. These early works have been widely studied for their importance to postcolonial and war literature, as well as for their status as historical documents charting the Angolan liberation and civil wars. I argue that Pepetela's works offer a political theory on Angolan identity, linking this with ideas about the transformative power of war, Marxism, the importance of anti-colonialism and the negative aspects of racism and tribalism. However, as I shall explore, this political theory expresses Pepetela's perspectives and anxieties *as a 'white' Angolan in an emerging postcolonial Angola*. Put differently, the political theory in his early writings are narratives wherein Pepetela contemplates how and why he belongs there. From this personal anxiety, Pepetela is urged to create a political theory about what it means to be Angolan – an idea of 'Angolanness' (*Angolanidade*) – and how one can transform oneself to belong to a nation. Hence, what I offer as new in this chapter is my deciphering of a narrative of belonging by a 'white' individual regarding the Angolan nation in connection with a political theory of Angolan identity. I do not wish to claim that this attempt to make sense of Pepetela's belonging to the Angolan nation is necessarily conscious or deliberate; instead, I wish simply to affirm that by looking at his novels written during this period – *Muana Puó, The Adventures of Ngunga, Mayombe* and *The Rope* (Pepetela 1980, 1973, 1969) – this political theory can be linked to his question of belonging to Angola. In fact, I think many implications I draw in this chapter are not thought by Pepetela himself (e.g. the views on personhood and war). However, I think his thought is extremely rich and its value goes beyond what the writer intended to convey.

The chapter has four sections. In the first section, I describe Pepetela's account of ethnic conflict during the Angolan liberation and civil wars and his suggestions for ways to address this. Here, I explain Pepetela's typology of tribalism and racism and how he sees these as barriers to anti-colonial liberation. In the second section, I situate Pepetela's life and work in a historical context and demonstrate that it is reasonable to argue that he was – as a white man – anxious and reflective about living in Angola. That is, the political and historical context suggests that this was likely to have been a preoccupation of Pepetela's during that time. In the third section, I put forward my argument that he is trying to find a way to belong by showing how his texts reveal that, despite being white, he endorses Angolanness alongside African culture and value systems. Mainly, I contend that two arguments are at stake in his novels: on the one hand, to be Angolan is to be an anti-colonialist, which in turn, means to endorse African culture and elements of Marxism; on the other, this political theory explains why he, a privileged white man, has a place in Angola. In the fourth section, I reinforce these arguments by contending that Pepetela sees war as a *transformative ritual* that gives individuals personhood and belonging in a specific community. By arguing this, he simultaneously indicates his own belonging to the emerging postcolonial Angolan nation, as he was a guerrilla fighter during the Angolan liberation war.[1]

Tribalism, racism and anti-colonialism

Racism, tribalism and anti-colonialism during Angola's liberation and civil wars are recurrent topics in Pepetela's early fiction. In this section, I wish to demonstrate that Pepetela presents racism and tribalism as moral problems and barriers to liberation from colonialism and neocolonialism, suggesting that a shared consciousness against Portuguese colonialism should be the mark of the Angolan nation (Chabal 1996). In other words, this shared consciousness unites Angolans and ought to characterize the emerging postcolonial Angolan nation. In Pepetela's work, tribalism refers to ethnic conflict between African people from different ethnicities, which Pepetela calls 'tribal groups'. For instance, a recurrent conflict in his work is played out in the tension between Ovibumdos and Kimbundus, two Angolan tribes. The concept of 'tribe' is never defined, and in some cases, there are not even significant fundamental differences between the groups. Still, the term refers to the social categories that Portuguese colonialists applied to differentiate indigenous groups in Angola. Racism, on the other hand, refers to the conflict between individuals who are perceived as members of different races. Pepetela's work depicts this conflict between black and white people and mixed-race and black people.

Muana Puó is a metaphorical text in which the characters are bats and crows. And, yet, the text is entirely about racism and how it is intertwined with ideas about classism. The crows eat the honey produced by the bats; the crows constantly pit the bats against each other, making them believe that they are bats of different shapes and colours. The bats can overcome the crows only when they see the world differently and realize their shared identity. However, not all bats are precisely the same, so what unites them is not simply that they are bats but that they are commonly positioned in relation to the crows. This refers to how Angolans need to understand their own collective identity, stretching beyond racial or tribal categories and how failing to do so can undermine their liberation (Pepetela 1969).

Mayombe is a story about the tribal and racial conflicts among MPLA guerrilla soldiers in the Angolan liberation war. Throughout the book, Pepetela describes how the soldiers distrust and act against each other based on racial or tribal hatred. A clear example is when a soldier called 'Ingratitude' steals money from a civilian. 'Fearless', the operation commander punishes him and returns the money to the civilian, a fair act; however, it is not seen this way by all the characters in the story. The soldier 'Miracle', for instance, who is from a different tribe to Fearless, reflects on this matter: 'Did you see how the commander worried about giving money back to that traitor from Cabinda? I'll tell you why. He is from the Kikongo tribe, and they are the cousins of the Cabinda people. And did you see how angry he was with Ingratitude? Because Ingratitude is a Kimbundo!' (Pepetela 1980: 47). As this passage shows, Miracle perceives the punishing of Ingratitude and return of the stolen money as Fearless trying to punish a member of a tribe he dislikes, thereby privileging a member of a tribe that he is close to. Actions are, therefore, judged not by their intrinsic moral goodness or badness but by the ethnicity of the agents. There is, in other words, a constant racialization of discourse by the soldiers. Fearless is the character through whom Pepetela attempts to illustrate what the right actions to address tribalism and racism might be. He is portrayed as a brave, generous and intelligent man who has fought on many fronts against the Portuguese. Fearless routinely engages in speeches and conversations with his soldiers, reiterating that racial and tribal differences are a legacy of Portuguese colonialism. What unites Angolans in this is the shared consciousness of their oppression under the Portuguese colonial system. This includes individuals from all races and tribes who have been exploited by the Portuguese colonial empire. To be an Angolan, Fearless suggests, is to be someone who understands the history of oppression, opposes it and contests it.

The moral climax wherein Pepetela illustrates his main moral lessons is in one of the final scenes of *Mayombe* in which Fearless sacrifices his life for that of the MPLA's Political Commissary, who was supposedly from an enemy tribe (Cordeiro-Rodrigues and Chimakonam 2022). At the end of the book, their guerrilla is attacked and trapped in his headquarters by the Portuguese colonialists. The situation demands that either Fearless or the Political Commissary survive; Fearless, in an act of courage and self-sacrifice, kills the Portuguese colonialists at the cost of his own life, thereby saving the Political Commissary. The act is one of courage that impresses everyone, making them question the ridiculous tribal and racial nature of attachment when, in fact, what matters is to act in ways that promote the good of the community because they are all the same. Through the voice of Fearless, Pepetela attempts to demonstrate how ethnic tensions are a barrier to liberation and encourage self-harm. Only by realizing one's common identity as the colonially oppressed can colonialism be overcome. The shared identity goes beyond race or tribe; it is again the idea that the state of mind against Portuguese colonialism can be identified as the common feature of Angolan identity.

The Rope is a short story about the Angolan civil war. It features two teams who are playing tug of war. The team that pulls hardest wins the prize: power over Angola. The 'American', 'Holden', 'Savimbi', 'Chipenda' and the 'South African Racist' are on one team. The leaders of this team are the American and the South African Racist, while the others are simply following orders. On the other side are five people from different races and ethnic groups – a Kimbundu, an Ovimbundu, a Tchokuê, a mixed-race person and a white person. The members of this second team do not have a leader and neither do they have personal names, instead calling themselves 'The Angolan People'. The other character is called 'Likishi', a Tchokuê dancer who judges the fight. Initially, the Angolan people are united and start winning. The American keeps humiliating Holden, Savimbi and Chipenda, calling them stupid and useless. The game then suddenly changes when Savimbi and Chipenda go and speak to members of the Angolan People, poisoning them with tribalism and racism. They influence them into believing they will eventually betray each other owing to their racial or tribal affiliations. This disruptive discourse makes The Angolan People lose several times over. However, understanding what is going on, the Tchoukuê dancer intervenes, explaining that they should not be poisoned by beliefs of racial and tribal differences and should instead unite for the good of the people. On hearing this, the Angolan People win because they have heard that they are all the same and that the words of Savimbi and Chipenda are simply a spell used to segregate the Angolan nation (Pepetela 1980). The main lesson in *The Rope* is how one should ignore racial and tribal differences to instead focus on similarities and zones of commonality.

The fact that the winning team members do not identify themselves by their real names but rather by 'The Angolan People' highlights how similarities are more important and how unification overpowers differences. How behaviour can be changed according to beliefs or disbeliefs about racial and tribal differences suggests how important it is to create a national understanding of these similarities. The similarities, however, cannot be racial or tribal, as the members of the winning team are from different tribes and races; instead, they endorse an anti-colonial political position against the Portuguese.

The Adventures of Ngunga is a story about the life of 'Ngunga', a young MPLA soldier. The book was initially written to teach military ethics to MPLA guerrilla soldiers. Ngunga is the moral compass that evaluates the goodness or badness of other characters. Those who disappoint Ngunga are those who pretend to be generous but who are, in fact, individualistic and self-interested. For instance, 'Kafuxi' is the leader of a small black community who pretends to help the MPLA but refuses to give food to soldiers. The characters are moral exemplars who have names signalling generosity and solidarity and who behave in ways that include sacrifice and that benefit the good of the community. In particular, Ngunga admires the soldier called 'Our Struggle', who has on various occasions sacrificed himself for the good of the community (Pepetela 1973: 25). Although the book rarely mentions racism and tribalism, the moral standard is one of inclusion and promotion of the common good, which thereby rejects tribal or racial ideas. This sense of inclusion and the common good, in turn, relates to the independence of the Angolan nation from years of Portuguese colonialism.

In this regard, two core ideas are present throughout Pepetela's early fiction. The first is that the Angolan nation is strongly divided by racism and tribalism. This problem must be addressed as it poses a barrier to a successful liberation and the construction of a solid and united new Angolan nation. It is impossible to be liberated without overcoming these forms of hatred; it is a necessary condition to address them for the sake of true liberation. The second is that what unites people from different tribes and races is their shared consciousness against Portuguese colonialism. The anti-colonial positioning that occurs despite one's racial and tribal identity defines Angolanness. Angolanness consists in this state of consciousness that realizes the wrongs of colonialism and wishes to construct an independent Angolan nation. As such, it endorses the idea that all ethnic and racial groups are equal, imagining a nation with features of all the Angolan people, thereby embracing and reclaiming aspects of traditional African culture with the rejection of colonialism. Hence, there is a sense of identity rooted in local cultural Angolan practices and a certain degree of cosmopolitanism to the extent that diversity is endorsed.

Being white in an emerging postcolonial Angola

The theory I have just advanced is not often defended in relation to Pepetela's writings. In this section, I argue that by looking at the historical context and life of Pepetela, it is reasonable to say that part of his motivation to write these novels was to try to make sense of his white identity in emerging postcolonial Angola. Put differently, this section explains what it was like to be white at the time at which Pepetela wrote these novels. By connecting this to Pepetela's life, it is reasonable to suggest that his novels reveal the concern of a white person's belonging in an emerging postcolonial Angola. This contextualization, in turn, reinforces the theory that Pepetela is offering a political theory about Angolan identity.

The Portuguese arrived on the Angolan coast for the first time in 1483/1484, under the command of the Portuguese explorer, Diogo Cão (Birmingham 2016). It was only in 1575, however, that settler colonialism started, mainly in order to further the Atlantic Slave Trade on the west coast of Africa (Birmingham 2016). Charles Boxer has compiled substantial evidence from official government documents, clerical documents and correspondence between colonial elites, suggesting that the Portuguese were particularly cruel towards indigenous Africans, incentivizing hatred between African tribes. By way of illustration, Boxer identifies that Portuguese colonialists spread myths about other tribes being cannibals, thereby explaining to the indigenous of Angola that the Portuguese presence was a necessary protection against these other tribes. In addition, there are substantial reports of the rape of many African women by European men who travelled to the Angolan colony without their wives. At the time, there were many slave trade routes to Brazil and mainland Portugal, with

African people working either on plantations or in homes; this situation lasted until 1875 (Boxer 1973).

By the end of the nineteenth and the beginning of the twentieth century, the Portuguese economy began to decline. This was the result of many factors but was mainly related to Brazil's independence as a colony (Birmingham 2016). Following this, poverty began increasing substantially on the mainland, while in urban centres, anarchist and republican movements against the Portuguese monarchy started to grow in abundance (Rosas 2018a). Moreover, the Portuguese population felt rather humiliated by the successful 1890 British ultimatum against the Portuguese government's attempt to link the territories of Angola and Mozambique in the 'Project of the Pink Map'. These tensions and discrediting of the Portuguese monarchy eventually led to the regicide of Charles I in 1908 and the establishment of the First Republic in 1910 (Guimarães 2017). Despite being less conservative than the monarchy, the First Republic still underscored the importance of white superiority in Africa. In particular, it viewed the settlement in Africa as a civilizing mission that the Portuguese ought to carry out and incentivize. This surely was a reflex of the economy still being in decline and the need to send the Portuguese away from the mainland (Rosas 2018b). The strategy of sending colonizers to Africa, however, was insufficient in boosting the Portuguese economy and the disapproval rates ran high in the First Republic. Then, on 28 May 1926, there was a *coup d'état* which established a military dictatorship, shortly followed by the proto-fascist government *Estado Novo* (Rosas 2018a).

During the *Estado Novo*, more settlement colonialism was incentivized. The African colonies, particularly Angola, were described by *Estado Novo*'s propaganda as a promised land where Portuguese dreams could be realized. *Estado Novo* established many laws reinforcing European power and division among local tribes. The '*Estatuto do Indigenato*' ('Statute of the Indigenous People') of 1929 underlined the legal inferiority of indigenous peoples, establishing that non-Europeans could not be full citizens and specifying crimes only indigenous peoples could commit (Rosas 2018a; Bethencourt 2014).

The act also established that the forced labour of African people was justified, especially for public enterprises and the payment of taxes (Rosas 2018b). Then, the 'Colonial Act' of 1930 limited economic expansion of the colonies, stipulating that all economic activity needed to be regulated by the Ministry of Colonies on the Portuguese mainland (Bethencourt 2014). In 1933, a new law called the *'Carta Orgânica do Império Colonial Português'* ('Letter From the Portuguese Colonial Empire') was decreed, establishing that the Portuguese should maintain the civilizing mission of conserving and developing indigenous African populations. They understood this mission to consist of eradicating local languages and what they considered to be barbarous African practices, forcing Africans to work to educate them out of their supposedly lazy nature (Bethencourt 2014).

Such racist colonial discourse and policy were common and acceptable until the mid-twentieth century, but this changed at the beginning of the 1950s as a result of a series of events (Bethencourt 2014: 123). First, these colonial discourses were strongly connected with ideas of racial superiority, and after the end of the Second World War, these ideas became less popular in Europe. In particular, the atrocities of Nazi Germany and its racist ideology provided a negative mirror in which other Europeans could positively reflect. Second, the emergence of the language of equality and freedom emerging from the civil rights movement in the United States also shaped discourses of the time, thus influencing views on the legitimacy of colonialism. Third, there was strong support for decolonization emerging from China and the Soviet Union, powerful nations with resources to ideologically, discursively and materially support the decolonization movements (Bethencourt 2014: 42). By the 1960s, most African countries had been decolonized. Nevertheless, still under the dictatorship of *Estado Novo*, Portugal did not wish to give up its colonies. There was, however, substantial international pressure on Portugal to return some power to the Angolans. Rather than doing this, however, the dictatorship attempted to reform the official discourse and political system, so that they could justify their presence in Africa

(Boxer 1973). While before there had been an explicit discourse on the superiority of whites and the inferiority of blacks, the official discourse was now about how Portuguese colonialism was different from other types of colonialism. The *Estado Novo* engaged in rhetoric claiming that the Portuguese were good colonizers who aided the development of the colonies (Birmingham 2016). Moreover, as part of this change, the *Estado Novo* officially renamed the colonies 'provinces' to signal that these were simply extensions of the Portuguese mainland (Chabal et al. 2002). It was only in 1961 that the discriminatory laws were revoked (Boxer 1973).

The strategy of gaining international support and mitigating internal opposition, however, failed. The United Nations and especially the United States imposed a variety of economic sanctions on Portugal, while internally, many liberationist movements grew, leading to a colonial war in Angola (1961), Guinea-Bissau (1963) and Mozambique (1964) (Chabal et al. 2002). The movements in Guinea-Bissau and Mozambique mobilized quite successfully; this was not the case in Angola, however, and there were significant divisions among liberationists, especially in connection with ethnicity and class. The National Liberation Front of Angola (FNLA) under the leadership of Holden Roberto mostly drew support from the Bakongo tribe of northern Angola, while the National Union for the Total Independence of Angola (UNITA) led by Jonas Savimbi was mostly supported by the Ovimbundu people from central Angola; finally, the MPLA had a wider range of support, but this mostly came from peasants and the working classes in southern Angola as well as some educated African elites from Luanda. These three fronts were strongly associated with ethnic groups, meaning that rather than collectively fighting the Portuguese, they often launched military operations against each other (Birmingham 2016; Chabal et al. 2002). The war ended suddenly with the Carnation Revolution in Portugal on 25 April 1974, after which Angola became independent on 11 November 1975. In the first elections, the MPLA won, but other political parties, especially the UNITA, were sceptical of the elections.

The pre-existing ethnic tensions between groups and the contestation of the elections led to a civil war that ended only in 2002. This had three main fronts: the FNLA, the MPLA and the UNITA (Birmingham 2016; Chabal et al. 2002). The FNLA and UNITA (especially the latter) had discourses that were very strongly anti-white and more directed at specific tribal identities (Fernado 2012; Chabal et al. 2002).

Taking this on board, the image of white colonizers in Angola at the time of Pepetela was an overwhelmingly negative one. White people had substantially contributed to and benefitted from the exploitation of black people, and the latter were not only aware of this but – fed by anti-colonial and Marxist ideologies – significantly opposed to it. For them, the history of white people in Angola is a history of oppressing black people; hence, white people were generally seen with distrust and as invaders. All this was inflamed by the strong anti-white discourse of Savimbi, who pointed out that the inclusion of white people in the emerging postcolonial Angola, as the MPLA had it, meant that black people would not be liberated. Savimbi linked white people's presence with Portuguese racist white rule, albeit ironically, he was supported by the apartheid government of South Africa. In short, white colonialists were understood by many as enemies, invaders and outsiders; they were seen as culturally different from indigenous Angolans (Fernado 2012; Chabal et al. 2002).

As a white man who benefitted from the colonial system but who simultaneously wished for an independent Angola, Pepetela felt the need to justify his belonging to the Angolan nation. Put differently, the historical context of white oppression and the anti-white discourse of some political forces forced him to justify his place in an emerging postcolonial Angola. In other words, given that Pepetela was white in an emerging postcolonial Angola, he tries to find ways to negotiate the structural contradictions of his position by way of the heritage of Angola's racially ordered colonial past. From this perspective, he was a socially privileged individual who, just by virtue of his identity, benefitted from discriminatory measures and participated in an oppressive system. Although this shows that the environment was indeed unwelcoming for white people and that those who wanted to stay felt a need to justify their position, it does not yet demonstrate that Pepetela wished to belong to the emerging postcolonial Angola. This can be confirmed by looking at some of Pepetela's biographical details. First, he was born in Benguela in 1941, the most racially mixed of all cities in colonial Angola, and having lived here, he saw part of his identity as bound up in this melting pot, for as a child he had the chance to interact with people from different ethnic groups (Chaves and Macêdo 2010). Indeed, Pepetela has affirmed that it was as a child in Benguela that he first noticed the economic differences between white people and black people in colonial Angola, and that later, in high school, when he moved to the then Sá da Bandeira (now Lubango) – a much more segregated city – this feeling was solidified (Chaves and Macêdo 2010). Moreover, Pepetela could have left Angola to live in mainland Portugal as many white people did; instead, he stayed in Angola, which is revealing of his genuine desire to fully belong to the emerging postcolonial Angolan nation (Mata 2012b).

In addition, note that Pepetela's identity could only belong to an emerging postcolonial Angola. Broadly speaking, the political positioning of white Angolans with respect to independence can be divided into three kinds. First, those strongly opposing the independence of the colonies and wanting to keep Portuguese rule. Second, those supporting independence but understanding this as giving power to white settlers living in Angola. Third, those supporting independence and in support of giving power to the indigenous people of Angola. The third group were a minority and included Pepetela among their number. Hence, Pepetela challenged the emotional standards of the dominant white Angolan community, which landed him in a situation without many white Angolans with whom he might identify. Moreover, many black Angolans were distrustful of him (Kapuscinski and Glowczewska 2001).

In addition, the desire to belong, his personal anxieties, experience and situatedness as a white Angolan supporting independence can be found in some of the interviews Pepetela gave about his work. In one interview, Pepetela affirms that *Muana Puó* and *Mayombe* were written out of a personal need to exteriorize his feelings (Chaves and Macêdo 2010). They were a form of catharsis aiding him in thinking through the fact of war and racial tensions. *Muana Puó* was written in 1969, a period just before Pepetela decided to join the struggle in Angola, and is possibly a reflection piece for himself on what to do. *The Rope* was written during the civil war, a time when Savimbi's anti-white discourse was significant and potentially fermenting anti-white sentiment in part of the population. In fact, a topic addressed throughout *The Rope* is how white people are suspected of being fake allies (Pepetela 1980). Pepetela was confronted at various times about this because there were not only internal MPLA discourses against white solidarity, but also a significant anti-white discourse from UNITA, especially during the civil war. Likewise, *Mayombe* was written during Pepetela's time as a guerrilla fighter in Cabinda, and he stated that even though the characters are fictional, many of the events described refer to real situations (Mata 2012b). For instance, he mentions in *Mayombe* how white and mixed-race people feel that they need to do more to prove that they belong to Angola. Indeed, *Mayombe* was written at a time when many MPLA soldiers believed that white people should not be included in the struggle for liberation.

To summarize, Pepetela's historical context in the emerging postcolonial Angola was one in which white identity was understood by many as the enemy. Specifically, because of the history of Portuguese colonialism and its cruelty towards black people, coupled with the fact that UNITA espoused an inflammatory anti-white discourse, white Angolans wishing to stay in Africa felt the need to justify their presence (Kapuscinski and Glowczewska 2001). It is this situation that is reflected in Pepetela's work and life: both a desire for independence and an anxiety to justify his position.

Africanizing identity, Marxism and embracing Angolanness

In the previous section, I showed that the context in which Pepetela has written as well as his biographical details indicate why he may have felt the need to consider why he belonged to Angola. Here, I wish to point out one of the ways in which he demonstrates his endorsement of and participation in African and, more specifically, Angolan identity. I shall argue that he demonstrates his Angolan identity (Angolanness) by supporting aspects of African culture and Marxist ideology. To clarify, the idea of Angolanness is a version of the *négritude* and black consciousness movements from francophone and anglophone Africa. Many African intellectuals have emphasized the distinctiveness and value of African culture. Indeed, such movements were important throughout Africa and were conducive to properly conceptualizing postcolonial African nations (George 2021). Under the leadership of Agostinho Neto, the MPLA sought to express Angolanness by endorsing African elements that were banned, degraded and repressed by Portuguese colonialism; this included – to name only a few – religious rituals, Afrocentric ideologies, frameworks of thought dances, names and literary expressions. In his work, Pepetela attempts very precisely to reveal that, despite his whiteness, he values and endorses African culture and Angolanness, thereby signalling that he belongs to the Angolan nation (Chabal 1996).

In particular, Pepetela construes Angolanness through at least three dimensions: it is marked by *holding a state of consciousness* against Portuguese colonialism (an anti-colonialist consciousness), an endorsement and valuing of African culture and a Marxist understanding of liberation. The anti-colonial mindset rendered as a characteristic for Angolanness is, as explained above, omnipresent in Pepetela's texts. He constantly mentions that what characterizes those who act morally is that they support anti-colonialism, which in turn allows him – as a white individual – to perceive himself as belonging to the emerging postcolonial Angolan nation. At the same time, it also allows him to criticize those who may look like they belong, but actually do not. In *The Rope*, he describes Savimbi and Holden as supporting colonialism and, thereby, as not belonging to Angola. This anti-colonial state of mind, however, allows for some fluidity in the conception of belonging; indeed, those who change their state of mind can either endorse or stop endorsing Angolanness.

One feature of Pepetela's fiction that reveals the endorsement and valuing of African culture is the heroism of African characters in his narratives. This heroism acts as a symbolic gesture for endorsing Angolanness; that is, picturing African people as heroes suggests that the African way is morally good, thereby supporting the Africanization of institutions. Moreover, as these heroes were guerrilla fighters against colonialism it also shows an endorsement of anti-colonialism. This is particularly telling when contrasted with the dominant narrative in Portuguese colonial discourse, especially in the fictional realm, where European people were often depicted as saviours and African people as less intelligent and cowards. This is noticeable, for instance, in children's stories at the time when African people were constantly ridiculed, whereas white people appeared as the heroes (Chabal 1996). In Pepetela's narrative, there is a complete inversion of this rhetoric: African people are often framed as heroes, while Europeans are either enemies or people who contribute (but not lead) to the liberation of Angola. Take, for instance, *The Rope*, in which the white people on the Angolan team equally contribute to success in the war. Moreover, in the same story, the judge Likishi is a traditional African dancer, which shows that traditional African values are the moral compass to be endorsed. Likewise, in *The Adventures of Ngunga*, the hero is a young African man who fights against both European colonialists and all those corrupted by colonialism. Likewise, in *Mayombe*, Fearless is an African man who is the hero of the narrative. This framing of African individuals as heroes is a radical change in support of Angolanness and, simultaneously, a rejection of Portuguese colonial discourses stating that African people are incapable of governing themselves.

Pepetela also engages in a discourse that signals his belief in an emerging postcolonial Angola through his support of the Africanization of societies. The values of community, solidarity and unity that Pepetela mentions were constitutive of a Pan-African ideology and dominant political view at the time. These were held by African liberators who defended unity between Africans as a way of overcoming colonialism and neocolonialism. For instance, Amílcar Cabral from Guinea-Bissau insisted on the value of unity, Julius Nyerere on 'Ujamaa' (treating others as family) and Nelson Mandela on 'Ubuntu' (treating others with love and care as if they were a continuation of ourselves). In Kimbundo, a Bantu language from the central north of Angola, the equivalent expression is 'Etu Mudyetu', which means that one ought to always behave with kindness and humanity. By mentioning the centrality of these values, Pepetela is simultaneously signalling his rejection of values from the Global North and his support for an Africanized Africa.

Finally, Pepetela attempts to show his Angolanness through his *nom de plume*. Pepetela's birth name is Portuguese (Artur Carlos Maurício Pestana dos Santos), but he decided to symbolically sign his work with a Kimbundo word '*Pepetela*', which means 'eyelash'. The symbolic gesture of dropping his original name to endorse an African one is quite meaningful. First, it shows that he shared the knowledge and revulsion of many Africans regarding Portuguese colonialists changing indigenous people's original names to Christian names, and he is aware of how these original names have become valuable in African culture. Second, by using a Kimbundo word, Pepetela challenged one of the European discourses of the time affirming that European people should not speak like African people. In colonial Portugal, the expression 'speaking like a black' was often used in a negative way. To speak like a black person meant that one did not know how to speak, such that white people ought never to do so. Adopting a Kimbundo name meant rejecting this discourse of black inferiority and instead valuing black discourse. Third, adopting a name in an African language demonstrates how he valued and integrated African culture in his life. Adopting a *nom de guerre* was a tradition in Bantu African war codes, and Pepetela's decision to also adopt such a name symbolizes how much value he places on Africanity. The choice of name, therefore, is revealing of his desire to make part of an emerging postcolonial Angola free from Portuguese colonial rule (Chaves and Macêdo 2010).

These symbolic endorsements of African culture suggest that Pepetela's theory of Angolanness is, as stated above, linked with having an anti-colonial state of mind. But what does it actually mean to have an anti-colonial state of mind? In short, it refers to a state of mind whereby individuals reverse colonial values of subjugation and humiliation of colonized cultures and, instead, uphold and praise the culture of the colonized. What this means in the particular case of Angola is that to hold Angolanness is to value the culture and endorse it by refusing colonial legacies, substituting them for truly African ones.

To have an anti-colonial state of mind is also to endorse a Marxist ideology (which at the time Pepetela wrote these novels meant supporting MPLA's ideology). Pepetela has no doubt been influenced by Marxism. At a young age, he was introduced to Marxist texts by his uncle (Chaves and Macêdo 2010). In 1958, he moved to Portugal to pursue university studies in engineering. In 1961, the war for the liberation of Angola erupted, and *Estado Novo* started to force young males to join the war effort (Mata 2012b). Because Pepetela believed in independence for Angola, he did not complete his degree and instead fled to Paris and later Algeria. In Algeria, he pursued studies in sociology; Algeria was already independent and much of the curriculum had been decolonized. Instead, it was now filled with the anti-colonial thought of the National Liberation Front in Algeria (Mata 2012b; Chaves and Macêdo 2010; Peres 2003). Moreover, the most widely studied sociopolitical thinkers in the Global South at that time were Frantz Fanon and Harold Wolpe, who were strong supporters of Marxist liberationist views of Africa (Santos 2014). In both *Mayombe* and *Muana Puó*, just like in *The Rope*, Marxist language is used as a symbolic tool to gain international support. In fact, in *Muana Puó* and *Mayombe*, the idea of class consciousness appears as a crucial part of MPLA discourse. In *Muana Puó*, the description of exploitation, particularly of how it can be overcome, is an allusion to the Marxist idea which depicts the capitalist bourgeoisie benefitting from workers' labour only to lead to their own demise. In another play, the *Revolution of the House of the Idols*, there is a tension between what the elites and the people want; Pepetela, of course, sides with the people.

African personhood and war as transformative

Pepetela also attempts to make sense of his belonging to an emerging postcolonial Angola by intertwining the African concept of personhood with the idea that war has a transformative effect on the individual (Cordeiro-Rodrigues and Chimakonam 2022). In Pepetela's novels, war is revealed as a means by which to achieve or create national unity; through the act of war, there is a transformation of the individual (and so of the collective) into something else. In Pepetela's narratives, war is seen as creating a feeling of common identity. In the case of *Mayombe*, the soldiers are all from different ethnicities and are in constant conflict because of this. This symbolizes how a lack of unity exists in the emerging Angolan nation. However, it is also through the act of war that these ethnic differences and prejudices are gradually dissolved into a sense of common identity. In *The Adventures of Ngunga*, it is also made clear that there is a transformative process underway throughout the novel. Initially, Ngunga has never been a soldier and does not pay much attention to social reality, but when he must enter the war, he realizes the importance of unity and disdains those who are individualistic. In *The Rope*, the sense of unity of The Angolan People is fragile as it becomes disrupted by the words of Savimbi and Holden; it is only at the end of the war that a real sense of unity emerges. Finally, in *Muana Puó*, the bats transform themselves into humans only after war against the crows.

Hence, one of the purposes of these novels is to show precisely how an anti-colonial war can transform individuals, help to overcome difference and create unity. Indeed, this is confirmed in an interview in which Pepetela stated, 'If war has anything positive, it's that when different people socialize, it creates a sense of unity' (Unimesantos 2018). The idea that war is necessary for transformation is corroborated by other African thinkers such as Kwame Nkrumah, Frantz Fanon and Amílcar Cabral. For instance, Cabral, one of the most influential thinkers on Lusophone liberation, stated that war was able to create a national consciousness among the people of Guinea-Bissau: 'With regards to our country, armed struggle not only eliminated tribal conflict, but also is totally transforming our people' (Cabral 1974: 71).

The reason why war is thought about in this way is related to the African idea of personhood. In African thought, what a person is does not refer to the physical or psychological characteristics of a lone individual, but is inextricably linked to the surrounding community. Indeed, the identity of an individual can be understood only alongside the collectivity in which the individual is situated. For it is the community that defines the person, rather than the isolated individual. Moreover, personhood is not something that everyone possesses. Instead, persons become persons only after a process of incorporation. Personhood is something achieved rather than acquired through birth (Menkiti 2018). It requires a long process of social and ritual transformation until one acquires the excellences that make someone a person. Hence, according to this view, some people could fail to become a person (Molefe 2019; Gyekye 2011). Therefore, Africans tend to emphasize rituals of incorporation and learning the social rules of a community in order to attain social self-hood. Thus, war conducted around a morally right idea (namely, anti-colonialism) can foster precisely this value. The individuals acquire personhood through rituals of war for the purpose of achieving a high moral value: the anti-colonial independence of Angola (Cordeiro-Rodrigues and Chimakonam 2022).

How does this apply to Pepetela's theory of Angolanness? First, as mentioned in the previous section, a significant aspect of Angolanness is the endorsement of African concepts and values. Pepetela is here endorsing an African conceptual value system and framework – the idea of personhood, war as transformative – and thereby showing his allegiance to Africa and African liberationist discourses. Second, and perhaps most importantly, we must recall that Pepetela was not only a writer, for he also voluntarily joined the war on the side of the MPLA, refusing to fight on the side of the Portuguese. Hence, by defending the theory wherein war forms both personhood and a sense of community, by implication, Pepetela argues that be belongs to this community, that despite his white identity he has also been through the transformative process necessary to become a person and a part of the community, which can be shared with other guerrilla fighters. In fact, by changing his birth name to his *non de guerre* Pepetela signals precisely this process of transformation through war. He is someone who has become a person by participating in war, who undertook a transformative communal ritual, one that gave him personhood and made him into an important member of the community. Thus, Pepetela expresses his belonging to an emerging postcolonial Angola to the extent that he has also been through this transformative process. In short, for Pepetela, war is transformative and therapeutic, having the power to create a new identity through a ritual wherein individuals realize their commonality, their binding to a community and their belonging to a certain group.

Conclusion

Pepetela's fiction has been widely studied by scholars. In this chapter, I have interpreted Pepetela's work as a narrative wherein he tries to understand his place – as a white person – in postcolonial, emerging Angola. In turn, this leads to a political theory of Angolan identity that includes Marxist ideology, anti-colonialism and the idea of war as transformative. This view offers a new insight into Pepetela's work to the extent that it deciphers meanings within the text that are so closely related to his identity that they may even have gone unnoticed by Pepetela himself.

9

Agostinho Neto: Revolution, art and liberation

Introduction

Born in 1922 in Ícolo e Bengo, Luanda, Agostinho Neto is without a doubt one of the most important names in twentieth-century Angolan history (Laranjeira 2016; Rodrigues 2016; Medina 2016a, 2016b). The first president of independent Angola from 1975 to 1979, he is also lauded for his poetry. The community in which he grew up was very simple, based mostly on horticulture and fishery, and dominated by Methodists who were significantly influenced by American Methodists. His father, Agostinho Pedro Neto (to whom Neto looked up as a model), was a reverend and had an important role in the religious community. Neto went to primary school at a Methodist church, where his mother worked. In 1924, when Neto was only two, a military dictatorship was introduced in Portugal after a *coup d'état*, which resulted in António de Oliveira Salazar later seizing power in 1932. Consequently, a quasi-fascist political regime emerged (*Estado Novo*), and it was this regime that Neto would so avidly fight against and eventually help to overthrow (Infopédia Porto Editora 2022; Medina 2016a, 2016b).

Neto was a good student and generally stood out in this respect. The Portuguese government gave him a scholarship, and he went to study at a prestigious high school called '*Liceu Salvador Correia*'; in 1934, he moved together with his parents to Luanda. However, he had to interrupt his studies on account of the financial situation at home; this resulted in him taking longer to finish high school (Medina 2016a, 2016b).

It was also around this time that Neto began becoming interested in questions about Angolan independence and the African condition. In 1938, a young man committed suicide by jumping from the Diogo Cão bridge, the provocative factor being the fact that he was not allowed to walk in 'white areas'. This event had an extremely strong impact on Neto, and in his poetry, he began to explore the African condition in Angola. Between 1938 and 1946, he published essays and poems in newspapers such as *O Estandarte* (The Banner) and *O Farolim* (The Lighthouse). There, he criticized how Angolans were physically and spiritually oppressed by Portuguese colonialism. In fact, many of the political ideas that he more explicitly defended later in his life are already at work in his early poetry (Medina 2016a, 2016b; Laranjeira 2016). Neto moved to Portugal in 1947 to study medicine at the University of Coimbra and then at the University of Lisbon. He spent thirteen years in Portugal and became very involved in 'associativism' (*associativismo*). He also had the opportunity to meet several African intellectuals, such as Amilcar Cabral and Pinto de Andrade. In 1958, he married Maria Eugénia Neto, a Portuguese poet and journalist he met in these cultural circles. The marriage itself was seen as a defiance at the time, owing to their different ethnicities (Medina 2016a, 2016b).

After Pinto de Andrade, Neto became the president of the MPLA. The Carnation Revolution in Portugal in April 1974 eventually led to Angola's independence on 11 November 1975. Neto became its first president after independence. In that year, he was awarded the Lenin Peace Prize, a prize given by the Soviet Union to individuals who worked towards strengthening peace between peoples. He died in Moscow in 1979 from liver cancer and was succeeded temporarily by Lúcio Lara and then by José Eduardo dos Santos. His birthday, 17 September, is celebrated in Angola as the national hero day (Infopédia Porto Editora 2022; Laranjeira 2016; Medina 2016a, 2016b; Rodrigues 2016).

The political ideas in this chapter reflect many of these moments in Neto's life. This chapter is divided into the following sections. In the next section, I describe Neto's views on colonialism and imperialism: how it is harmful, how it is expressed, what varieties of it are prevalent and how to overcome it. In the section following that, I shall outline his theory of art. The third section will explain Neto's views on just war theory and military ethics.

Angolan liberation and the many shades of oppression

All humans have the desire and the right to be free and to have the tools to liberate themselves from a society that kills their humanity: this was the fundamental belief Neto held. All people have the right to live in a society where they can function as human beings and in which institutions do not remove a person's humanity (Carreira 1996; Neto 1987, 1975). This concept of humanity is very common in African thought. African philosophers often understand humanity as the capacity to develop a certain form of character with specific communal virtues (Ewuoso 2021; Ewuoso and Hall 2019; Metz 2010). This view is similar to human rights discourses in the West, but the African perspective is different insofar as it combines individual rights with communal rights (Chimakonam and Agada 2020; Metz 2010). Any society or action that systematically undermines the development of these virtues is to be considered morally bad (Cordeiro-Rodrigues 2021; Metz 2013; Gyekye 2011).

During the time in which Neto wrote, the main concern was to liberate Angolans from an oppressive regime. Neto's understanding of this oppression was holistic; he did not view the Angolan problem simply as a struggle for independence from the Portuguese. Instead, for Neto, the proper way to understand the Angolan liberation struggle was in terms of the power structures of the world order. For Neto, the Angolan struggle was but one of the many networks of events happening in world politics. In short, world politics has different local manifestations, and the Angolan situation was to be understood as a local expression of a global phenomenon (Carreira 1996; Neto 1987, 1977a, 1976, 1974).

Locally, African countries suffer either from paleo-colonialism or neocolonialism. Paleo-colonialism for Neto is the old kind of colonialism, where oppression is clear, direct and assumed. In paleo-colonialist societies, there is an assumed self-perception of the colonizer as superior to the colonized, and policies do not try to hide the oppression. As examples of this, Neto refers to Portuguese fascism before 1974 and apartheid South Africa. But as Neto clearly states, most of the colonialism today does not have such a direct expression and instead operates subtly. This new form of colonialism, or neocolonialism, hides its real oppressive intentions, which are masked by superficially liberating discourses and actions but in practice aim at subjugating African peoples (Neto 1987, 1974). Neto is clearly inspired here by Kwame Nkrumah's views on neocolonialism, stating that colonialism has changed to a system that controls Africans through political and economic dominance without settlement (Nkrumah 1974).

These forms of colonialism, however, are only local expressions of a much greater problem: imperialism. Imperialism is the system that feeds everything else, such that, for Neto, it is the main enemy of Angolans – and more specifically, the main enemy is the type of imperialism represented by the United States. Portugal is then rendered only as the direct enemy – the one on the field barring liberation – but Portugal is not the main enemy, for it is not the most fundamental force driving oppression (Neto 1974). This entails that the problem in Angola is not inherently racial; for Neto, the reason why Angolans are oppressed is not because of racism. Note that Neto does not dismiss racism in Angola; he clearly thinks that racism exists, as can be seen in his poetry. But the *fundamental problem* is not racial for Neto, but, rather, is bound up with the power hierarchies caused by an imperialistic capitalist system (Neto 1987, 1975, 1974): 'The problem is not and has never been, purely racial; race is simply an argument used for domination of a class over the other' (Neto 1979: 9, my translation).

In this regard, the real problem according to Neto is to do with class; race is simply a discursive tool to mask this more fundamental issue. To demonstrate this, he points out that the European proletariat suffers from a similar form of oppression as African people in Africa.

The focus of the struggle, therefore, should switch from fighting Europeans in Africa to fighting imperialists (the owners of the means of production) in Africa (Neto 1979, 1977a, 1976, 1975, 1974). This focus was particularly relevant at the time Neto was writing because some of his competitors (e.g. UNITA) strongly focused on the racial question as the main drive for their struggle (Chabal et al. 2002).

Underlying Neto's view is an important element of African thought: the idea that everything is interconnected (Jecker and Atuire 2021; Cordeiro-Rodrigues 2021; Gyekye 2011). It is common in African philosophy to think the world as one, wherein all events are causally connected (Cordeiro-Rodrigues 2020). This view is also partly reflected in Neto's solution. During his period as president, for instance, Neto insisted on having a global network of revolutionaries as he believed it is only through a joint revolutionary change that Angolan independence can become meaningful. Angola, in other words, could not become fully independent if there is oppression elsewhere; liberation needs to be universal (Neto 1987, 1974). Indeed, Neto attempted to create close ties with Cuba, the Soviet Union and many African and Arab countries (Medina 2016a, 2016b). It is important to note how aligned this is to the thought of African intellectuals such as Desmond Tutu and Nelson Mandela, who maintained that the end of racist systems required the liberation of both the oppressor and the oppressed (Tutu 2000; Mandela 1995).

How can the wrongs of colonialism be corrected, according to Neto? As a Marxist thinker, he was clearly influenced by revolutionary leaders who were popular at the time such as Che Guevara, Fidel Castro, Mao Zedong and Vladimir Lenin. The revolution against colonialism is simultaneously against imperialistic capitalist forces; a revolutionary struggle that requires class unity and coordination. For Neto, the Angolan struggle against Portuguese colonialism should be led by the proletariat and the peasants. It is only through these two groups working together that revolution can be achieved (Neto 1987, 1976, 1975).

Urban areas of Angola had a significant number of proletariat who could unite against oppression. But Portugal's colonialism was significantly marked by attempting to produce agricultural goods (especially cotton) through the exploitation of Africans; thus, the inclusion of peasants was crucial for a successful revolution. In addition, Neto considered that the proletariat should have a leading role in the organization. There is nothing intrinsically better about the proletariat, but, according to Neto, this class has gained a unique experience in resisting capitalism and therefore has the know-how and experience of revolutionary organization (Neto 1979, 1977a, 1976). Note how similar this view is to Mao's understanding of revolution, wherein both peasants and the proletariat have a crucial role (Tse-Tung 2014). However, in his texts, Neto never acknowledges this Maoist influence, simply insisting on not making race the main issue. Contrary to other movements, like the UNITA, which emphasized the racial dimension, Neto and the MPLA attempted to resist this tendency, so as to organize the struggle in terms of ideology and class (Chabal et al. 2002).

The policies that ought to be implemented to achieve independentist goals concern land distribution and welfare rights. Neto considered that the returnees (European people born in Africa who fled to Portugal when Angola became independent) did not have an automatic right to come back to Angola and should leave many of their possessions behind. Their land and property was to be appropriated by local Africans, but this comes with certain duties. Everyone should be invested in making the country better, such that once they appropriate the land, they need to work and maximize production (Neto 1987). From Neto's viewpoint, the development of Angola was mainly dependent on increasing production, and this was why he emphasized the communal duty of those appropriating land. Furthermore, he did not believe in individual property. Ultimately, the land belongs to society and not to particular individuals, such that those who appropriate it are entitled to it only to the extent that they use it for the benefit of the larger society (Neto 1987, 1979, 1975).

There is, in fact, a larger ideology and project of nationalization underlying this idea. From Neto's point of view, everything that referred to basic welfare rights should be nationalized to satisfy the Angolan population's basic needs, such as key industries, healthcare and teaching. Neto believed that everyone needs to learn how to read and write as well as have access to housing and healthcare. Bureaucracies should be simplified, and sometimes, he suggests that they should even be totally eliminated in order to facilitate access to these goods (Neto 1987).

This all required a major change in mindset. Neto was frustrated by the fact that many people were reluctant to appropriate land that colonizers used for exploiting Africans, but at the same time were willing to sabotage revolutionary advances for independence. The only way to change this was to have an ideological rejuvenation led by the MPLA, which would bring a revolutionary mindset, freeing individuals from mental slavery. For Neto, a great part of this work was to be done by intellectuals like poets (Neto 1987, 1980, 1977b).

African art, poetry and literature

Neto was himself a poet. He wrote three acclaimed books: *Sacred Hope*, *Dawn* and *Renouncing the Impossible*. These books focus on several themes such as love and solitude, but, most importantly, they attempt to explore, understand and address the suffering of African people in Angola. Neto uses his poetry as a tool to denounce the wrongs of colonialism, but also as a method of incentivizing a decolonized spirit and mind. As such, Neto's poetry can be considered a historical document which connects the theory with the practice of liberation by exploring the frustrations, anxieties and desires of oppressed people (Laranjeira 2016). In his poetry, Neto tries to illuminate the voice of Angolans, showing how they suffer. This can be found, for instance, in his poem 'Sábado nos musseques' ('Saturday in the *Musseques*').[1] In this poem, Neto wishes to denounce the poverty endured by Africans, especially in a context where Portuguese colonialism is trying to justify its presence in Africa as a 'good colonizer'. The good colonizer allegedly civilizes and treats the colonized equally, helping with their development. Neto denounces this as false. This can be seen in another poem entitled '*Civilização Ocidental*' ('Western Civilization'). In this poem, Neto emphasizes the negatives of colonialism, showing that it does not bring benefits and that it is, indeed, harmful. The civilizing mission is simply a myth. In addition, he adds a criticism to the colonial mindset of some of the colonized: he is critical of those Africans who praise colonialism but do not see the evils it introduces into their lives. Indeed, in his poetry, Neto tries to provide reasons for decolonization and independence and often uses his own experience of transformation as a model for what others might do to liberate themselves (Laranjeira 2016; Teixeira Medeiros 2015).

Neto also attempts to show how valuable Angolan culture is, giving a special role to the African drums (Teixeira Medeiros 2015). In important ways, Neto's intentions are like Assis Júnior's, which I explored in Chapter 6. But there is a fundamental difference: while Júnior was not explicitly in favour and, in fact, might even have opposed Angolan independence, Neto was clearly pro-independence and an anti-colonialist. What unites them is the idea that there is a need for change and that the integration of African elements in Angola is crucial for this change to be successful.

The use of poetry coheres with Neto's theoretical views on the role of art. For him, the artist (and he is mostly thinking about the writer) has a duty to address the social issues that surround them. Thus, the Angolan artist also has a duty to address their circumstances through art. What all this means, more precisely, is that art should serve the people (i.e. it needs to be an instrument for people's liberation). Art cannot be dissociated from – and in fact, is only morally justified if it serves – the good of the people (Neto 1987, 1980, 1977b).

How can art actually do this? Neto routinely visited cultural associations to give speeches, and he considered it important to be in touch with artists on a regular basis. Colonialism partially involves diminishing African artistic expression, according to Neto, such that one way to enact liberation is to reverse this diminution. Hence, part of the way that the Angolan artist ought to address social issues is by producing art that integrates and reflects Angolan culture *positively*. It should express the lives of African people and their condition to try and offer African-led solutions to Angolan problems. It should tell the history of Angola in an accurate way, rather than with the colonial bias with which it has been told before. It is also important for poets to be aware of the problems highlighted by the political party, which can guide them on these issues (Neto 1987, 1980, 1977b).

There is an underlying assumption in what Neto is stating. He strongly believes that art has a performative effect, significantly impacting people's lives and influencing how they act, such that it is possible through art to change the cultural mindset. The cultural mindset of a society is significantly determined by the society's art, according to Neto. It can work, however, in a negative or positive way. During colonialism, art was instrumentalized to further colonial goals. Now revolutionaries could use art positively by helping the revolution's goals. Art could be used to liberate Angola from colonialism, neocolonialism and the imperialistic forces underpinning them (Neto 1987, 1980, 1977b). In fact, during the time of Neto's presidency, he was very supportive of Pepetela's literary works, partly because he believed them to be instrumental in forming the right form of consciousness (Mata 2012b; Chaves and Macêdo 2010).

Finally, an important aspect of Neto's views involves the language of transmission of art – that it should be conducted in African languages rather than in Portuguese. Neto does not really explain in detail why this is the case, but it is possible to guess this based on the context of Portuguese colonialism. The imposition of the Portuguese language was an important way of curtailing African forms of expression. As Neto believed that art should reflect African culture and express the African condition, it seems that the best way to do this was through the native language of individuals, which, in this context, was usually not Portuguese. In other words, the expression of art in African languages is a more genuine way to authentically understand and pass the message of what the African condition is (Neto 1980, 1977b). This view is, therefore, shared with other African intellectuals, such as Ngũgĩ wa Thiong'o, who at a certain point of his career decided to cease writing in English and instead started to write in his own language, Kikuyu, precisely for the reasons enunciated here (Ngugi 2009).

To sum up, there are four core ideas in Neto's aesthetical thought. The first is that art has the power to change society. It is able to modify the world by changing mindsets, which will then act accordingly. Second, this role of art entails that artists have a duty to conduct artistic work in ways that benefit society (or 'the people' as Neto prefers to say). Art ought to be oriented towards promoting society's good. Third, Angolan artists should endorse this idea to help the construction of an independent Angola. Finally, this artistic expression should, as much as possible, be carried out in African languages rather than the colonizers' language (Neto 2016, 1987, 1980, 1977b).

War and military ethics

At the time that Neto composed most of his political writings, war was part of daily life (Medina 2016a, 2016b). War is a very difficult – perhaps the most difficult – action to justify on moral grounds. After all, it involves many wrongs: killing innocents, invading countries, using violence and harming others (Walzer 2015, 2006; Mcmahan 2011). Neto understood that it is important to have reasonable justifications for war. But what were they? For Neto, war was justified because of the oppression Africans suffered at the hands of the Portuguese. Colonialism corrupted the colonized subject's material, psychological and social existence (Neto 1987, 1977a, 1974).

Furthermore, war was justified because colonialists refused to change. It is well known that the Portuguese government refused to give independence to the colonies when all other European powers were doing so (Chabal et al. 2002). Instead, it decided to change its language, so as to classify African colonies as 'provinces' rather than 'colonies'. Thus, the war against Portugal was justified on the grounds of being the last resort: Portuguese politicians were intransigent and did not want to negotiate independence, such that the only option left was war (Neto 1987). This kind of justification for war as a last resort and as a response to oppression is common in African thought (Cordeiro-Rodrigues 2022, 2018; Badru 2019). Nelson Mandela, for instance, contended that the reason why the ANC decided to engage in violence was because of the lack of responsiveness of the apartheid government to peaceful means (Hyslop 2014; Mandela 1995, 1967).

Neto, however, did not write much about this. He wrote much more about military ethics: the duties of the armed forces (Cook and Syse 2010). Neto repeats throughout his texts that the armed forces cannot be apolitical. They need to have a political consciousness and clearly understand what moral and political problems are at stake. Soldiers cannot simply be professional workers following orders but must be critical thinkers who cultivate the right ideology. One implication of this is that mercenaries are ruled out as legitimate agents in war. Involvement in war requires an ideological motivation, and those with none, such as mercenaries, must not be involved; individuals who have a financial motivation for entering war are not morally permitted to do so (Neto 1987).

But soldiers cannot support just any ideology; it must be the right ideology. According to Neto, this right ideology is provided by the party. Neto incentivized intellectuals to help people develop this consciousness (Neto 1987, 1980, 1977b). One of the books mentioned in the previous chapter on Pepetela – *The Adventures of Ngunga* – is an example of this. The book was written as a handbook for soldiers and conformed to the ideology that Neto wanted to spread at the time. Given this ideological requirement, the armed forces should be subordinated to the party, for it is the party which maintains sovereignty because it represents the people. So, in practice, the armed forces exist solely to serve the people (Neto 1987).

Taking this on board, the members of the armed forces need a multiplicity of virtues and duties. First, they should not have a racist or tribalist mindset. They need to understand their fellows as humans who deserve respect regardless of ethnic difference. Accordingly, they should not behave in ways that privilege certain groups over others (Neto 1987). This concerns Neto because there was a perception that military and political decisions were made in favour of some groups over others, and he hoped to eliminate this (Mabeko-Tali 2018). Second, members of the armed forces need to have class consciousness. They need to be aware that they are fighting imperialism and, as such, are all part of a group oppressed by imperial forces. Their actions should be directed to the liberation of classes from oppression. Core to this is a sense of unity and solidarity with all the oppressed people of the world (Neto 1987). Third, they need to cultivate a spirit of sacrifice. The times were not easy, and without everyone's personal effort victory would be more difficult (Neto 1975). There is, therefore, a need for the private investment of each person, and given the circumstances, the armed forces were called upon to endorse this even more. Fourth, their duty is not simply to fight, but also to educate people by example. When the MPLA was fighting against Portugal, the soldiers needed to behave in ways that showed them to be a real alternative to the Portuguese and not another force that abused its power; in other words, the armed forces should act in solidarity with the people, acting in kind, helpful and liberating ways, rather than continuing the injustice that the colonialists committed. This will help convince the people of the importance of the struggle and, thereby, help them form a revolutionary consciousness (Neto 1987).

Neto insisted that these struggles were not isolated from the rest of the world. Hence, he often sought out international solidarity with other countries. He created alliances with several countries inside and outside Africa, such as the Soviet Union, Cuba, Ghana and Tanzania. He was very critical of African countries that did not foster solidarity with the people. Neto was a pan-African; he believed that these African countries had even more special duties towards fellow Africans. He insisted, however, that the armed forces should also be prepared to defend their territory against neighbouring African countries (Neto 1987). Neto does not mention Napoleon in his writings, but his posture resembles the Napoleonic principle, 'if you want peace, prepare for war'.

Conclusion

Neto played a crucial role in the anti-colonial struggle in Angola and is one of the most important figures in its liberation. Having been the first president of an independent Angola, he has also significantly shaped the country's history. In this chapter, I have aimed to provide an overview of Neto's thought, from the years of his anti-colonialist struggle to his presidency. His views did not change throughout that time, and there is clearly some considerable continuity. In earlier years, his concerns were primarily related to independence and denouncing colonialism. However, his focus changed when he became Angola's president, when he needed to worry about sovereignty and development. Regardless of one's focus, however, Neto's role is marked by a Marxist and anti-colonialist ideological groundwork that aimed to liberate Africans and build a common identity.

# 10

Angolan political thought and the indefatigable heartbeat of African philosophy

Introduction

In this book, I have examined the history of Angolan political thought by focusing on key figures from the fifteenth to the twentieth century. While this has required long and patient overviews of historical events, contexts, language, biographies and so forth, my aim has not been solely historical but also partisan and philosophical. My intention has been to defend African philosophy as a legitimate and valuable enterprise and to denounce its exclusion from philosophical discourse on political grounds. In so doing, I have tried to show what African philosophy is and has been. But I have not yet made an argument for the generalization of my statements regarding Angolan political thought to African philosophy as a whole. Although this book has concerned Angola, I believe that its claims are generalizable to a certain degree. When I say this, I mean that evidence about Angolan thought is informative about African philosophy. I shall first outline Angolan thought in the next section. Then, I will make the case for the generalization to African philosophy in the following section. In the subsequent sections, I will respond to the objections (mostly methodological) that may be raised against my argument.

Angolan thought in a nutshell

Starting with Afonso I of Kongo and ending with Neto, it is clear that all these thinkers have opposed colonialism. King Afonso I resisted the ways that Europeans wanted to dominate the Kingdom of Kongo and tried to oppose it and create his own and independent power network. Queen Njinga manipulated rituals and played different roles with great plasticity in order to defy colonial rule. The form of resistance they offered, however, cannot be properly classified as decolonial. By 'decolonial', I mean a perspective that is informed by pursuing the liberation of all colonized subjects. This decolonial turn only starts appearing (but not fully yet) with da Silva Mendonça, who offers a proto-universalist perspective for protecting all Christian subjects (including Africans) from slavery. Before that, King Afonso I and Queen Njinga seemed to be more preoccupied with the elite. da Silva Mendonça also seems a bit preoccupied with this, but not to the same degree. Kimpa Vita, however, revolutionizes this perspective by offering a truly inclusive thought which aims at protecting all African subjects, independently of their class membership. Kimpa Vita looks, in my interpretation, at the metaphysical and social implications of colonialism and its ideology and subverts it. Its subversion is by offering an inclusive metaphysics with inclusive social implications. There seems to be a step back during the late nineteenth and early twentieth century. Creole intellectuals seem to be a bit more accepting of colonial rule, but they have also challenged it. They did not reject colonialism entirely, but they resisted colonial forces trying to suppress the African subject. Their approach, generally speaking, was to make colonialism more inclusive, but not to abandon it. The true change comes with Marxist thinkers in the mid-twentieth century: Pinto de Andrade, Pepetela and Neto. Their theories are distinct in many ways, as has been demonstrated in the respective chapters. But in common, they have a decolonial drive of liberating Angola from colonial forces, as they see no benefits in colonialism. They aim for an Angola ruled by true Angolans, and they tend to understand 'Angolan' as someone with a specific state of mind. They all consider that the use of force (war) is justified for them to achieve this goal. Finally, they tend to think that racism is a manifestation of a larger problem and that the solution for an independent Angola cannot be to perpetuate racial categories. In short, all these thinkers addressed in this book opposed colonialism, although in different degrees and ways; their thoughts are thoughts of resistance to the extent that they are spelt out as defiance to colonial rule. There is a certain degree of historical continuity in the writings of these five centuries; but to see this continuity, it is necessary to abstract enough and look at these philosophies as a large array of forms of resistance to colonialism.

From Angolan thought to African philosophy's heartbeat

Africa is a continent of pain. Much of this pain has been caused by external forces that have brought new technologies of control, humiliation and destruction (Oro 2012; Mbembe 2017). Sometimes the strategy has been to import new oppressive social dynamics; at other times, domination has been achieved through the exploitation of existing local grievances. The result, in any case, has been the creation of an image of the African as the inferior and uncivilized other who requires the guidance and aid of non-Africans. 'African' has meant disease, lack of reason, destruction and so forth. African thought has therefore been marked precisely by the urge to resist this oppression and to materially and conceptually liberate Africa from the tools of the oppressor. African philosophy has an indefatigable heartbeat: it has survived many attempts to ensure its disappearance by way of the elimination of Africans as subjects. African philosophy is therefore defined as a form of resistance and, in this light, I very much agree with Pinto de Andrade, who understands the term 'African' as an ideological word for liberation. This does not mean, however, that the term 'African' should always be used interchangeably with 'decolonial'.

Contrary to what some authors appear to contend (Asante 2013; Chimakonam and Ogbonnaya 2021), the mere fact that something is African does not ensure that it is decolonial (in the contemporary sense of the term), as the examples of King Afonso I, Queen Njinga and proto-nationalist Creoles have shown. Likewise, race is a poor criterion for determining whether something or someone is African. While 'European' intellectuals such as Pepetela have been incisively decolonial and pro-African in thought, other thinkers whom I have explored in this book have simply employed racial binaries for the sake of convenience. In a recent article, Metz (2022) points out similarities between the young Marx and African philosophy and suggests that there are very important similarities between the ethics of each, such as a shared communal ethos. While Metz does not propose an explanation for this, and while I doubt that he would agree with my argument, I believe that these similarities are not a simple coincidence. Marxism developed within a context of capitalist oppression and Marxist ideas therefore reflect a spirit of revolt against these conditions. Likewise, the spirit of resistance of African philosophy can be explained with recourse to the history of oppression perpetuated by colonialism.

This spirit of resistance has taken very different forms throughout its history and is also different in different places in Africa. Until the beginning of the twentieth century, there was no radical opposition to colonialism and European rule. Before that, any such views are better understood to have been 'proto-anti-colonial'. There are several reasons for this change. First, it was only in the twentieth century, under the influence of the Soviet Union, that Marxist and revolutionary ideologies began to proliferate internationally. This enabled the dissemination of a language of resistance for which there had previously been no available vocabulary. There was also material support from the Soviet Union for these movements to grow and spread (Keller 1987; Drew 2003, 2015, 2017). Second, the First World War had a great (though often underappreciated) psychological effect worldwide, leading to a change in the image of Europe. While Europe had previously been relatively successful in promoting the idea of its superiority and civilization, the atrocities of the First World War dealt a significant blow to this notion. Third, the Second World War brought to Europeans what Europeans had brought to Africa: the horrors of systemic racial hierarchies.[1] The anti-Nazi sentiment that was born in Europe with the Second World War led to a change in attitudes towards race and the idea of racial hierarchies that eventually made racism politically incorrect, though without in fact ending it (Olivier and Cordeiro-Rodrigues 2017).

Abusive generalization and the selection of evidence

The key objections that can be raised against my view are methodological. That is, the main way to contest my argument is that I have committed some methodological mistakes which led me to the wrong conclusions. Hence, it is important to return to some methodological issues which I already initiated in the introduction of this book. The obvious objection to my argument is that I have abusively generalized the case of Angola to the whole of Africa and have not presented sufficient evidence to support such a strong conclusion – that I would in fact need evidence from every African country to prove my point. Were this the case, my argument would be especially problematic since the discipline of African studies and the invention of Africa have been precisely marked by this kind of generalization, with the goal of oppressing Africa (Mudimbe 1990).

There are several possible replies to this objection; however, an initial clarification of purpose is perhaps in order. I do not claim to have identified the essence of African philosophy. Indeed, I believe that essentialist views on identity are harmful and reflect power-seeking and populist attempts to monopolize intellectual and material resources (Benhabib 2015; Phillips 2009). As such, they do not help the African continent and are likely to be beneficial only for those who claim them. What I have instead tried to do here is to offer a historically informed account of a tendency in African thought. By looking at representative thinkers in Angola across five centuries, I have attempted to make a generalization about the development and continuity of African philosophy. However, I fully accept that this does not encompass all African philosophies and simply represents a salient current within African thought, though one for which there is significant historical evidence.

Yet why make the generalization to African philosophy at all? First, I would note that this is precisely what the discipline of history does: it works with inductive methodologies and tries to generalize to make larger points. But, of course, historians need to be open to evidence and to accept that their theories may fail should a better narrative appear. The key is to abandon historical realism and accept that these theories may just be educated guesses as to what has occurred. Second, as Michel Foucault has pointed out, sometimes historians and social scientists are overly constrained by certain concepts that frame their research (Foucault 2002). The concept of 'Angolan' is, to a certain extent, an artificial one and the generalization challenges pre-established conceptual frames that were, in fact, imposed by colonialism. In this light, it is important not to forget that some of the thinkers studied in this book are also part of the history of the Congo, the Democratic Republic of the Congo and even Brazil and Portugal.

Third, as pan-Africans rightly point out, there are important similarities in the histories of African peoples (Eze 2013). There is, in fact, historical evidence suggesting that, despite their differences, experiences of colonialism have something in common. Looking, for example, at the thought systems of the Zulu in South Africa, the Bemba from northern central Zambia and the Kede in Nigeria, it is clear that they adapted in response to colonial rule (Pritchard and Fortes 2015). Also, racial hierarchies, exploitation and so forth were common in different parts of Africa and did not just arrive with Europeans. As Tidiane N'Diaye has pointed out, before the Europeans arrived, there was already a history of the enslavement of Africans dating from the seventh century (N'Diaye 2017). Before that, it is clear from the available sources that the Ancient Greeks and Romans despised Ethiopians and mocked Egyptians (Isaac 2006; Jr 1971). My point is that there are good reasons to believe that the generalization is true because of the dynamics of resistance to oppression and exclusion present throughout Africa. Fourthly, the way I set up my argument does not imply homogeneity. To claim that African philosophy is a philosophy of resistance allows a great scope for difference. Indeed, as this book shows, there is a significant difference amongst Angolan forms of resistance throughout history. Fifthly, my claim intends to be informative and indicative rather than definitive. I am fully aware that all that is Angolan is African, but not that all that is African is not Angolan. Thus, what my argument does is not to state this; instead, what it states is that looking at Angolan political thought sheds light on some basic and important traits of African philosophy, such as resistance to colonialism, and that there are good reasons to think this is similar in other parts of Africa due to the history of colonialism. Thus, what my view defends is that the African continent is internally diverse and yet an organic whole.

A second possible objection to my argument is that, because I have selected political writings as the focus of this book, I am bound to suggest that Angolan and African philosophy are united by a spirit of resistance. Thus, had I chosen more metaphysical work as my focus, my conclusion might have been substantially different. This objection, however, neglects much of the significance of metaphysics and of other non-normative philosophical disciplines in Africa (including in Angola), which are similarly marked as forms of resistance to dominant ideologies. The problem of evil, for example, is addressed from an African viewpoint, as a decolonial enterprise (Cordeiro-Rodrigues and Chimakonam 2023). They are what Albert Camus called 'metaphysics of rebellion' (Camus and Brague 2015; Camus 1992): ways to resist imposed metaphysical views that have oppressive implications. Examples of this include the following: Ada Agada and Aribiah Attoe's metaphysical systems (Attoe 2022; Agada 2021); Jonathan Chimakonam's (2019) system of African logic; and Desmond Tutu's theology and philosophy of religion (Tutu 2011, 2000, 1988; Tutu and Allen 2011). Among my examples, both Queen Njinga and Kimpa Vita clearly understood the importance of holding metaphysical views that are less oppressive for Africans. More generally, the discipline of philosophy in Africa is not seen as a purely intellectual enterprise, but rather as a practical discipline to inform one's way of life (Cordeiro-Rodrigues 2021a ;Nyerere 1969; Nkrumah 1996).

Methodology and the Cambridge School

In the introduction, I announced that one of my influences was the Cambridge School of Intellectual History. To recall, philosophers like Skinner and Dunn are very sceptical about what can be said regarding a certain text. They consider that a robust comprehension of the context, linguistic knowledge, audience and what is indeed in the text are crucial to understand the meaning of the text. From this vantage point, the possible criticism of my interpretation is that I fail to give both the right context and an analysis of the linguistic devices that the thinkers I studied might have used. Put differently, I potentially extrapolate too much from the original text without knowing enough of their intentions to be able to accurately put forward my interpretation.

One objection that I wish to raise in response to this potential criticism is that although trying to understand the linguistic context of the time in which a text was written is undoubtedly valuable, the importance placed by Skinner on this is over-exaggerated. The process of writing is not an obviously conscious and intention-driven one, at least not as much as Skinner views it. Instead, it is both a conscious *and* unconscious process, whereby individuals place words to bring out meaning, some of which they are aware of and others of which they are not. In fact, even, for example, Pepetela recognized this about his own work; he stated in one of his interviews that during the process of writing and rereading his work he encountered ideas that perhaps were hidden, which reflected influences in his life that he did not fully realize (Parekh and Berki 1973). In this regard, my first reply to this potential criticism is that the linguistic aspect is exaggerated and that it is not necessary – nor entirely *possible*! – to establish intention in this way in order to provide a valid argument for my interpretation.

Although I do not think that it is necessary to pursue the strict methodology required by Skinner, I also contend that my argument meets the requirements imposed by his theory anyway. That is, my analysis does seek the situatedness and linguistic context outlined by Skinner. First, I provide an historical overview of each thinker's context. But, as Skinner contends, this is insufficient. Yet my interpretation also meets the second requirement to bring out how it is linguistically possible given the time at which the thinker was writing. For example, I explore with whom Creole proto-nationalists, Neto, Pepetela and all the others had contact with at the time, how they shared similar ideas and what debates were the most common. I also consider the personality and identity of the authors by looking at their biographical details and interviews, their audience and the relations between these by showing who the texts were written for as well as their political affiliations. Of course, contemporary writers like Pepetela or Neto are not as distant from our contemporary analysis as is the case with the writings of earlier thinkers, and the meaning is more accessible. Yet I did what was possible regarding earlier thinkers like King Afonso I.

The death of the author

In this section, I shall address a potential objection inspired by the work of French philosophers, such as Roland Barthes and Michel Foucault (Foucault 2020; Gallix 2010; Barthes, Krauss and Hollier 2005). The objection is that a good interpretation ought to promote the death of the author. Particularly, they argue that to connect an author to a text is to constrict one's reading to a limited experience and meaning of the text. Alternatively, if the author is absent from the text, then a doorway to a variety of meanings is opened for deciphering the text. For without the author, the text is not confined to the author's intention, which thus opens up the reading. Barthes suggests that the death of the author is simultaneously the birth of the reader: death opens the possibilities of reading a text otherwise destroyed by the intentionality of the author. Applied to my analysis, the objection states something like the opposite of the previous objection from the Cambridge School, that by including so much biographical and contextual information around the four books I analyse, I limit the variety of textual meanings that I can derive (Foucault 2020; Barthes, Krauss and Hollier 2005).

In response to this criticism, a preliminary note is that Foucault and Barthes do not necessarily defend that one interpretation is better than the other, but that the concept of the 'author' is a constraint to the way we interpret a text. Furthermore, the singular focus on a text is also problematic and can close other possible meanings. In Barthes's and Foucault's approaches there is a tendency to project only the readers' own interests, views and preoccupations into the text that they are reading. Thus, this strategy entails a projection of a reader's expectations about what the text says; it is, therefore, also a limitation. Moreover, it is not just an issue of self-projection, but also of anachronism: readers may be strongly influenced by the biases of their own epoch and limit their reading to this. A second reply is that the methodology developed by Barthes and Foucault is not necessarily incompatible with the more historically informed approach that I use, specifically in terms of opening the meaning of texts. There is, therefore, some merit in the textualists' proposal, for by ignoring the author, new meanings emerge and the text is enriched. And yet by including the author, her context and identity, it is also possible to identify new meanings in the text that were not captured before. Hence, the optimal reading of the text does not seem to be one that is purely textualist *or* purely historical, but rather one that can encompass both approaches. In this book, I have specifically tried to open the multiplicity of meanings made possible through the inclusion of historical context, but this does not foreclose other scholars from exploring different meanings of the text by ignoring these factors. In other words, it is not the case that a historically informed reading like mine necessarily blocks other kinds of reading (Beaumont 2018). It is still possible for the text to be sustained in open reinterpretation, despite some of these being potentially more historically informed than others.

On top of this, there is a specific methodological problem with this approach in relation to African intellectual history. As I will mention later regarding the sage philosophy methodology, routinely, African intellectual history has made invisible the African subject as an author (Oruka 2022). This is very much related to racism, where the African person disappears as a capable individual who is able to produce intellectual work. The African person is brutalized and disappears as a subject (Mbembe 2020, 2017; Morrison 1992). Although I think that Foucault's and Barthes's work is, broadly speaking, liberating, in this case, the disappearance of the author unintentionally furthers the disappearance of the African as a subject. This is why it is important to use a methodology which does not assume an ideal world and, instead, is informed by empirical aspects of subjugation, oppression, discrimination and so forth (Cordeiro-Rodrigues 2018b; Mills 2005).

The Archaeology of Knowledge and colonialism

In his *The Archaeology of Knowledge*, Foucault challenges historical work that is grounded on concepts which make little sense and that predispose scholars to frame their thought in certain ways. Foucault rightly affirms that we need to be critical of these concepts. Indeed, the challenge of the concept of the 'author' is precisely part of this critical methodology. Taking this on board, the objection could be raised that my research has been strongly influenced by the concept of 'colonialism' and of colonialism as a bad thing. But this is the wrong way to start. In an article which was retracted from the *Third World Quarterly*, Bruce Gilley argued that the idea that colonialism was a bad thing needs to be rethought (Gilley 2017). Also, the Mozambican-born academic Gabriel Mithá Ribeiro summarizes his book *O Colonialismo Nunca Existiu* (*Colonialism Never Existed*) as follows:

Colonialism never existed, racism does not exist anymore, collective violence is a fabrication – three thesis that sum up my book. Firstly, this is because the legacy of history indicates to several processes of colonization, but the labelling of these processes as 'colonialism' is simply carried out for the purpose of political instrumentalization. Secondly, the historical context of racism in the nineteenth and twentieth centuries (…) are clearly distinct from the reality in the twenty-first century. Social and historical phenomena are not immutable or eternal; rather, they transform themselves and some terms become dated. Thirdly, collective violence is conditioned and directed by ideological variables, even if they look scientific. (Mithá Ribeiro 2013: 9–10) (my translation)

It is difficult to debate with scholars who have nothing in common with us. The differences are so broad that it is difficult to even engage with what is being stated. But starting with the Foucauldian aspect of the argument, my interpretation of what Foucault says is not that we necessarily need to abandon the existing conceptual tools but that we need to be critical of them, so that they do not overinfluence our interpretation. It is impossible to do social research without any concepts. So the question is not whether I used a conceptual framework, but whether the concept of 'colonialism' and my assumption that it is bad is a flawed methodological approach.

In reply, the evidence that colonialism is a real thing is so overwhelming that it is difficult to understand how it is possible to deny it. And the fact that it involved slavery, racism and so forth makes it hard to see what is good about it. Gilley tried to make a cost-benefit analysis of colonialism. It is unclear that a cost-benefit analysis would be the right form of evaluation for this question. But in addition to this, Gilley fails to offer a balanced and lengthy assessment of the relevant evidence to make such a statement. Regarding Mithá Ribeiro's argument, it seems that, in fairness, his thesis is not so much to deny a historical fact, but rather whether we can call it 'colonialism'. I am a bit skeptical of this labelling strategy, which seems to try to find a more acceptable term for a morally wrong action. But let's suppose, for the sake of argument, that Mithá Ribeiro is right that colonialism did not exist and Gilley is correct that colonialism was not that bad. Would these affect my argument? It would not because my claim is that there is a *philosophy of resistance* against a force that tries to bring change. I do think the change is morally bad and colonial, but my argument does not depend on my evaluation of colonialism or that we call it 'colonialism'.

African methodologies and other readings of African philosophy

Another possible criticism that could be raised is that I have used Western methodologies to study Africa and this methodology. Imposing a non-African methodology to study Africa will inevitably lead to a colonial result (Chimakonam 2019). The colonizer's tool will never dismantle oppression (Lorde 2018). This is because it is grounded in colonial assumptions, which will clearly determine the result negatively for Africans. Hence, I should have instead engaged, for example, with *ezumezu* logic or with sage philosophy, which are truly African methodologies (Oruka 2022; Chimakonam 2019). Furthermore, I need to confront my understanding of African philosophy with different readings of the same; my argument is strong only if my narrative is more convincing. This includes *ezumezu* as well, but also the most prominent interpretation, Metzian philosophical anthropology and ethics (Metz 2007).

There are several replies to this potential criticism. As I have been trying to argue throughout this book, the binarism between what is African and what is Western is flawed. This is a binarism which is, in fact, a colonial imaginary legacy that creates opposing categories and demonizes one of the categories. But the best way to respond is to look at alternative methodologies specifically. Take a prominent one in Africa these days: *ezumezu* logic. Roughly, the *ezumezu* logic has, in my interpretation, two core features. One is the idea of continuity and complementarity of the world – that is, it holds a holistic understanding of social reality. The other is a three-valued logic, where propositions can have a third value besides true and false. Taking this on board, the advocate of *ezumezu* logic could raise two arguments against my view. Firstly, that I have used the wrong methodology because it is not African. Secondly, I have failed to see a key feature that captures the way African thought has developed better than mine. Particularly, the idea of complementarity and continuity is what differentiates and characterizes African thought as different.

My reply to these objections comes together. Firstly, to claim that this is *only* African would be a mistake because elsewhere there have been philosophies with similar characteristics. The philosophy of Heraclitus is one of continuity and complementarity, and it has even sometimes been understood as implying a three-value logic (Heraclitus 1981). Furthermore, the *ezumezu* logic is in many ways similar to Graham Priest's pluri-valent logic (Priest 2021). By stating this, I do not mean to question the importance and authenticity of the *ezumezu* logic. Instead, my point is that the binary that radically opposes African and Western methodologies misrepresents how these intersect. If this is true, the idea that one Western methodology can *never* dismantle African oppression is clearly false. Indeed, Marxism, which is a theory hailing from the West, underlies many African anti-colonial movements that helped dismantle oppression (Allison Drew 2017).

On top of this, *ezumezu* is not a historiographical method. Using it throughout the book as the main methodology would not help me understand statements from the past as it does not give sufficient tools for knowing how to examine such statements. For example, the *ezumezu* logic could not give me tools to understand if the proto-nationalists were expressing their support for colonialism or were simply afraid of being censored. The only way to know this is to have historiographical tools that allow an interpretation that gives the reader a narrative that might reveal approximately what happened.

Regarding the point that I miss something fundamental (complementarity and continuity) about African philosophy, I also reject this objection. To start, if the argument were to be put this way, it seemed to be searching for some kind of essence, which, as explained before, is an approach I reject. But in addition to this, my approach has integrated aspects of complementarity and continuity. This is most obvious in the chapter on Kimpa Vita where I clearly use African ontology to understand her form of Christianity. The underlying framework of interpretation is an Asouzian understanding of the world.[2] Just like Innocent Asouzu's viewpoint, in that chapter, there is an understanding of the world that sees '[entities in the world] are all the units and combinations necessary in the conceptualization of an entity or of the whole... all existent realities relate to each other in the manner of mutual service' (Asouzu 2005: 286). Thus, this book includes certain aspects of complementarity and continuity underlying the theoretical analysis. This means I do not necessarily reject the *ezumezu* interpretation, but I think there is something even more fundamental about Angolan and African thought than its complementarity and continuity.

How about the Metzian reading of African philosophy? A Metzian interpretation instead could contend that the spirit of communion is what best captures African philosophy and that I have failed to see this. Metz (2007) understands that solidarity and identification – jointly understood as social harmony or friendship – offer a good philosophical anthropology of African thought. He also thinks it is the best moral theory. Metz has offered a moral theory grounded on his perspective that offers a view which may be better than mainstream ethical theories like Kantianism and utilitarianism. I agree with Metz that the African communal theory is promising and can compete with mainstream ethical theories. What I disagree with is that this is an accurate philosophical anthropology. I would argue that the spirit of communion, as Metz defends it, is a development of the twentieth-century African Marxism. There were already elements of it before that which allowed such development, but it is clear that, say, King Afonso I did not really think communion was a good. There is, therefore, ample evidence that that form of communion has not been always widely shared. Put differently, there is a lack of historical continuity in African thought if it is interpreted as a communitarian philosophy; nonetheless, if it is understood as a form of resistance to colonialism, African philosophy can be said to have a certain degree of continuity.

With respect to sage philosophy, the reply to the criticism cannot be the same. Sage philosophy was born as a response to two kinds of methodologies which Henry Oruka (the main proponent of sage philosophy) considered to be biased. On the one hand, Oruka considered that ethnophilosophy, as told by non-Africans, was a simplification and misrepresentation of African wisdom, which reduced African philosophy to folk beliefs and eliminated individual subjects as intellectuals. On the other hand, Oruka thought that professional philosophy excluded African forms of wisdom which were at least as good as professional philosophy. These included, for example, the wisdom from elders of the community. Resultantly, Oruka carried out the project of interviewing African sages and write about their wisdom (Oruka 2022).

Although Oruka was not trying to carry out historiographical work, his methodology is, in fact, very similar to oral history, which is a method often used to study Africa. I do not oppose oral history and/or sage philosophy as a methodology. Although I do not use it directly, many of the references where I ground my work do, in fact, use it; therefore, this book's output partly depends on and benefits from this kind of methodology. Having said that, I doubt this could be the primary methodology for this project. While Oruka was trying to outline mostly philosophical systems in the present with roots in the past, I tried to understand the ideas of the past. To understand the past better, the closer the primary sources, the better. To rely on contemporary intellectuals' memory is too distant and potentially too altered from the original meaning to be reliable, specifically in the context of Angola, where 60 per cent of the population is under twenty-four and has not experienced direct colonialism (Gorjão Henriques 2015). Thus, the information they can give seems very unreliable and influenced by a colonial mindset. Indeed, as a recent study by Joana Gorjão Henriques on postcolonial Angola suggests, there is still a significant degree of colonial mindset in postcolonial Angola (Gorjão Henriques 2015). Consequently, using this colonial framework could potentially influence the project negatively.

Learning from the past, building the future

A spectre is haunting Europe and the world – the spectre of neo-fascism and populism. In these times, those who are committed to the values of diversity, equality and freedom must unite. This book has shown that resistance against inegalitarian and racist ideologies is more likely to succeed where there is a degree of unity and identification that goes beyond appearances, as well as a sense of solidarity and common destiny. In order for change to happen, these commitments must be made at a personal as well as an institutional level. The poetic words of the Lutheran pastor Martin Niemöller regarding the uprise of the Nazi regime offer an insightful perspective on unity. He warned that ignoring injustice may eventually backfire and that we must understand oppression as a continuous activity against which the oppressed must unite (Niemöller 1946).

The history of Angolan political thought reveals further that struggles against colonialism have been more successful where there has been less conflict among the oppressed, who may today be African, Asian, Latinx, European, indigenous, working class and so forth. It is important to understand how these oppressions fuel each other. The experience of these revolutionaries offers invaluable guidance for future struggles. It is possible to learn from Africa's history of pain and resistance and use it to be a lesson to the world.

Notes

1 Introduction

1 It cannot be stated that Pepetela uses racist terms because they did not have negative meanings at the time he wrote and Pepetela is certainly not a racist. He has in fact contributed quite significantly and positively for racial equality in Angola.
2 Potentially, according to the definition used in this book, Hesiod and Homer could also be considered philosophers.

2 King Afonso I of Kongo: Slavery, power and a Christian revolution

1 This originally appeared in the Portuguese *Monumenta Missionaria Africana* (Brásio 1952: 38). I follow the English translation by John Thornton here.
2 There is a discussion in the field of whether slavery existed before the arrival of Europeans. This debate does not challenge that there were forms of servitude before the Europeans' arrival, but considers that this ought not to be thought of as slavery. I disagree with this and think that this is a form of domination that implies that it be considered slavery, despite it having differences from the Atlantic Slave Trade. I use the term 'slavery' to refer to this form of servitude.

3 Queen Njinga: Resistance without ideology

1 Queen Njinga has been known by many names throughout history and was not always known as a queen. For the sake of clarity, however, I shall refer to her here as 'Queen Njinga'.

4 Lourenço da Silva Mendonça: Towards universalism and abolitionism

1 Lingna Nafafé (2022) claims that this was a criminal case, but I shall not discuss this here.
2 The term '*pardo*' referred to mixed-raced individuals.
3 The term '*preto*' is today used as a racial slur in Portugal. Nonetheless, it does not necessarily have this meaning in the letter.
4 Lingna Nafafé is slightly ambiguous on this point, however, and he may not have a very different opinion from mine. Nonetheless, he challenges the view of slavery as precolonial.

5 Kimpa Vita and subversive Christianity: Challenging colonialism from within

1 See, for instance, Montecuccolo (1965).
2 I coin this term to better specify Kimpa Vita's intention, not merely to appropriate the prayer into the broad array of cultures and languages of Africa but into the culture and language of Kongo.

6 Creole anti-colonialist and proto-nationalist voices in Angola

1 An important note on terminology in this chapter. The context in which these authors wrote was one of exceptionally blunt racism, which makes contemporary inclusive terminology difficult to use when outlining the debates with which they engaged. Hence, I am forced to use terms that in some contemporary contexts are considered discriminatory, although in other contexts they are not; these include 'creole', 'black', and 'white'. I use these terms so as to accurately read my source material, but where possible, I use terms that are more inclusive in the contemporary context, such as 'African' and 'European settlers'.

2 'Antes de tudo, o castigo severo do branco por motivo de simples offensa ao preto, sendo deprimente do homem, é consequentemente desautorador da raça, e secundariamente é attentatorio da autonomia pátria'.
3 'Metter em ferros d'El rei um preto que delinquiu, assassinando, roubando, ferindo, offendendo a moral publica por acções ou palavras, não é aplicar um castigo, é antes incita-lo ao crime ... Pois qual é o ideal do preto senão comer sem trabalhar? ... Qual é a sua lei, a sua norma de vida, o seu superior anhelo? Não somos apologistas dos castigos corporaes ... mas umas palmatoadas não matam ninguém'.
4 The author used the word 'black' (*preto*) and I use the term to refer to the passage, but in the following, I shall use the term 'African' in its place, as this is the more correct word to use in this context. I will use the term 'black' again when the term is required for clarification.

7 Mário Pinto de Andrade: Colonialism, African nationalism and liberation

1 Pinto de Andrade is highly influenced by the black consciousness movement and therefore he uses the term 'black' more often than 'African'. To make sense of his argument, I try to follow his designation here.

8 Pepetela: Angolanness, African personhood and transformative war

1 In this chapter, I need to use very specific terminology to make sense of Pepetela. But it is terminology which does not fit very well with contemporary ways of referring to ethnic diversity. The discussion about race and whether 'black' or 'white' people belong to Angola is one of the key topics of his work. Likewise, the tensions between 'tribes' and the feeling of 'tribalism' are a significant concern for Pepetela. To make it clear what Pepetela is talking about and to be faithful to the text, I use the terms 'black', 'white', 'tribes', and 'tribalism', while always being conscious of the

negative connotations of such terms today. Pepetela, of course, did not use these terms negatively as these were not really a problem at his time.

9 Agostinho Neto: Revolution, art and liberation

1 The term '*musseque*' refers to poor Angolan African neighbourhoods, whose closest English translation would be 'slums'.

10 Angolan political thought and the indefatigable heartbeat of African philosophy

1 I do not mean to suggest that ethnic conflict did not exist in Africa prior to colonialism. My point is, rather, that the scale of such conflict increased significantly upon the arrival of Europeans.
2 Innocent Asouzu's philosophy is one of the main philosophical inspirations for *ezumezu* logic.

References

Afonso, Louis Jadin, and Mireille Dicorato. 1974. *Correspondance de Dom Afonso; roi du Congo, 1506–1543*. Mémoires in-8o (Académie royale des sciences d'outre-mer. Classe des sciences morales et politiques). Bruxelles: Académie royale des sciences d'outre-mer.

Agada, Ada. 2019. *Consolationism and Comparative African Philosophy: Beyond Universalism and Particularism*. 1st edition. Abingdon: Routledge.

Anonymous. 1901. 'Contra Lei, Pela Grey'. *Gazeta de Loanda* 1 (4).

Aquinas, Thomas. 1981. *The Summa Theologica of St. Thomas Aquinas*. Translated by Fathers of the English Dominican Province. London: Burns Oates and Washbourne.

Archer, Maria. 1935. *Cadernos coloniais – Ninho de Bárbaros*. Edições Cosmos.

Asante, Molefi Kete. 2000. *The Egyptian Philosophers: Ancient African Voices from Imhotep to Akhenaten*. 1st edition. Chicago: African American Images.

Asante, Molefi Kete. 2013. *Afrocentricity: Imagination and Action*. Pulau Pinang: Multiversity & Citizens International.

Aschenbrenner, Anne. 2015. *Social Darwinism and Its Consequences for 19th Century Society*. GRIN Verlag.

Asouzu, Innocent. 2005. *The Method and Principles of Complementary Reflection in and Beyond African Philosophy*. LIT Verlag Münster.

Attoe, Aribiah David. 2022. *Groundwork for a New Kind of African Metaphysics: The Idea of Predeterministic Historicity*. Palgrave Macmillan.

Badru, Ronald Olufemi. 2019. 'An African Philosophical Account of Just War Theory'. *Ethical Perspectives* 26 (2): 153–81. https://doi.org/10.2143/EP.26.2.3286746.

Balandier, Georges. 1968. *Daily Life in the Kingdom of the Kongo, from the 16th to the 18th Centuries*. 1st edition. Pantheon.

Barnes, Jonathan. 1982. *The Presocratic Philosophers*. 1st edition. London: Routledge.

Barthes, Roland, Rosalind Krauss and Denis Hollier. 2005. *The Neutral: Lecture Course at the College de France*. New York: Columbia University Press.

Beaumont, Tim. 2018. 'A Perennial Illusion? Wittgenstein, Quentin Skinner's Contextualism and the Possibility of Refuting Past Philosophers'. *Philosophical Investigations* 41 (3): 304–28. https://doi.org/10.1111/phin.12196.

Benhabib, Seyla. 2015. *The Claims of Culture: Equality and Diversity in the Global Era*. Princeton, NJ: Princeton University Press.

Bernal, Martin. 1987. *Black Athena: The Afroasiatic Roots of Classical Civilization*. 1st edition. New Brunswick, NJ: Rutland Local History & Record Society.

Bethencourt, Francisco, ed. 2007. *Portuguese Oceanic Expansion, 1400–1800*. Illustrated edition. Cambridge: Cambridge University Press.

Bethencourt, Francisco. 2014. *Racisms: From the Crusades to the Twentieth Century*. Reprint edition. Princeton, NJ: Princeton University Press.

Bewaji. 1998. "Olodumare: God in Yoruba Belief and the Theistic Problem of Evil," *African Studies Quarterly* 2 (1). https://www.africabib.org/rec.php?RID=P00008026.

Bhattacharyya, Sambit. 2020. 'Atlanticism, the Slave Trade, and the Westward Expansion of Western Europe'. In *A History of Global Capitalism: Feuding Elites and Imperial Expansion*, edited by Sambit Bhattacharyya, 27–43. Cham: Springer International. https://doi.org/10.1007/978-3-030-58736-9_3.

Birmingham, David. 1998. *Kwame Nkrumah: The Father of African Nationalism*. USA: Ohio University Press.

Birmingham, David. 2016. *A Short History of Modern Angola*. 1st edition. Oxford: Oxford University Press.

Birmingham, Professor David, and David Birmingham. 2000. *Trade and Empire in the Atlantic 1400–1600*. 1st edition. London: Routledge.

Bjerk, Paul. *Julius Nyerere* (Ohio Short Histories of Africa). Ohio University Press. Kindle edition.

Black, Jeremy. 2015. *The Atlantic Slave Trade in World History*. New York: Routledge.

Bocage, Manuel Maria Barbosa du. 1870. *Poesias eroticas, burlescas e satyricas*. Lisbon INCM – Imprensa Nacional Casa da Moeda.

Boddice, Rob. 2016. *The Science of Sympathy: Morality, Evolution, and Victorian Civilization*. University of Illinois Press.

Bois, W. E. B. Du. 2020. *The Souls of Black Folk by W.E.B. Du Bois*. Independently published.

References

Bonavena, E. 2000. 'As origens do nacionalismo africano (leitura crítica de Mário Pinto de Andrade)'. In *Mário Pinto de Andrade, um intelectual na política*, edited by Inocência Mata and Laura Cavalcante Padilha, 181–96. Lisboa: Edições Colibri.

Boxer, C. R. 1973. *The Portuguese Seaborne Empire 1415–1825*. New edition. Harmondsworth: Penguin.

Boxer, C. R. 1985. *Women in Iberian Expansion Overseas, 1415–1815: Some Facts, Fancies, and Personalities*. New York: Oxford University Press.

Boxer, Charles Ralph. 1958. *Portuguese and Dutch Colonial Rivalry, 1641–1661*. Centro de Estudos Históricos Ultramarinos.

Boxer, Charles Ralph. 1969. *Four Centuries of Portuguese Expansion, 1415–1825: A Succinct Survey*. Berkeley: University of California Press.

Brásio, António. 1952. *Monumenta Missionaria Africana: África Ocidental (1471–1531)*. Agência Geral do Ultramar.

Brásio, António (org). 1982. *Monumenta Missionaria Africana. Volume 13. África Ocidental (1666–1685)*. Academia Portuguesa da História. https://repositorio.ul.pt/handle/10451/34717.

Cabral, Amilcar. 1969. *Revolution in Guinea: African People's Struggle*. Edited by Richard Handyside. 1st edition. London: Stage 1.

Cabral, Amílcar. 1974. *Guiné-Bissau: nação africana forjada na luta*. Novo Aurora.

Cabral, Amilcar. 2016. *Resistance and Decolonization*. London: Rli.

Cadornega, Antonio de Oliveira de. 1681. *História geral das guerras angolanas*. Divisão de publicações e biblioteca, Agência geral das colónias.

Caldeira, Arlindo Manuel. 2013. *Escravos e traficantes no império português: o comércio negreiro português no Atlântico durante os séculos XV a XIX*. Esfera dos Livros.

Camus, Albert. 1992. *The Rebel: An Essay on Man in Revolt*. Reissue edition. New York: Vintage.

Camus, Albert, and Rémi Brague. 2015. *Christian Metaphysics and Neoplatonism*. Translated by Ronald Srigley. 1st edition. South Bend, IN: St. Augustines Press.

Carreira, Iko. 1996. *O pensamento estratégico de Agostinho Neto: Contribuição histórica*. 1a. edition. Lisboa: Publicações Dom Quixote.

Castelo, Cláudia. 1998. 'O modo português de estar no mundo': o lusotropicalismo e a ideologia colonial portuguesa (1933–1961)*. Edições Afrontamento.

Cavazzi, Giovanni Antonio. 1965. *Descrição histórica dos três reinos do Congo, Matamba e Angola*. Junta de Investigações do Ultramar.

Centro de Estudos Angolanos Grupo de Trabalho História e Etnologia. 1965. *História de Angola*. Afrontamento.

Chabal, Patrick, ed. 1996. *The Post-Colonial Literature of Lusophone Africa*. 1 edition. Evanston, IL: Northwestern University Press.

Chabal, Patrick, David Birmingham, Joshua Forrest and Malyn Newitt. 2002. *A History of Postcolonial Lusophone Africa*. Bloomington: Indiana University Press.

Chaves, Rita, and Tania Macêdo. 2010. *Portanto... Pepetela*. 1ª edição. Cotia: Ateliê Editorial.

Chimakonam, Jonathan O. 2018. 'Africans Are Not Black: The Case for Conceptual Liberation'. *African Identities* 16 (3): 365–9. https://doi.org/10.1080/14725843.2018.1473149.

Chimakonam, Jonathan O. 2019. *Ezumezu: A System of Logic for African Philosophy and Studies*. 1st ed. 2019 edition. New York: Springer.

Chimakonam, Jonathan O., and Ada Agada. 2020. 'The Sexual Orientation Question in Nigeria: Cultural Relativism Versus Universal Human Rights Concerns'. *Sexuality & Culture* 24 (6): 1705–19. https://doi.org/10.1007/s12119-020-09705-9.

Chimakonam, Jonathan O., and L. Uchenna Ogbonnaya. 2021. *African Metaphysics, Epistemology and a New Logic: A Decolonial Approach to Philosophy*. 1st ed. 2021 edition. Cham: Palgrave Macmillan.

Claeys, Gregory. 2000. 'The "Survival of the Fittest" and the Origins of Social Darwinism'. *Journal of the History of Ideas* 61 (2): 223–40. https://doi.org/10.2307/3654026.

Claro, Regina Célia Soares. 2009. 'Letras negras em folhas brancas: a construção da nação em Angola por Assis Júnior (1917–1935)'. *África*, no. 24–26 (December): 428–38.

Cook, Martin L., and Henrik Syse. 2010. 'What Should We Mean by "Military Ethics"?' *Journal of Military Ethics* 9 (2): 119–22. https://doi.org/10.1080/15027570.2010.491320.

Cordeiro-Rodrigues, Luis. 2018a. 'African Views of Just War in Mandela and Cabral'. *Journal of Speculative Philosophy* 32 (4): 657–73.

Cordeiro-Rodrigues, Luis. 2018b. 'Animal Abolitionism Revisited: Neo-Colonialism and Morally Unjustified Burdens'. *Journal of Agricultural and Environmental Ethics* 31 (4): 499–510. https://doi.org/10.1007/s10806-018-9742-7.

Cordeiro-Rodrigues, Luis. 2020. 'Toward a Decolonized Healthcare Ethics: Colonial Legacies and the Siamese Crocodile'. *Developing World Bioethics* 20 (3): 118–19. https://doi.org/10.1111/dewb.12273.

Cordeiro-Rodrigues, Luís. 2021a. 'African Higher Education and Decolonizing the Teaching of Philosophy'. *Educational Philosophy and Theory* 0 (0): 1–14. https://doi.org/10.1080/00131857.2021.1945438.

Cordeiro-Rodrigues, Luís. 2021b. 'Afro-Communitarianism and the Duties of Animal Advocates within Racialized Societies: The Case of Racial Politics in South Africa'. *Journal of Bioethical Inquiry*, July. https://doi.org/10.1007/s11673-021-10112-4.

Cordeiro-Rodrigues, Luis. 2021. 'Mutability and Relationality: Towards an African Four-Dimensionalist Pan-Psychism'. *Religions* 12 (12): 1094. https://doi.org/10.3390/rel12121094.

Cordeiro-Rodrigues, Luis. 2022. 'Public Health and Christian Theism in Africa: An Approach to Evil and Religious Belief in the Afterlife'. *Indian Journal of Medical Ethics*, May, 01–06. https://doi.org/10.20529/ijme.2022.036.

Cordeiro-Rodrigues, Luís. 2022b. 'Christianity in the Kingdom of Kongo and Western Theism: A Comparative Study of the Problem of Evil'. *Philosophia Africana* 21 (1): 13–27. https://doi.org/10.5325/philafri.21.1.0013.

Cordeiro-Rodrigues, Luis, and Emanuele Achino. 2017. 'A Case Study on Moral Disengagement and Rationalization in the Context of Portuguese Bullfighting'. *Polish Sociological Review* 199 (1): 315–27.

Cordeiro-Rodrigues, Luis, and Jonathan O. Chimakonam. 2020. 'The South African Land Question in Light of Nelson Mandela's Political Thought'. *African Studies* 79 (2): 250–65. https://doi.org/10.1080/00020184.2020.1806037.

Cordeiro-Rodrigues, Luís, and Jonathan O. Chimakonam. 2022. 'The Logical Problem of Evil and African War Ethics'. *Journal of Military Ethics* 0 (0): 1–14. https://doi.org/10.1080/15027570.2022.2158949.

Cordeiro-Rodrigues, Luis, and Jonathan O. Chimakonam. 2023. 'The Problem of Evil from a Decolonial Viewpoint'. *Philosophia (Philippines)* 24 (January). https://doi.org/10.46992/pijp.24.1.a.4.

Cordeiro-Rodrigues, Luís, and Cornelius Ewuoso. 2021b. 'An Afro-Communitarian Relational Approach to Brain Surrogates Research'. *Neuroethics*, August. https://doi.org/10.1007/s12152-021-09475-7.

Cordeiro-Rodrigues, Luís, and Thaddeus Metz. 2021. 'Afro-Communitarianism and the Role of Traditional African Healers in the COVID-19 Pandemic'. *Public Health Ethics* 14 (1): 59–71. https://doi.org/10.1093/phe/phab006.

Corrado, Jacopo. 2007. 'The Rise of a New Consciousness: Early Euro-African Voices of Dissent in Colonial Angola'. Vol. 5, No. 2. https://digitalis-dsp.uc.pt/jspui/handle/10316.2/25350.

Corrado, Jacopo. 2008. *The Creole Elite and the Rise of Angolan Protonationalism: 1870–1920*. Cambria Press.

Costa, João Paulo Oliveira e, José Damião Rodrigues, and Pedro Aires Oliveira. 2014. *História da expansão e do Império português*. A Esfera dos Livros.

Crowley, Roger. 2015. *Conquerors: How Portugal Forged the First Global Empire*. Random House Publishing Group.

Darwin, Charles. 2020. *The Autobiography of Charles Darwin*. W. W. Norton & Company; Reissue edition.

Darwin, Charles, and Oliver Francis. 2017. *On the Origin of Species: Charles Darwin*. Macmillan.

Darwin, John. 2009. *The Empire Project: The Rise and Fall of the British World-System, 1830–1970*. Cambridge: Cambridge University Press. https://doi.org/10.1017/CBO9780511635526.

Davidson, Basil. 1980. *Black Mother: Africa and the Atlantic Slave Trade*. New edition. Harmondsworth: Penguin.

Davis, Angela Y. 2019. *Women, Race & Class*. Penguin.

D'Azevedo, Pedro A. 2019. *As Cartas do Padre Antonio Vieira: Offerecidas ao Archivo da Torre do Tombo*. Forgotten Books.

Dias, Augusto. 1935. *Cadernos coloniais – Benguela*. Edições Cosmos.

Drew, A. 2003. 'Bolshevizing Communist Parties: The Algerian and South African Experiences'. *International Review of Social History*, August, 167–202.

Drew, Allison. 2015. 'Visions of Liberation: The Algerian War of Independence and Its South African Reverberations'. *Review of African Political Economy* 42 (143): 22–43. https://doi.org/10.1080/03056244.2014.1000288.

Drew, Allison. 2017. 'Comparing African Experiences of Communism'. In *The Cambridge History of Communism: Volume 2: The Socialist Camp and World Power 1941–1960s*, edited by Norman Naimark, Silvio Pons and Sophie Quinn-Judge, 2:518–43. The Cambridge History of Communism.

Cambridge: Cambridge University Press. https://www.cambridge.org/core/ books/cambridge-history-of-communism/comparing-african-experien ces-of-communism/931E7E227992886E39BA7B67E20835C9.
Duffy, James. 1961. *Portuguese Africa*. Cambridge: Harvard University Press.
Dunn, John, and John M. Dunn. 1996. *The History of Political Theory and Other Essays*. Cambridge: Cambridge University Press.
Eisenberg, José. 2003. 'António Vieira and the Justification of Indian Slavery'. *Luso-Brazilian Review* 40 (1): 89–95.
Eltis, David, and David Richardson. 1997. 'The "Numbers Gam" and Routes to Slavery'. *Slavery & Abolition* 18 (1): 1–15. https://doi.org/10.1080/01440399708575200.
Encyclopaedia Britannica. 2022. 'Afonso I | King of Kongo Kingdom | Britannica'. The Encyclopaedia Britannica. 2022. https://www.britannica.com/biography/Afonso-I-king-of-Kongo-kingdom.
Espírito Santo, Alda. 2000. 'Sobre Mário Pinto de Andrade – um depoimento possível'. In *Mário Pinto de Andrade, um intelectual na política*, edited by Inocência Mata and Laura Cavalcante Padilha, 37–42. Lisboa: Edições Colibri.
Ewuoso, C., and S. Hall. 2019. 'Core Aspects of Ubuntu: A Systematic Review'. *South African Journal of Bioethics and Law* 12 (2): 93–103. https://doi.org/10.7196/SAJBL.2019.v12i2.679.
Ewuoso, Cornelius. 2021. 'Patient Confidentiality, the Duty to Protect, and Psychotherapeutic Care: Perspectives from the Philosophy of Ubuntu'. *Theoretical Medicine and Bioethics* 42 (1–2): 41–59. https://doi.org/10.1007/s11017-021-09545-0.
Eze, M. 2010. *The Politics of History in Contemporary Africa*. 2010th edition. Palgrave Macmillan.
Eze, Michael Onyebuchi. 2013. 'Pan Africanism: A Brief Intellectual History'. *History Compass* 11 (9): 663–74. https://doi.org/10.1111/hic3.12074.
Faria, António. 2000. 'Mário Pinto de Andrade, espelho da revolução africana num espaço português'. In *Mário Pinto de Andrade, um intelectual na política*, edited by Inocência Mata and Laura Cavalcante Padilha, 153–72. Edições Colibri.
Fernado, Emídio. 2012. *Jonas Savimbi No lado errado da História*. Leya.
Ferreira, Manuel. 1982. 'Metamorfose e Premonição'. In *Poesia negra de expressão portuguesa*, edited by Francisco José Tenreiro and Mário de Andrade, 13–36. Lisboa: Livraria Escolar Editora.

Figueiredo, Isabela. 2018. *Caderno de memórias coloniais*. 1ª edição. Todavia.

Fish, Bruce, and Becky Durost Fish. 2002. *Angola, 1880 to the Present: Slavery, Exploitation, and Revolt*. Infobase Publishing.

Foucault, Michel. 2002. *Archaeology of Knowledge*. 2nd edition. London: Routledge.

Foucault, Michel. 2020. *Power: The Essential Works of Michel Foucault 1954–1984*. S.l.: Penguin Classics.

Fouéré, Marie-Aude, ed. 2015. *Remembering Julius Nyerere in Tanzania. History, Memory, Legacy*. Dar es Salaam, Tanzania: Mkuki Na Nyota Publishers.

Freyre, Gilberto. 1936. *Casa-grande & senzala: formação da familia brasileira sob o regimen de economia patriarchal*. Schmidt.

Gallix, Andrew. 2010. 'In Theory: The Death of the Author'. *The Guardian*, 13 January 2010, sec. Books. https://www.theguardian.com/books/booksb log/2010/jan/13/death-of-the-author.

George, Olakunle. 2021. *A Companion to African Literatures*. 1st edition. Hoboken, NJ: Wiley-Blackwell.

Geraldo de Oliveira, Vicente. 2000. 'A dialéctica como via de libertação em Mário de Andrade: a literatura como arma de luta'. In *Mário Pinto de Andrade, um intelectual na política*, edited by Inocência Mata and Laura Cavalcante Padilha. Lisboa: Edições Colibri.

Gilley, Bruce. 2017. 'The Case for Colonialism'. *Third World Quarterly* 0 (0): 1–17. https://doi.org/10.1080/01436597.2017.1369037.

Gonçalves, António Custódio. 1999. 'Identidades culturais e emergência do nacionalismo angolano (c. 1885–c. 1930)'. *Africana Studia*, no. 2. https://ojs.letras.up.pt/index.php/AfricanaStudia/article/view/7072.

Gorjão Henriques, Joana. 2015. 'Angola: "Houve independência mas não descolonização das mentes."' PÚBLICO. 1 November 2015. https://acervo.publico.pt/mundo/noticia/houve-independencia-mas-nao-descoloniza cao-das-mentes-1712736.

Gorjao Henriques, Joana. 2017. *Racismo em Português. O Lado Esquecido do Colonialismo*. Tinta da China.

Grande Entrevista Com Pepetela. n.d. Accessed 20 April 2020. https://www.youtube.com/watch?v=cr_iXEIIuoE.

Graness, Anke. 2015. 'Introduction'. *Philosophia Africana* 17 (1): 1–9. https://doi.org/10.5325/philafri.17.1.0001.

Graness, Anke. 2016. 'Writing the History of Philosophy in Africa: Where to Begin?' *Journal of African Cultural Studies* 28 (2): 132–46. https://doi.org/10.1080/13696815.2015.1053799.

Gray, Richard. 1987. 'The Papacy and the Atlantic Slave Trade: Lourenco Da Silva, The Capuchins and the Decisions of the Holy Office'. *Past & Present* 115 (1): 52–68. https://doi.org/10.1093/past/115.1.52.

Gray, Richard. 1997. 'The Kongo Kingdom and the Papacy | History Today'. 1997. https://www.historytoday.com/archive/kongo-kingdom-and-papacy.

Guerra, Henrique. 1980a. 'Prefácio'. In *O segredo da morta: romance de costumes angolenses*, by António de Assis Júnior, 11–26. Lisboa: Edições 70.

Guerra, Henrique. 1980b. 'Prefácio'. In *Relato dos acontecimentos de Dala Tando e Lucala*, by António de Assis Júnior, 11–37. Lisboa: União dos Escritores Angolanos.

Guimarães, Paulo Eduardo. 2017. 'Anarquismo, violência e protesto popular durante a Primeira República em Portugal'. BookPart. Almedina. April 2017. http://dspace.uevora.pt/rdpc/handle/10174/21405.

Gyekye, Kwame. 2011. 'African Ethics'. In *The Stanford Encyclopedia of Philosophy*, edited by Edward N. Zalta, Fall 2011. Metaphysics Research Lab, Stanford University. https://plato.stanford.edu/archives/fall2011/entries/african-ethics/.

Hamilton, Russell G. 1975. *Literatura africana, literatura necessária: Angola*. Edições 70.

Hardin, Russell. 1995. *One for All: The Logic of Group Conflict*. Princeton, NJ: Princeton University Press.

Hastings, Adrian. 1996. *The Church in Africa, 1450–1950*. Oxford: Clarendon Press.

Hawkins. 2008. *Social Darwinism European Thought: Nature as Model and Nature as Threat*.

Heraclitus. 1981. *The Art and Thought of Heraclitus: An Edition of the Fragments with Translation and Commentary*. Edited by Charles H. Kahn. Cambridge: Cambridge University Press.

Heywood, Linda M. 2019. *Njinga of Angola: Africa's Warrior Queen*. Reprint edition. Cambridge, MA: Harvard University Press.

Heywood, Linda M., and John Thornton. 2007. *Central Africans, Atlantic Creoles, and the Foundation of the Americas, 1585–1660*. Cambridge: Cambridge University Press.

Hickson, Michael W. 2013. 'A Brief History of Problems of Evil'. In *The Blackwell Companion to the Problem of Evil*, 1–18. John Wiley. https://doi.org/10.1002/9781118608005.ch1.

Hilliard, Constance. 1997. *The Intellectual Traditions of Pre-Colonial Africa*. Boston, MA: McGraw-Hill Education.

Hohlfeldt, Antonio, and Caroline Corso de Carvalho. 2012. 'A imprensa angolana no âmbito da história da imprensa colonial de expressão portuguesa'. *Intercom: Revista Brasileira de Ciências da Comunicação* 35 (December): 85–100. https://doi.org/10.1590/S1809-58442012000200005.

hooks, bell. 2014. *Ain't I a Woman: Black Women and Feminism*. 2nd edn. New York: Routledge.

Hountondji, P. J. 1996. *African Philosophy, Second Edition: Myth and Reality* (2nd edn). Indiana University Press.

Hua, Wei. 2022. 'Augustine, Ancestors and the Problem of Evil: African Religions, the Donatists, and the African Manichees'. *Filosofia Theoretica: Journal of African Philosophy, Culture and Religions* 11 (1): 131–8. https://doi.org/10.4314/ft.v11i1.9.

Hyslop, Jonathan. 2014. 'Mandela on War'. In *The Cambridge Companion to Nelson Mandela*, edited by Rita Barnard, 162–81. Cambridge: Cambridge University Press. https://doi.org/10.1017/CCO9781139003766.010.

Infopédia Porto Editora. 2022. 'Agostinho Neto – Infopédia'. infopedia.pt – Porto Editora. 2022. https://www.infopedia.pt/apoio/artigos/$agostinho-neto.

Isaac, Benjamin. 2006. *The Invention of Racism in Classical Antiquity*. Princeton, NJ: Princeton University Press.

Jackson, John P., and David J. Depew. 2017. *Darwinism, Democracy, and Race: American Anthropology and Evolutionary Biology in the Twentieth Century*. Routledge.

Jacob, Sheila Ribeiro. 2010. 'A Imprensa Livre E O Despertar Da Vida Literária Angolana No Século Xix'. *Miscelânea: Revista de Literatura e Vida Social* 8: 96–107.

Jecker, Nancy, and Caesar Atuire. 2021. 'Out of Africa: A Solidarity-Based Approach to Vaccine Allocation'. *Hastings Center Report* 51 (3): 27–36. https://doi.org/10.1002/hast.1250.

Jones, Greta. 1980. *Social Darwinism and English Thought: The Interaction Between Biological and Social Theory*. Humanities Press.

Jordan, Manuel. 1999. *The Kongo Kingdom*. New York: Franklin Watts.

Jr, Frank M. Snowden. 1971. *Blacks in Antiquity: Ethiopians in the Greco-Roman Experience*. Cambridge, MA: Belknap Press: An Imprint of Harvard University Press.

Júnior, António de Assis. 1949. *Dicionário kimbundu-português*. Argente, Santos.

Júnior, António de Assis. 1985. *Relato dos acontecimentos de Dala Tando e Lucala*. União dos Escritores Angolanos.

Júnior, António de Assis. 2004. *O segredo da morta: romance de costumes angolenses*. Edições Maianga.

Kajibanga, Víctor. 2000. 'Mário Pinto de Andrade. Subsídios para o estudo biográfico do seu retrato social e intelectual'. In *Mário Pinto de Andrade, um intelectual na política*, edited by Inocência Mata and Laura Cavalcante Padilha, 197–224. Lisboa: Edições Colibri.

Kandjimbo, Luís. 2000. 'Mário Pinto de Andrade, Agostinho Neto, a geração literária de 48 e o problema do slogan Vamos descobrir'. In *Mário Pinto de Andrade, um intelectual na política*, edited by Inocência Mata and Laura Cavalcante Padilha, 53–70. Lisboa: Edições Colibri.

Kapuscinski, Ryszard, and Klara Glowczewska. 2001. *Another Day of Life*. Translated by William R. Brand and Katarzyna Mroczkowska-Brand. New York: Vintage.

Keller, Edmond J. 1987. *Afro-Marxist Regimes: Ideology and Public Policy*. 1st edition. Boulder, CO: Lynne Rienner.

Kenny, Anthony. 2006. *Ancient Philosophy: A New History of Western Philosophy, Volume 1*. 1st edition. Oxford: Oxford University Press.

Kiros, Teodros. 2004. 'Zera Yacob and Traditional Ethiopian Philosophy'. In *A Companion to African Philosophy*, edited by Kwasi Wiredu, 183–90. Wiley.

Kupperman, Karen Ordahl. 2012. *The Atlantic in World History*. Illustrated edition. New York: Oxford University Press.

Lagamma, Alisa. 2015. *Kongo: Power and Majesty*. Illustrated edition. New York: Yale University Press.

Laranjeira, Pires. 1995. 'Literaturas africanas de expressão portuguesa: formação e desenvolvimento das literaturas'. https://repositorioaberto.uab.pt/handle/10400.2/5240.

Laranjeira, Pires. 2016. 'Introdução'. In *Agostinho Neto – Obra Poética Completa*, 13–24. Luanda: Fundação Dr. António Agostinho Neto.

Lopes, Carlos. 2000. 'Bibi, o intelectual orgânico'. In *Mário Pinto de Andrade, um intelectual na política*, edited by Inocência Mata and Laura Cavalcante Padilha, 33–6. Lisboa: Edições Colibri.

Lorde, Audre. 2018. *Master's Tools Will Never Dismantle The*. Penguin Classics.
Mabeko-Tali, Jean-Michel. 2018. *Guerrilhas e Lutas Sociais – O MPLA Perante Si Próprio*. 1ª edição. Lisboa: Mercado de Letras.
Macamo, Elísio. 2015. 'The Belated Phoenix: The Practice of Philosophy in Portuguese-Speaking Countries of Africa'. *Philosophia Africana* 17 (1): 11–25. https://doi.org/10.5325/philafri.17.1.0011.
Madureira, Luís. 2021. 'Lusophone Southern African Literature (Angola, Mozambique)'. In *A Companion to African Literatures*, 267–82. John Wiley. https://doi.org/10.1002/9781119058199.ch17.
Magalhães, Joaquim Romero. 1997. 'Africans, Indians, and Slavery in Portugal'. *Portuguese Studies* 13: 143–51.
Mandela, Nelson. 1967. "I Am Prepared to Die' – Nelson Mandela Foundation'. https://www.nelsonmandela.org/news/entry/i-am-prepared-to-die.
Mandela, Nelson. 1995. *Long Walk to Freedom: The Autobiography of Nelson Mandela*. New edition. London: Abacus.
Manning, Patrick. 1990. 'The Slave Trade: The Formal Demography of a Global System'. *Social Science History* 14 (2): 255–79. https://doi.org/10.2307/1171441.
Manso, Maria de Deus Beites. 2016. *História da Companhia de Jesus em Portugal*. Lisboa: parfit. https://www.wook.pt/livro/historia-da-companhia-de-jesus-em-portugal-maria-de-deus-beites-manso/18617941.
Martin, G. 2012. *African Political Thought*. 2012th edition. New York: Palgrave Macmillan.
Martins, Joaquim Pedro Oliveira. 1921. *As raças humanas e a civilisação primitiva: por J. P. Oliveira Martins*. A. M. Pereira.
Mata, Inocência. 2012a. *A rainha Nzinga Mbandi: história, memória e mito*. Edições Colibri.
Mata, Inocência. 2012b. *Ficção e História na Literatura Angolana O caso de Pepetela*. Lisbonne: Edições Colibri.
Mata, Inocência, and Laura Cavalcante Padilha. 2000. 'Dez anos sem Mário Pinto de Andrade (1990–2000)'. In *Mário Pinto de Andrade, um intelectual na política*, edited by Inocência Mata and Laura Cavalcante Padilha, 13–17. Lisboa: Edições Colibri.
Mata, Inocência, Laura Cavalcante Padilha and Moema Parente Augel. 2000. 'Mantenhas para Mário de Andrade. Notas sobre a presença de Mário

Pinto de Andrade na Guiné-Bissau'. In *Mário Pinto de Andrade, um intelectual na política*, 119–30. Lisboa: Edições Colibri.

Mattos, Hebe. 2006. '"Pretos" and "Pardos" between the Cross and the Sword: Racial Categories in Seventeenth Century Brazil'. *European Review of Latin American and Caribbean Studies*, no. 80 (April): 43–55. https://doi.org/10.18352/erlacs.9654.

Mbembe, Achille. 2017. *Critique of Black Reason*. Durham, NC: Duke University Press Books.

Mbembe, Achille. 2020. *Brutalisme*. Paris: LA DECOUVERTE.

Mbiti, John S. 1990. *African Religions & Philosophy*. 2nd revised and enlarged edition. Oxford: Heinemann.

Mbiti, John S. 2015. *Introduction to African Religion, Second Edition*. 2nd edition. Long Grove, IL: Waveland Press.

Mcmahan, Jeff. 2011. *Killing in War*. Reprint edition. New York: Oxford University Press.

Medina, Osvaldo. 2016a. *Agostinho Neto – De Cabeça Levantada*. Luanda: Fundação Dr. António Agostinho Neto.

Medina, Osvaldo. 2016b. *Agostinho Neto – Todos Para o Interior*. Luanda: Fundação Dr. António Agostinho Neto.

Menkiti, Ifeanyi. 2018. 'Person and Community – a Retrospective Statement'. *Filosofia Theoretica: Journal of African Philosophy, Culture and Religions* 7 (2): 162–7. https://doi.org/10.4314/ft.v7i2.10.

Mesquita, António Pedro. 2006a. *Liberalismo, democracia e o contrário: um século de pensamento político em Portugal (1820 – 1930)*. Editora Sílabo.

Mesquita, António Pedro. 2006b. *O pensamento político português no século XIX: uma síntese histórico-crítica*. Impr. Nacional-Casa da Moeda.

Metz, Thaddeus. 2010. 'Human Dignity, Capital Punishment, and an African Moral Theory: Toward a New Philosophy of Human Rights'. *Journal of Human Rights*, February, 9 (1): 81–99. http://www.tandfonline.com/doi/abs/10.1080/14754830903530300.

Metz, Thaddeus. 2013. 'The Virtues of African Ethics'. In *The Handbook of Virtue Ethics*, edited by Stan van Hooft, 276–84. Acumen.

Metz, Thaddeus and Motsamai Molefe. 2020. 'Traditional African Religion as a Neglected Form of Monotheism', *The Monist*.

Miller, Joseph C. 1972. 'The Imbangala and the Chronology of Early Central African History'. *Journal of African History* 13 (4): 549–74.

Miller, Joseph C. 1975. 'Nzinga of Matamba in a New Perspective'. *Journal of African History* 16 (2): 201–16.

Miller, Joseph C. 1976. *Kings and Kinsmen Early Mboundu States in Angola*. Clarendon Press.

Mills, Charles W. 2005. '"Ideal Theory" as Ideology'. *Hypatia* 20 (3): 165–84.

Moeller, Hans-Georg, and Paul J. D'Ambrosio. 2017. *Genuine Pretending: On the Philosophy of the Zhuangzi*. New York: Columbia University Press.

Mohanty, Manoranjan. 1978. *The Political Philosophy of Mao Tse-Tung*. Macmillan.

Molefe, Motsamai. 2019. *An African Philosophy of Personhood, Morality, and Politics*. Springer.

Montecuccolo, Giovanni Antonio Cavazzi de. 1965. *Descrição Histórica Dos Três Reinos Do Congo, Matamba e Angola (Istorica Descrizione de'tre Regni Congo, Matamba et Angola, Portug.) Pelo P.João António Cavazzi de Montecúccolo*. Lisboa: Junta de Investigações do Ultramar.

Moreno, Helena Wakim. 2014. 'Voz d\'Angola clamando no deserto: protesto e reivindicação em Luanda (1881–1901)'. Text, Universidade de São Paulo. https://doi.org/10.11606/D.8.2014.tde-27062014-112505.

Morrison, Toni. 1992. *Playing in the Dark: Whiteness and the Literary Imagination*. First Printing edition. Cambridge, MA: Harvard University Press.

Mudimbe, V. Y. 1990. *The Invention of Africa: Gnosis, Philosophy and the Order of Knowledge*. Bloomington: James Currey.

Mullett, Michael. 1999. *The Catholic Reformation*. 1st edition. London: Routledge.

Nafafe, Jose Lingna. 2019. 'Lourenco Da Silva Mendonca: The First Anti-Slavery Activist?' *Modern Marronage* (blog). 2019. https://mmppf.wordpress.com/2019/03/12/loure nco-da-silva-mendo nca-the-first-anti-slav eryactivist/.

Nafafé, José Lingna. 2022. *Lourenço Da Silva Mendonça and the Black Atlantic Abolitionist Movement in the Seventeenth Century*. New edition. Cambridge: Cambridge University Press.

Nandy, Ashis. 2009. *The Intimate Enemy: Loss and Recovery of Self under Colonialism*. 2nd edition. New Delhi: OUP India.

National Museums Liverpool. 2021. 'Diet and Food Production for Enslaved Africans'. National Museums Liverpool. 2021. https://www.liverpoolmuseums.org.uk/diet-and-food-production-enslaved-africans.

Nazareth Soares Fonseca, Maria. 2000. 'Mário Pinto de Andrade e a questão das literaturas nacionais'. In *Mário Pinto de Andrade, um intelectual na*

References 193

política, edited by Inocência Mata and Laura Cavalcante Padilha, 71–86. Lisboa: Edições Colibri.

N'Diaye, Tidiane. 2017. *Le génocide voilé: Enquête historique.* Paris: FOLIO.

Neto, Agostinho. 1974. *Quem é o Inimigo? Qual é o Nosso Objectivo?* NA: Edições Maria da Fonte.

Neto, Agostinho. 1975. *Construamos o Socialismo.* Luanda: Colecção Resistência.

Neto, Agostinho. 1976. *Operários e Camponeses no Poder.: Good Soft Cover | Livraria Castro e Silva.* Luanda: Colecção Resistência. https://www.abebooks.com/OPER%C3%81RIOS-CAMPONESES-PODER/30648079090/bd.

Neto, Agostinho. 1977a. *Avancemos na Revolução Com o Partido da Classe Operária.* – *Livraria Castro e Silva.* Luanda: Colecção Resistência. https://www.castroesilva.com/store/sku/3004AR441/avancemos-na-revolucao-com-o-partido-da-classe-operaria.

Neto, Agostinho. 1977b. *Sobre a Literatura.* NA: Cadernos 5 da Oficina.

Neto, Agostinho. 1979. *Estamos Num Momento Historicamente Decisivo Para a Libertação Da África.* Luanda: RPA – Rep. Popular de Angola.

Neto, Agostinho. 1987. *Textos Políticos Escolhidos 2.* Luanda: DIP.

Neto, Agostinho. 2016. *Agostinho Neto – Obra Poética Completa.* Luanda: Fundação Dr. António Agostinho Neto.

Neto, António Agostinho. 1980. *--Ainda o meu sonho--: discursos sobre a cultura nacional.* Edições 70.

Ngugi, Wa Thiong'o. 2009. *Decolonising the Mind: The Politics of Language in African Literature.* Oxford: James Currey.

Niemöller, Martin. 1946. 'Martin Niemöller: "First They Came for the Socialists ..."', https://encyclopedia.ushmm.org/content/en/article/martin-niemoeller-first-they-came-for-the-socialists.

Nkrumah, Kwame. 1974. *Neo-Colonialism: The Last Stage of Imperialism.* Reprint edition. Panaf LTD.

Nkrumah, Kwame. 1996. *Consciencism: Philosophy and Ideology for De-Colonization.* USA: Monthly Review Press.

Noronha, Eduardo. 1935. *Cadernos coloniais – Freire de Andrade.* Edições Cosmos.

Nyerere, Julius K. 1969. *Freedom and Unity: Uhuru Na Umoja: Essays on Socialism.* Dar es Salaam: Oxford University Press Tanzania Ltd.

Oliveira, Heloisa Tramontim de, and Cristine Görski Severo. 2019. 'Intelectuais, Lutas de Resistencia e Linguas em Angola'. *Revista*

TransVersos, no. 15 (April): 127–40. https://doi.org/10.12957/transversos.2019.42039.

Oliveira, Susan. 2010. 'A Voz de Angola clamando no deserto e a emergência dos ideais anticoloniais em Angola'. *Ipotesi – Revista de Estudos Literários* 14 (2): 45–51.

Olivier, Abraham, and Luís Cordeiro-Rodrigues. 2017. 'Racism, Speciesism and Suffering'. In *Animals, Race, and Multiculturalism*, edited by Luís Cordeiro-Rodrigues and Les Mitchell, 147–74. The Palgrave Macmillan Animal Ethics Series. Cham: Springer International Publishing. https://doi.org/10.1007/978-3-319-66568-9_7.

Olusegun Oladipo. 'Religion in African Culture: Some Conceptual Issues', in *Companion to African Philosophy*, ed. Kwasi Wiredu. Oxford: Blackwel, 2004, 355–63.

Oro, Aja. 2012. *Afrophobia – The Fear of Being an African*. Bookstand.

Oruka, Henry Odera. 2022. *Sage Philosophy: Indigenous Thinkers and Modern Debate on African Philosophy*. Brill. https://brill.com/display/title/3180.

Osofsky, Michael J., Albert Bandura and Philip G. Zimbardo. 2005. 'The Role of Moral Disengagement in the Execution Process'. *Law and Human Behavior* 29 (4): 371–93. https://doi.org/10.1007/s10979-005-4930-1.

Padilha, Laura Cavalcante. 2008. 'Literatura Angolana: Suas Cartografias e Seus Embates Contra a Colonialidade'. In *Lendo Angola*, edited by Laura Cavalcante Padilha and Margarida Ribeiro, 50–68. Porto: Afrontamento.

Paixão Franco, Pedro da. 1901. 'O Fanfarrão' 2.

Paixão Franco, Pedro da. 1911. *História de Uma Traição*. Luanda.

Pantoja, Selma. 2000. *Nzinga Mbandi: Mulher, Guerra e Escravidão*. Brasília: Thesaurus. https://catalog.library.vanderbilt.edu/discovery/fulldisplay/alma991007882809703276/01VAN_INST:vanui.

Pantoja, Selma. 2020. 'Njinga a Mbande: Power and War in 17th-Century Angola'. In *Oxford Research Encyclopedia of African History*. Oxford: Oxford University Press. https://doi.org/10.1093/acrefore/9780190277734.013.326.

Parekh, Bhikhu, and R. N. Berki. 1973. 'The History of Political Ideas: A Critique of Q. Skinner's Methodology'. *Journal of the History of Ideas* 34 (2): 163–84. https://doi.org/10.2307/2708724.

Parreira, Adriano. 1990. *Economía e sociedade em Angola na época da rainha Jinga (século XVII)*. Lisbon editorial estampa.

Parris, LaRose T. 2015. *Being Apart: Theoretical and Existential Resistance in Africana Literature*. University of Virginia Press.

References

Pepetela. 1969. *Muana Puó*. Alfragide, Portugal: Editora Dom Quixote.
Pepetela. 1973. *As Aventuras de Ngunga*. Lisboa: Imprint unknown.
Pepetela. 1980. *A Corda*. 2. ed. Cadernos Lavra & oficina; 3. Luanda: União dos Escritores Angolanos.
'Pepetela, o Guerrilheiro Escritor'. n.d. Pepetela, o Guerrilheiro Escritor. Accessed 20 April 2020. https://ensina.rtp.pt/artigo/pepetela-o-guerrilheiro-escritor/.
Pereira, Ana Leonor. 2010. 'The Reception of Darwin in Portugal (1865–1914)'. *Revista Portuguesa de Filosofia* 66 (3): 643–60.
Peres, Phyllis. 2003. 'Traversing PostColoniality: Pepetela and the Narrations of Nation'. *Luso-Brazilian Review* 40 (2): 111–17.
Phillips, Anne. 2009. *Multiculturalism without Culture*. Princeton, NJ: Princeton University Press.
Pimentel, Maria do Rosário. 1999. 'Aspectos do quotidiano no transporte de escravos no século XVII: do sertão africano à costa americana'. *Estudos Ibero-Americanos* 25 (2): 7–18. https://doi.org/10.15448/1980-864X.1999.2.25503.
Pinto, Alberto. 2016. *História de Angola Da Pré-História Ao Início Do Século XXI*. Lisboa: Mercado de Letras.
Pinto, Alberto, dir. 2021a. *A Guerra Civil Do Kongo – Alberto Oliveira Pinto – Lembra-Te, Angola Ep. 14*. https://www.youtube.com/watch?v=2mVPeXR-zaQ&list=PLVocLA75qjomYHor0kj-kr2Yv_yxFIU8d&index=16.
Pinto, Alberto, dir. 2021b. *A Morte de Kimpa Vita – Alberto Oliveira Pinto – Lembra-Te, Angola Ep. 20*. https://www.youtube.com/watch?v=-zwCoCoX1tE&list=PLVocLA75qjomYHor0kj-kr2Yv_yxFIU8d&index=24.
Pinto, Alberto, dir. 2021c. *Kimpa Vita Ressuscita Mbanza Kongo – Alberto Oliveira Pinto – Lembra-Te, Angola Ep. 19*. https://www.youtube.com/watch?v=R_ydQ2AEyyM&list=PLVocLA75qjomYHor0kj-kr2Yv_yxFIU8d&index=22.
Pinto de Andrade, Mário. 1953a. 'Ideologias de Libertação Nacional'. 1953. http://casacomum.org/cc/visualizador?pasta=04354.003.001#!1.
Pinto de Andrade, Mário. 1953b. 'Poesia Negra de Expressão Portuguesa'. In *Poesia Negra de Expressão Portuguesa*, edited by Francisco Tenreiro and Mário Pinto de Andrade, 47–52. Lisboa: África.
Pinto de Andrade, Mário. 1977. 'A Geração de Cabral'. 1977. http://casacomum.org/cc/visualizador?pasta=10192.001.008.
Pinto de Andrade, Mário. 1978. 'Prefácio'. In *Aimé Césaire Discurso Sonre o Colonialismo*, 5–29. Portugal: Sá da Costa.

Pinto de Andrade, Mário. 1980. 'Prefácio'. In *Antologia temática de poesia africana: Cabo Verde, São Tomé e Príncipe, Guiné, Angola, Moçambique. Na noite grávida de punhais. I*, edited by Mário Pinto de Andrade, 1–14. Praia: Instituto Caboverdeano do Livro.

Pinto de Andrade, Mário. 1986. 'Consciência Histórica, Identidade e Ideologia Na Formação Da Nação'. 1986. http://casacomum.org/cc/visualiza dor?pasta=04358.005.003.

Pinto de Andrade, Mário. 1988. 'Formação e Papel Histórico Dos Intelectuais Africanos'. 1988. http://casacomum.org/cc/visualiza dor?pasta=04358.005.002.

Pinto de Andrade, Mário. 1997. *Origens do nacionalismo africano: Continuidade e raptura nos movimentos unitários emergentes da luta contra a dominação colonial portuguesa, 1911–1961*. 1a. ed edition. Lisboa: Publicaçãoes Dom Quixote.

Pinto de Andrade, Mário. 2000. 'Literatura e nacionalismo em Angola'. In *Mário Pinto de Andrade, um intelectual na política*, edited by Inocência Mata and Laura Cavalcante Padilha, 21–30. Lisboa: Edições Colibri.

Pinto de Andrade, Mário de. 1975. 'Prefácio'. In *Antologia temática de poesia africana: O Canto Armado*, edited by Mário Pinto de Andrade, 1–14. Praia: Sá da Costa.

Pinto de Andrade, Mário, and Buanga Fele. 1955. 'Qu'est-Ce Que Le Luso-Tropicalismo?' 1955. http://casacomum.org/cc/visualizador?pasta=04330.008.006#!6.

Pinto de Andrade, Mário, and Marc Ollivier. 1974. *A guerra em Angola*. Seara Nova.

Pinto, João Paulo Henrique. 2017. 'Literatura e identidade nacional em Angola'. *Revista Hydra: Revista Discente de História da UNIFESP* 2 (3): 105–32. https://doi.org/10.34024/hydra.2017.v2.9104.

Plantinga, Alvin. 1974. *God, Freedom and Evil*. Grand Rapids, MI: William B. Eerdmans.

Pocock, J. G. A. 1989. *Politics, Language, and Time: Essays on Political Thought and History*. Chicago: University of Chicago Press.

Portal de Angola. 2016. 'Academia Angolana de Letras: Manifesto | Portal de Angola'. 2016. https://www.portaldeangola.com/2016/07/18/academia-angolana-de-letras-manifesto/.

Priest, Graham. 2021. *The Fifth Corner of Four: An Essay on Buddhist Metaphysics and the Catuṣkoṭi*. Reprint edition. Oxford: Oxford University Press.

Pritchard, E., and M. Fortes, eds. 2015. *African Political Systems*. Routledge. https://doi.org/10.4324/9781315683461.

Rabaka, Reiland. 2009. *Africana Critical Theory: Reconstructing the Black Radical Tradition, From W. E. B. Du Bois and C. L. R. James to Frantz Fanon and Amilcar Cabral*. Lexington Books.

Randles, W.-G.-L. 2002. *L'ancien royaume du Congo des origines à la fin du XIXe siecle*. Paris: Editions de l'Ecole des Hautes Etudes en Sciences Sociales.

Ribeiro, Gabriel Mithá. 2013. *O colonialismo nunca existiu!: colonização, racismo e violência: manual de interpretação*. Gradiva.

Ribeiro, Maria Cristina Portella. 2012. 'Ideias republicanas na consolidação de um pensamento angolano urbano, 1880 c.-1910 c.:convergência e autonomia'. https://repositorio.ul.pt/handle/10451/7937.

Rodrigues, Catarina Isabel Silva. 2016. *A Renúncia Impossível de Agostinho Neto*. Fundação Dr. António Agostinho Neto.

Rodrigues, Eugénia, and Mariana P. Candido. 2018. 'Cores, classificações e categorias sociais: os africanos nos impérios ibéricos, séculos XVI a XIX'. *Estudos Ibero-Americanos* 44 (3): 401–8. https://doi.org/10.15448/198 0-864X.2018.3.32129.

Rosas, Fernando. 1986. *O Estado Novo nos anos trinta: 1928–1938*. Ed. Estampa.

Rosas, Fernando. 2000. *Salazarismo e fomento económico (1928–1948)*. Editorial Notícias.

Rosas, Fernando. 2018a. *A primeira república, 1910–1926: como venceu e porque se perdeu*. Livraria Bertrand.

Rosas, Fernando. 2018B. *História a História*. Lisboa: Tinta da China.

Ross, Emma George. 2002. 'African Christianity in Kongo | Essay | The Metropolitan Museum of Art | Heilbrunn Timeline of Art History'. The Met's Heilbrunn Timeline of Art History. 2002. https://www.metmuseum. org/toah/hd/acko/hd_acko.htm.

Rubiés, Joan-Pau. 2005. 'The Concept of Cultural Dialogue and the Jesuit Method of Accommodation: Between Idolatry and Civilization'. *Archivium Historicum Societatis Iesu* 74 (147): 237–80.

Russell-Wood, A.j. 2008. 'The Portuguese Atlantic 1405–1808'. In *Atlantic History: A Critical Appraisal*, edited by Jack P. Greene, 81–110. Oxford: Oxford University Press.

Said, Edward W. 2014. *Culture and Imperialism*. New edition. Vintage Digital.

Santos, Boaventura. 2014. *Epistemologies of the South: Justice Against Epistemicide*. 1st edition. London: Routledge.

Schwartz, Stuart B. 1970. 'The "Mocambo": Slave Resistance in Colonial Bahia'. *Journal of Social History* 3 (4): 313–33.

Segal, Ronald. 1996. *The Black Diaspora: Five Centuries of the Black Experience Outside Africa*. 1st edition. New York: Farrar, Straus and Giroux.

Silva, António João de Sousa Rocha e. 2017. 'A Ciência Social também é negra! – O caso de Mário Pinto de Andrade'. February. https://run.unl.pt/handle/10362/20406.

Skinner, Quentin. 1969. 'Meaning and Understanding in the History of Ideas'. *History and Theory* 8 (1): 3–53. https://doi.org/10.2307/2504188.

Snethen, Jessica. 2009. 'Alfonso I [King] (?-1543)'. *Black Past* (blog). 10 June 2009. https://www.blackpast.org/global-african-history/king-alfonso-i-d-1543/.

Sowell, Thomas. 2006. *Black Rednecks and White Liberals*. New York: Encounter Books.

Strauss, Leo. 1988. *Persecution and the Art of Writing*. University of Chicago Press. edition. Chicago: University of Chicago Press.

Sunshine, Edward R. 2007. *A Just Defense of the Natural Freedom of Slaves: All Slaves Should Be Free (1682) by Epifanio De Moirans, a Critical Edition and Translation of Servi Liberi Seu Naturalis Mancipiorum Libertatis Iusta*. Lewiston: Edwin Mellen Press.

Sweet, Matthew. 2002. *Inventing the Victorians*. New edition. London: Gardners Books.

Swinburne, Richard. 1998. *Providence and the Problem of Evil*. Oxford: Oxford University Press.

Sykes, Gresham M., and David Matza. 1957. 'Techniques of Neutralization: A Theory of Delinquency'. *American Sociological Review* 22 (6): 664–70. https://doi.org/10.2307/2089195.

Tavares, Ana Paula. 1999. 'Cinquenta Anos De Literatura Angolana'. *Via Atlântica*, no. 3 (December): 124–31. https://doi.org/10.11606/va.v0i3.49012.

Teixeira Medeiros, Taísa. 2015. 'Conscientização e Luta Em Sagrada Esperança – PDF Download Grátis'. *Revista Ao Pé Da Letra* 17 (2): 151–5.

Tempels, Placide. 2010. *Bantu Philosophy*. Orlando, FL: HBC.
Thornton, John. 1981. 'Early Kongo-Portuguese Relations: A New Interpretation'. *History in Africa* 8: 183–204. https://doi.org/10.2307/3171515.
Thornton, John. 1983. *The Kingdom of Kongo: Civil War and Transition, 1641–1718*. 1st edition. Madison: University of Wisconsin Press.
Thornton, John. 1991. 'Legitimacy and Political Power: Queen Njinga, 1624–1663'. *Journal of African History* 32 (1): 25–40. https://doi.org/10.1017/S0021853700025329.
Thornton, John. 1998. *The Kongolese Saint Anthony: Dona Beatriz Kimpa Vita and the Antonian Movement, 1684–1706*. Cambridge: Cambridge University Press.
Thornton, John. 1999. *Warfare in Atlantic Africa, 1500–1800*. 1st edition. London: Routledge.
Thornton, John. 2018. 'The Origins of Kongo: A Revised Vision'. In *The Kongo Kingdom: The Origins, Dynamics and Cosmopolitan Culture of an African Polity*, edited by Inge Brinkman and Koen Bostoen, 17–41. Cambridge: Cambridge University Press. https://doi.org/10.1017/9781108564823.002.
Thornton, John. 2020. *A History of West Central Africa to 1850*. Cambridge: Cambridge University Press.
Tindó Secco, Carmen Lúcia. 2000. 'Mário Pinto de Andrade: o didatismo ético, político e literário'. In *Mário Pinto de Andrade, um intelectual na política*, edited by Inocência Mata and Laura Cavalcante Padilha, 109–18. Edições Colibri.
Tooley, Michael. "The Problem of Evil," in *The Stanford Encyclopedia of Philosophy*, ed. Edward N. Zalta, Spring 2019 (Metaphysics Research Lab, Stanford University, 2019), https://plato.stanford.edu/archives/spr2019/entries/evil/.
Trindade, Luís, Francisco Louçã and Fernando Rosas. 2016. *História e memória: 'última lição' de Fernando Rosas*. Tinta da China.
Tse-Tung, Mao. 2014. *Selected Works of Mao Tse-Tung: Volume 1*. Beijing, People's Publishing House.
Tsri, Kwesi. 2016a. 'Africans Are Not Black: Why the Use of the Term "Black" for Africans Should Be Abandoned'. *African Identities* 14 (2): 147–60. https://doi.org/10.1080/14725843.2015.1113120.

Tsri, Kwesi. 2016b. *Africans Are Not Black: The Case for Conceptual Liberation*. 1st edition. London: Routledge.

Tutu, Desmond. 1988. 'Letter from Desmond Tutu to P W Botha A Letter to Pretoria | South African History Online'. https://www.sahistory.org.za/arch ive/letter-desmond-tutu-p-w-botha-letter-pretoria.

Tutu, Desmond. 2000. *No Future without Forgiveness*. New edition. New York: Image.

Tutu, Desmond. 2011. *God Has a Dream: A Vision of Hope for Our Times*. Ebury Digital.

Tutu, Desmond, and John Allen. 2011. *God Is Not A Christian*. Ebury Digital.

UNESCO. 2014. 'Njinga Mbandi | Women'. 2014. https://en.unesco.org/ womeninafrica/njinga-mbandi-1.

Unimesantos. 2018. 'Bate-Papo Com Pepetela'. Accessed 20 April 2020. https://www.youtube.com/watch?v=CL3PKRs3RZE.

Van Inwagen, Peter. 2008. *The Problem of Evil: The Gifford Lectures Delivered in the University of St Andrews in 2003*. Oxford: Oxford University Press.

Vários/União dos escritores Angolanos. 1984. *Voz de Angola clamando no deserto*. Edições 70.

Walzer, Michael. 2006. *Arguing About War*. New edition. New Haven, CT: Yale University Press.

Walzer, Michael. 2015. *Just and Unjust Wars: A Moral Argument with Historical Illustrations*. 5th edition. New York: Basic Books.

Wilson, Lindy, Bereket Habte Selassie, Georges Nzongola-Ntalaja, and Ernest Harsch. 2015. *African Leaders of the Twentieth Century: Biko, Selassie, Lumumba, Sankara*. USA: Ohio University Press.

Wiredu, K. 1997. "Toward Decolonizing African Philosophy and Religion," Undefined, https://www.semanticscholar.org/paper/Toward-Decoloniz ing-African-Philosophy-and-Religion-Wiredu/ee5d85952984bf35ca0af 6925b5c4c45bf774480.

Young, Jason R. 2011. *Rituals of Resistance: African Atlantic Religion in Kongo and the Lowcountry South in the Era of Slavery*. 1st edition. LSU Press.

Index

Afonso I of Kongo 2, 7, 15–28, 56, 58–61, 158, 160, 165, 171
Africanity 72, 91, 92, 137
Angolanness 122, 123, 127, 135–8, 140
anti-colonial 6, 7, 12, 13, 20, 30, 46, 77–91, 96, 97, 109, 110, 115, 117, 122–41, 150, 165, 170

Cambridge School of intellectual history 10, 11, 164, 166
creoles 4, 13, 77–98, 158, 160, 165

da Silva Mendonça 6, 13, 47, 58, 158

Foucault 112, 165–8

identity 3, 11, 42, 56, 67, 68, 90, 92, 98, 108–19, 122–41
imperialism 80, 105, 144, 146, 154

Kimpa Vita 6, 7, 59–175, 158

liberation 3, 74, 89, 95, 102, 106, 111–27, 131, 134–40, 149–55, 158–9

Marxism 103, 112–23, 132, 138, 141, 147, 155, 158, 160, 170

Metz 6, 7, 26, 160, 169–71

Neto 2, 7, 13, 135, 143–55, 158, 165
Njinga, 6, 8, 13, 29–49, 56, 59–60, 66–70, 158, 160

Pan-African 6, 13, 136, 154, 162
Pepetela 4, 7, 13, 118, 121–41, 151, 153, 158, 160, 164, 165
Pinto de Andrade, 6, 7, 13, 99, 101–19, 144, 158

racism 80, 89, 94, 95, 109, 122, 127, 146, 159, 161, 167, 168
resistance 1, 12, 13, 29, 30, 46, 51, 54, 81, 85, 97, 112, 158, 159, 163–9, 173
ritual 26, 36, 37, 39–44, 70, 123, 135, 140, 141, 158

slavery 13, 18, 21, 22, 41, 51–8, 72–5, 81–3, 88, 105, 107, 158, 168
Strauss 7–11

war 2, 13, 15–22, 31, 34, 35, 45, 50, 53, 55, 59–61, 64, 69, 81–4, 102, 106, 112 119–27, 132–41, 152–62

www.ingramcontent.com/pod-product-compliance
Lightning Source LLC
Chambersburg PA
CBHW052115300426
44116CB00010B/1667